THE CLINICAL PRACTICE OF
CAREER ASSESSMENT

INTERESTS, ABILITIES, AND PERSONALITY

RODNEY L. LOWMAN

American Psychological Association
Washington, DC

Published by
American Psychological Association
1200 Seventeenth Street, NW
Washington, DC 20036

Copies may be ordered from
APA Order Department
P.O. Box 2710
Hyattsville, MD 20784.

This book was typeset in Palatino by Harper Graphics, Waldorf, MD.

Printer: Edwards Brothers, Ann Arbor, MI
Cover designer: Beth Schlenoff
Technical/Production Editor: Christine P. Landry

Library of Congress Cataloging-in-Publication Data

Lowman, Rodney L.
    The clinical practice of career assessment : abilities, interests, and personality / Rodney L. Lowman.
        p.   cm.
    Includes bibliographical references and index.
    ISBN 1-55798-106-X (hard cover) : $37.50.—ISBN 1-55798-119-1 (soft cover) : $19.50
        1. Vocational interests—Testing.   2. Occupational aptitude tests.
3. Psychology, Industrial.   I. Title
    [DNLM: 1. Counseling.   2. Models, Psychological.   3. Psychological Tests.   4. Vocational Guidance.   HF 5381 L918c]
    HF5381.5.L68   1991
    153.9'4—dc20
    DNLM/DLC
    for Library of Congress   91-4545
                                                                                       CIP

Printed in the United States of America.
First edition

To Linda Richardson Lowman and
Marissa Richardson Lowman

Contents

Foreword

The clinical practice of career counseling has lacked a sterling text for a long time. The pioneering texts focused only on a single inventory or domain, such as Darley's (1941) clinical aspects of and interpretation of the Strong Vocational Interest Blank or Darley and Hagenah's (1955) *Vocational Interest Measurement*. Since these early clinically oriented publications, there has been a long succession of test manuals and textbooks that have focused on single inventories or domains, but no one has attempted to integrate the three-domain strategy (interests, personality, and abilities) exemplified in Rodney L. Lowman's book, *The Clinical Practice of Career Assessment: Abilities, Interests, and Personality*.

Lowman has taken the guts of three separate (perhaps "isolated" is a more fitting word) types of literature and created an integrated model or strategy for the conduct of career counseling. His integration is not a simple eclecticism. He has used the theoretical work in these divergent domains and his clinical experience as a career assessor to develop an assessment strategy that is comprehensive, explicit, and psychologically sound.

His plan for clinical practice is clearly presented and illustrated with vignettes as well as inventory and test data. He proposes and illustrates some principles for integrating data within and across the domains of abilities, interests, and personality; a concluding chapter proves to be an unusually explicit set of ideas for giving feedback to clients and for report writing.

Counseling and clinical psychologists, whatever their level of training experience, should learn something new from this guide. I did. Graduate students and researchers will find a treasure trove of ideas for new and old research problems. The extensive reference list is also an unusual collection of recent and old work. This book is a major contribution to a quiescent area of practice.

JOHN HOLLAND

Preface

Somewhere it had to stop. An author can be proud of a work and still find it incomplete. That is how I feel about this book, a longer term project than I had imagined and one that I release now not without some ambivalence but overall with great satisfaction.

The model of career assessment I present here is called the *interdomain career assessment model*. Like most new models in psychology, it is not all that new, but it aims to integrate the three major areas I consider most important in career assessment: abilities, interests, and personality characteristics. It is not possible to cover everything career relevant and important about each of these areas, much less their integration, in a book of this length. Perhaps it is not possible in a single book of any length.

Instead, you will find here a solid introduction to issues important in the assessment of career-related issues and some indication of where to go to find out more. I sought a balance between the theoretical and the applied, a balance that I think was attained. Above all, this book is intended to counter the simplistic practices that are too often passed off as career assessment, particularly by those who have had little exposure to or understanding of career or workplace dynamics but who have a firmly held (and unfortunately not always misplaced) notion that there is a pot of gold to be found in others' work concerns.

If you are a practicing clinician, the primary intended audience of this book, reading this material will not make you rich, but it may stimulate you to find new applications of your clinical skills that you may find professionally interesting and intellectually challenging. In addition, if you are a good marketer *and* a good practitioner of the models presented here you may become, if not rich, richer. If you are a practicing career assessor who takes your craft seriously, I invite you to join in this excursion on career assessment and to compare your own experiences and data with the models presented here. If you are at all serious about performing career assessments that are valid and useful, and if you also seek intellectual stimulation in your work, then you are probably professionally lonesome. Anyone who is fighting the sad state of practice that dominates the field of career assessment today will need a few allies.

This book is intended to introduce practicing psychologists and graduate students in psychology to the pleasures of a neglected area of clinical assessment. Career assessment is not neglected in the sense that psychologists are avoiding work in this area, but there is a need for the development of a more rigorous science and richer clinical literature.

Career choice and change are profoundly important issues in today's age. Whenever a culture presents its members with occupational choice, the possibility of career mismatches will allow opportunity for correction. Psychologists have much value to offer individuals who are in career distress. Yet, few of the writings published on career topics have approached career assessment as an area appropriate for clinical practice with all of the professional practice issues that must be taken into account.

Many researchers are skeptical about individual assessments, at least for personnel selection (e.g., Ryan & Sackett, 1987). Such skepticism is too frequently warranted when one considers what often passes for career assessment or counseling. "Professionals" (not all of whom, thankfully, are psychologists) who should not be administering tests to animals, much less to humans, can and do present themselves as "career counselors" to an often unsuspecting public. Many appear to be highly successful, if income is a criterion, but the future of their clients' careers may be less secure.

This book is directed toward improving the quality of career assessment and to helping assessors think much more profoundly about what they do and how they do it. Because tomorrow's professionals are today's students, I sincerely hope that the book will find an audience among interested graduate students. Let us teach new and old professionals alike that those who conduct career assessments have an important responsibility to their clients: for accuracy, for excellence, and for integration.

Acknowledgments

I completed this book under trying circumstances. A cross-country relocation (yes, some men really do move for their wife's career concerns) occurred midstream, and a number of new and prior commitments, not the least of which was founding the Career Development Laboratory, all competed for scarce time and attention.

There are many professionals whose work has influenced me and the ideas presented here, although none is obliged to accept their acknowledgment. I am conceptually and intellectually indebted to Howard Gardner, Raymond Cattell, John Holland, Richard Sternberg, Douglas Bray, Johnson O'Connor, and Linda Gottfredson, among others. The images of psychometric sophistication provided by my graduate school teachers Frank Schmidt, Jack Hunter, and Neal Schmitt served as good superego controls when my clinical impulses started to get too far out of balance. Although their influence was more tangential, Richard Hackman, Dave Berg, and others of the mostly dispersed Yale group are some of the best clinicians (disguised as organizational psychologists) I know. Harrison Gough provided, unintentionally I suspect, many ideas that helped focus my thinking on some of the career issues in personality assessment, even though our correspondence was mostly related to matters somewhat removed from career assessment.

Carl Frost, a mentor in graduate school at Michigan State University, taught me much about the clinical method of thinking in career and organizational contexts; his influences have proved long-lasting. I was also affected, in my years at the University of Michigan, by the high professional standards of organizational consulting practice modeled by my colleagues Stan Seashore and Corty Cammann. More recently, Dave Mills and the American Psychological Association (APA) Ethics Office and Committee (on which I served during much of the preparation of this book) supplied me with voluminous excuses for the slow finish of the manuscript. (I finished the book about a month after my last Ethics Committee meeting.) They also helped me to think more deeply about some of the ethical issues raised in doing career assessments. In addition, my clinical training at Michigan State University (especially the influence of Gershen Kaufman, Don Grummon, and Norm Abeles, among others), my work at the Texas Research Institute of Mental Sciences and Houston Child Guidance Center (especially the strategic models taught by Walt De Lange and Pat Brady), and many years of clinical practice with diverse patient populations have all contributed to my clinical understanding.

I was employed by Duke University Medical Center (the Division of Occupational Medicine and the Division of Medical Psychology) when the book was conceived; I wrote about one third of it while I was on staff at Duke. I also extend thanks to my present employer, the Career & Personal Development Laboratories, whose central offices are in Houston. Generous time from the Career & Personal Development Laboratories was provided to enable me to complete the book.

Special thanks go to Gary VandenBos, Executive Director of the APA Office of Communications and Publications, who was entirely and enthusiastically supportive of the book's concept and who provided many useful suggestions during various phases of its development. Brenda Bryant, previous Director of Book Acquisitions and Development at APA, and Julia Frank-McNeil, the present director of that department, provided much-needed administrative support and helped me to deliver the manuscript (more or less) on time. Not the least of Gary's and Brenda's contributions during the preparation of this book was their patience and forebearing. Mary Lynn Skutley, Book Acquisitions and Development Associate, and Christine P. Landry, Technical/Production Editor, also helped improve the book's readability.

I also wish to acknowledge the enthusiastic support from those psychologists and psychology trainees who have attended my classes and workshops on career assessment over the years, especially those sponsored by APA and Career Development Laboratory Workshops. The enthusiasm of these participants for the ideas in this book and their encouragement to record them in written form has been provocative.

Finally, two personal acknowledgments are warranted. Linda Richardson provided that delicate balance: a careful, sometimes critical, editorial reading of the manuscript on numerous occasions and a wife's support. I am indebted in so many ways both to Linda and to our daughter, Marissa Richardson Lowman, who suffered the absence of her father with little complaint while this book was in its middle and final stages. It is to Linda and Marissa that this book is dedicated.

RODNEY L. LOWMAN

.

1

Introduction

To her family and work associates, Velma was the model manager. She was assertive and conceptually facile, with just the right blend of social skills and tough-mindedness. She got things done without making people angry at her and, although she was one of the first female managers in a male-dominated industry, she was very well liked. Velma had attended one of the "right" MBA programs, had made rank in her company on schedule, and was earning a comfortable income. At 33, she had recently been engaged and there were no significant problems in her home life or with her many friends. Why, then, was Velma so unhappy?

The vague sense of dissatisfaction that she had first noticed 2 years earlier crept gradually but persistently into consciousness. This hard-driving, successful young woman did not know it, but she was in more career trouble than she had imagined. Her early successes masked an insidious discontent that she could either confront now or, with greater difficulty, later.

Compulsive in everything that she undertook, Velma sought professional assistance with the same attention to detail that had characterized all of her work. She narrowed her list of potential career counselors to three, interviewed each over the telephone, and chose one, a psychologist who had published extensively in the area of career assessment and development. She began the career evaluation with great energy, taking the extensive test battery that lasted for several days with few complaints. Her performance on the cognitive and intellectual measures was impressive, as was her purposefulness and intensity.

The psychological assessment process revealed that Velma had all of the intellectual and interpersonal abilities to be a manager except one: She was not interested in controlling people. However, she was very interested in helping others. Her considerable intellectual talents made it likely that she would be bored in a job that did not intellectually challenge her. In addition, unlike the modal successful manager, Velma was psychologically complicated.

Careful and tactful questioning about her family of origin history revealed that Velma had been raised in a home with an alcoholic father, where support and appreciation were tied to successful performance and where unconditional love was rarely expressed. Velma had long suppressed her emotional needs and was estranged from the degree to which her hard-driving nature masked a hurt, sad, and somewhat depressed young woman whose anger was forcefully directed into productive work.

Velma was not ready to change just then, but she was ready to listen. Like many people with such a background, she had never come to terms with the bitterness associated with her childhood. It would be many years before she could make fundamental changes in her need for personal control. Velma began to examine her work concerns as she slowly realized and accepted her personal needs as being significant. Fortunately, her therapist was sensitive to both her personal issues and her work issues and was able to identify the patterns that pervaded both aspects of her life. Near the end of her 30s, Velma was financially and emotionally secure enough to take off work for 2 years after the birth of a child. Thereafter, she was accepted into a graduate program in a helping profession and is currently completing her studies.

Even now, Velma is not "cured" of her need for personal control. She is still aggressive, hard-driving, and impatient with failure, both with her own and that of others. However, she is more self-accepting and happier, more challenged and fulfilled. She has even been able to laugh at herself. Velma is now more clearly aware of her anger and has become more direct in her dealings with her family of origin, although the relationships are still strained and perhaps always will be. However, as she has become more self-accepting, her performance in her career has changed. She has become more relaxed and, although she is still a striver, she is a more pleasant person to be with. Velma had always been an agreeable and likable person, but now she was someone with whom people could share the more intimate details of their lives, someone who could successfully help them.

When Velma looked back on her changes years later, she attributed her motivation to get help to her career assessment. It was that more than anything else that had pinpointed for her the degree of her emotional estrangement. Only through her career assessment and the work metaphor was she able to acknowledge her deep unhappiness and, for the first time, to face the gap between her public appearance and her underlying discontent.

This composite case is typical of many seen by psychologists for a career assessment. It is to psychologists and other professionals that persons dissatisfied and mismatched with their careers often turn. Sometimes (but too often not) they receive the help they need to chart a more suitable course.

As areas of professional practice, career assessment and career counseling represent important, exciting, and neglected domains. The practicing psychologist can use clinical skills to make an important contribution to this field. Although there is an ever increasing scientific base for understanding career choices and career changes, the psychological problems experienced by clients attempting to understand and act on their career concerns have been neglected. To be effective with such clients, psychologists must individualize their assessment process, must provide conceptual understanding of the issues experienced by the client, and, above all, must be sensitive to both the affective and the intellectual components inherent in any change process.

It is a risky undertaking to change one's career in midlife. Yet, the risk to one's mental health posed by remaining in an unsatisfying or aversive occupation may be even greater (although this risk may be less easily recognized by the client).

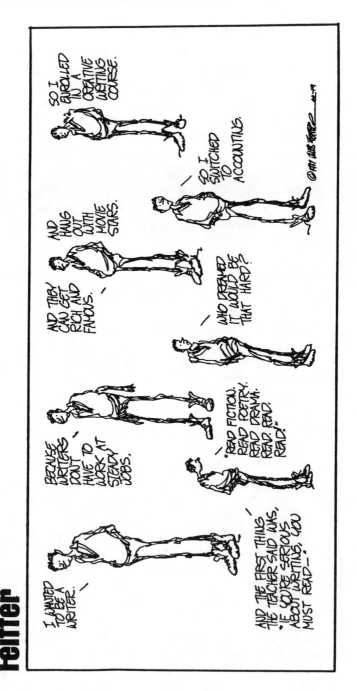

Career choices are so intricately enmeshed with a person's sense of personal identity that understanding and resolving career concerns or dilemmas may be crucial to a phase of successful psychotherapy or counseling. However, because many clinicians have not received adequate training in career assessment and counseling, they may interpret career dilemmas exclusively in terms of personal psychological dynamics or family of origin issues. For example, an underachieving male is acting out unresolved oedipal issues, or a woman about to reenter the workforce who must, on an interim basis, work as a secretary despite her executive abilities is fearful of success. Certainly, intrapsychic factors do influence career concerns, but the belief that occupational dilemmas are just one more arena in which psychodynamics are played out is inevitably limiting.

This is not to suggest that all clinicians are well suited for career assessment and counseling and can be easily trained to apply well-honed clinical skills to a new domain. Some psychologists will be ill suited to the pragmatic career field regardless of how much training they receive. For others, superficial knowledge may limit their usefulness. The field of career assessment and counseling badly needs an overhaul, at least partly because too many practitioners with marginal qualifications have been offering to the public services of questionable quality. The consumer only has to open the telephone directory or local newspaper to find a variety of resources purporting to offer competent assistance with career-related issues. Unfortunately, few of those people are trained or equipped to make a real or lasting contribution.

In contrast, expert career assessors of the type this book attempts to develop must be knowledgeable about vocational interests, well versed in theories of ability, skilled in the assessment of personality dynamics, and, most important, expert at the systematic integration of complex data from each of these domains. Such talents obviously require more than a passing familiarity with a few measures of interests and personality (typically the Strong Vocational Interest Blank and the Myers-Briggs Type Indicator).

Although this book was written for career assessors with a variety of backgrounds and theoretical orientations, it is directed mostly toward clinical and counseling psychologists who bring to the task of career assessment solid grounding in individual psychological dynamics and personality theory (the ability to "think clinically") who wish to extend this knowledge in a new direction. While presenting this information to professional audiences and graduate students throughout the country, I have realized that competent clinicians can, with proper training, become excellent career assessors and interventionists. On the other hand, psychologists who do not have a basic interest in personal psychological dynamics and the dynamics of individual change will find it more difficult to master the skills I discuss in this book. A good clinician can be trained to become a good career counselor; it is a more difficult task to help a nonclinician become sensitive to the interpersonal issues that are inevitably a part of the career counseling relationship. This book, then, is aimed at those professionals and graduate students who have a solid foundation in clinical psychological fundamentals and who have a real, if incipient, interest in the issues of career choice and change; it is also aimed at professionals who see the clinical practice of career assessment and counseling not only as a way to generate income and extend a private practice but also as an intellectually provocative challenge with great potential for positively affecting personal well-being and growth.

The Idiographic Approach

The theoretical models on which this book is based are not new, but the application of these theories has regrettably fallen out of favor among many career and personnel selection theorists. In an era in which intraoccupational differences have been minimized in the interest of validity generalization (Schmidt & Hunter, 1977; Schmidt, Hunter, & Pearlman, 1981), the approach I develop here is unabashedly idiographic. Some researchers (e.g., L. Gottfredson, 1986a, 1986b; Hunter, 1986) have argued for the reduction of critical variables predicting work performance to a very small number of factors, primarily intellectual. Recent literature suggesting that intellectual abilities account for virtually all variability in work performance is inconsistent with the idiographic approach, which argues for specificity and complexity rather than simplicity and generality in understanding individual differences in the workplace.

The career assessment and counseling of individuals requires individualized models. For example, although two candidates for a senior executive position may (and typically do) have similar patterns of intellectual abilities, their interests, personalities, and nonintellectual abilities may combine to make for decidedly different implementations of the role.

Career selection and development represents a complex, inevitably idiographic interaction of three major domains: *abilities, vocational interests,* and occupationally relevant *personality characteristics.* Encompassing both the trait-and-factor (D. Brown, 1984b) and the clinical integrative methodologies that accompany individual assessment techniques, I show in the following chapters that career assessment methodologies that are limited to a single domain (e.g., abilities) are of limited use to clients.

Significance of Career Choice

The choice of a career, which is decreasingly a once-and-forever decision, surpasses many other major life events in potential impact on a person's life. Career choice can dramatically influence an individual's social status, income, friends, and even core identity. That people who are unhappy in their work are also often generally unhappy with their lives suggests the importance of these issues to overall psychological well-being. The often subtly disguised physical and mental health issues associated with career concerns have been vastly underestimated (see, e.g., "Those Button-Down, Baby Boomer Blues," 1989).

The process of determining one's particular constellation of career characteristics (strengths and weaknesses) is comparable in some respects to the process of choosing a mate, both in complexity and in importance. Much trial-and-error learning about oneself is associated with both endeavors. Those who are successful in making a match with an occupation that is personally satisfying and consistent with identity goals are fortunate. For many people, the process of successful matching may take years. Every career choice and dilemma represents a potential plot twist in a life story filled with incipient longings and hopes. Competent career assessment and counseling can help clients to determine directions, but the process of integrating the data into emotional understanding and acceptance is typically much more extensive. Psychological conflict during such decision-making periods is inevitable, yet its magnitude is too often underestimated, even by psychologists.

This book takes a different strategy. It views issues of career choice and change in complex rather than simplistic terms, urging that the same care and precision with which a competent clinician approaches mentally troubled patients be applied to clients who are seeking career counseling. A good career counselor must have the skills of a good psychotherapist—able to understand and respond to the affective side of career concerns—and of a good scientist—able to contend with cognitive complexity and ambiguity. Effective career counselors must be prepared to help cushion disappointment and to assist clients in grieving the loss of inappropriate but cherished goals. They must put career information in a context that will fit clients' current understandings; they must also help to open self-doubting individuals to new possibilities that have previously been held unattainable. Career counseling inevitably requires both clinical and analytical skills.

Gone are the days when the career assessor, who would really rather be doing psychotherapy, merely completed a few paper-and-pencil instruments and tossed them back to the assessee. Today's career evaluator needs an array of skills, both theoretical and practical. Because of the clinical requirements, some scientific types have avoided the field because it is too applied; because of the scientific demands, many clinicians have rejected the area as being too sterile (i.e., too scientific). In fact, career assessment and development provides an unusually rich arena for the scientist–clinician who views therapeutic interventions as being more than an exercise in the irrational yet who views science that is removed from human applications as being painfully dull.

The Basic Model

Popular forms of career assessment have traditionally emphasized vocational interests and what might most appropriately be regarded as academic abilities. This probably resulted because most career counseling has taken place in university or high school counseling centers, where academic abilities are most germane. Of course, much career assessment has also been done in public agencies (especially the U.S. Employment Service), where the career concerns of blue-collar and pink-collar workers have been addressed, typically with the assistance of a test battery such as the General Ability Test Battery (GATB), which emphasizes cognitive abilities and a small number of physical abilities.

Clinical vocational assessors must collect and interpret information in three separable domains: abilities, interests, and personality characteristics. Comprehensive understanding, and therefore competent career assessment, rests on a careful examination of variables in each of those three areas. Although a greater contribution to career "success" may be made by one rather than the other of those domains (most typically, abilities are given primary attention), each of the three areas uniquely influences career performance and must be analyzed both separately and in conjunction with the other two. The aforementioned attempt to reduce all job performance factors to cognitive ability (especially intellectual ability) is inherently limiting. Any theory that maintains that the differential performance of garbage collectors, musicians, janitors, stevedores, and actors is attributable almost exclusively to intellectual factors is prima facie suspect.

Clinicians seeking to understand career dynamics bring to the task an inherent sensitivity to in-depth approaches. By and large, however, their training in occupational and organizational applications is limited. This book is directed toward that task. Although the information provided here is also pertinent in cases in which the primary client is a potential employer (e.g., for personnel selection among competing candidates), the main focus of this book is on career assessment and counseling with clients who are seeking help individually. Common types of referrals may include the midlevel executive, dead-ended in a career path, who is thinking of opening an independent firm; the recent college graduate who, despite 4 years of intensive training, is uncertain about the wisdom of a college major and is thinking of switching directions; and the former homemaker, who, in midlife, is ready to reenter a workforce that bears little resemblance to what it was 20 years previously.

Group differences in ability, interest, and personality do exist. The typical engineer presents a different profile in many important ways from a psychologist or teacher, even though the average intelligence test scores may be similar. Yet, within any occupational group (especially large ones), there will also be significant differences from one subspecialty to another and from one individual to another. A surgeon and a pediatrician or a trial lawyer and a corporate attorney share the commonalities of their respective professions but also have distinctive differences. The sometimes subtle variations within a single occupational group can prove useful in helping a person who is dissatisfied with his or her career make relatively minor changes that may have a significant impact on work satisfaction.

The Building Blocks

This book introduces the career assessor to three major domains regarded to be centrally important in conducting competent career assessments: vocational interests, human abilities, and occupationally relevant personality characteristics. These are certainly not the only factors important in career choice or change, but they surpass the global theories (see D. Brown, Brooks, and associates, 1984; Osipow, 1983) in providing a place to begin. After the psychologist thoroughly understands this base, he or she may later study issues such as career maturity, stage of career cycle, or ways in which occupational choice interacts with organizational settings (Hall & associates, 1987; London, 1985; Osipow, 1983, 1987).

Vocational Interests

The study of vocational interests is certainly not new. From Strong (1931, 1943) to Darley (1941) to Kuder (1965) to Holland (1985b), interests have been measured and theorized on.

What are vocational interests? They are predictors of the kinds of activities (work and nonwork) that people enjoy doing. Vocational interests identify the types of occupations that are likely to arouse motivation and to create feelings of satisfaction. Many sophisticated measuring devices currently exist, although most still need refinement.

Interests are variables that group people into a small number of career-relevant groups. Holland (1976, 1985a) contributed to the study of vocational interests by creating a unified theory to account for persistent findings of a recurring factor structure of occupational preferences. His theory continues to dominate the measurement of vocational interests today. However, much more work needs to be done to refine this theory of interests, particularly in advancing it beyond Holland's easily understood but somewhat clinically limiting six-factor typology. There needs to be a better understanding of the various subtypes that are possible and of the way in which secondary and tertiary interests interact with primary ones to predict career choice and satisfaction. Nonetheless, the theory of vocational interests is the most developed of the three major domains.

In chapter 2, I briefly review the history of vocational interest study, discuss Holland's (1976, 1985a) model of interests, and note recent literature on important aspects of vocational interest theory. Special attention is given to the relation between vocational interests and occupational choice factors. As in other chapters, this chapter includes many case examples to illustrate the constructs.

Abilities

Abilities refer to what one is able or potentially able to do rather than to what one has interest in doing. Vast amounts of literature have been directed by psychologists and other researchers to this domain in the last 50 years. The task of mapping cognitive abilities, especially intellectual abilities, has seen much accomplishment in the last decade (see R. B. Cattell, 1987, and Sternberg, 1982b, for recent reviews). Yet, for all of the taxonomic and topographical sophistication in mapping intellectual abilities, much more work is needed before a definitive portrait of the occupational significance of abilities is available.

Practicing clinicians and career counselors, who are not likely to create or validate new measuring devices, are largely limited to commercially available measures of abilities. Given the current state of commercially published measures, this is very limiting indeed. Although some very good tests of a variety of abilities exist, norms are often outdated and occupationally relevant validity coefficients are often in short supply. Areas of ability measurement that have apparently not promised commercially viable returns (e.g., social, artistic, and musical abilities) have remained largely undeveloped. In many cases, there are few even minimally acceptable measures from which to choose. In the measurement of abilities, an intellectual revolution is less needed than the tedious but important work of norming (or renorming) and validating existing measures of ability for occupational purposes. In chapter 3 I discuss the basic ability constructs with which the career assessor should be minimally familiar. I also present guidelines for evaluating tests to determine their appropriateness for clinical practice.

Occupationally Relevant Personality Characteristics

The conceptualization and measurement of personality variables have occurred almost independently of the study of occupational applications. Existing measures of personality have been applied somewhat mechanistically to speculate on the career fit or expected job performance of those with certain personality traits. Extraverts, for example, are assumed to be successful sales personnel or business managers, whereas introverts are assumed to be good scientists.

Much more needs to be known about personality as it relates to work before valid conclusions can be reliably drawn. For example, do the relatively stable characteristics of people (e.g., extraversion–introversion, masculinity–femininity, need for dominance) generalize to work settings? Or do the require-ments and expectations of work cause people to behave in prescribed ways even if they conflict with their dispositional tendencies? Psychologists know, for example, that psycho-pathology does not necessarily dispose people toward poor job performance (see Lowman, 1989), contrary to what many psy-chologists who conduct preemployment screening for psycho-pathology may assume. Chapter 4 presents important issues in the assessment of personality for work settings and outlines some of the current research needs.

As discussed in the first portion of this book, the clinical issues raised by each domain are complex. Yet, effective career assessment requires that psychologists put all of the pieces together to help the client translate psychological findings to pragmatic actions. Thus, integration of the interests, abilities, and personality characteristics measured is an important con-tribution of the assessor. Chapter 5 describes this complex pro-cess, which calls for clinical judgment and synthesis.

In the final chapter, I discuss other issues important in career assessment, especially those related to professional practice. I also discuss report-writing issues and the feedback of assess-ment results.

Career Assessment as a Clinical Activity

To counsel clients about career issues, the clinician must indeed counsel. Although career assessment is said to involve work with "normal" populations, personal reactions to career dilem-mas and concerns are wide ranging. For example, assessees may have self-perceptions that are inconsistent with their actual abilities, or they may be experiencing a conflict between am-bition and ability such that the drive to succeed blinds them to personal limitations. Alternatively, clients may need help punc-turing and reshaping erroneous fantasies, often unconsciously held, of their inability or ineptitude. In addition, many clients may be experiencing clinical depression or other psychological distress.

Clearly, the assessor must have more than detailed knowledge of each of the three domains discussed in this book. Comfort with the affective aspects of career assessment and feedback, sensitivity to the emotional nuances that inevitably accompany "objective" feedback, and the intelligence to entertain and explain personal psychological dynamics as they relate to career issues are all important in successful career assessment and counseling. Precisely because career issues define one's station in life and one's capacity to reach wished-for goals, they are issues that are emotionally charged and call for the skills of a competent clinician. Clinical competence is the foundation on which this new knowledge must be built. The aim of this book, then, is to assist good clinicians in becoming good career assessors.

2

The Clinical Assessment of Vocational Interests

Most applied psychologists have been exposed, if only as consumers, to vocational interest measurement. The assessment of interests is one of the cornerstones not only of career counseling but also of the standardized testing done by many high schools and colleges.

Vocational interests are often believed to be easily understood and applied. On the surface, they appear to be simple variables, bringing to mind the word *interesting*, in the sense of lightly preferred or easily dismissed or as in "That's interesting!" to refer to something that clearly is not. In contrast, vocational interests are very significant and indicate much more than the type of work that a person will find attractive or appealing. Many aspects of ability and personality are embedded within interest profiles and, contrary to the current common belief, interests are complex and clinically rich sources of information of great usefulness in career assessment and counseling.

Early Milestones

Vocational interests have long been studied. Good early reviews of the history of the construct of interests can be found in Crites (1981; also see Super & Crites, 1962, a dated but still good text on vocational appraisals).

The assessment of vocational interests provided one of psychology's early success stories. Vocational interests have been measured with exemplary psychometric sophistication and have shown ready practical applications. The pioneering nature of the early vocational researchers is well exemplified by Parsons's (1909) classic work, *Choosing a Vocation*, and by Strong's (1931, 1943) significant work developing a still-used vocational interest measure. Because of early measurement and classification success, the assessment of vocational interests is appropriately regarded as an important event in the application of psychological methods to real-world issues. That the measures have been less than ideal and that the need for individual counseling on the basis of these data is often underestimated do not detract from the substantial contribution made by the early pioneers who brought an empirical and scientific base to the measurement of vocational constructs.

The early vocational interest assessment devices, most notably that of Strong (1931, 1943), rank on par with early measures of intelligence for their impact on the practice of psychology and for their contribution to the scientific–professional model of psychological practice. These measures have typically required respondents to rate occupational, school, and recreational activities, which have been empirically validated by comparison with the differential responses of various occupational groups. This type of measurement set early standards for the practice of instrument development, although other early instruments also gained widespread use (e.g., Kuder, 1965). Although assessment instruments have been well grounded empirically, they have not been well grounded theoretically. Little apparent interest has been directed toward understanding why obtained differences came out as they did or toward determining how the expressed preferences could be integrated according to theory.

Because the initial work was approached as a pragmatic prediction problem, little attention was directed toward the creation of a vocational interest theory. In contrast, the theories that were developed (e.g., those of Roe, Super, Bordin, and others; see D. Brown, et al., 1984, for a recent summary) were theoretically consistent but were generally developed with little meaningful integration of empirical data. Not atypically, factor analysts and vocational interest theorists worked independently of each other, resulting in theory that was difficult to measure (e.g., Roe's, 1956) and empirical data that were hard to interpret.

It was a later theorist–empiricist, psychologist John L. Holland, who translated the empirical findings on vocational interests into a theory that meaningfully integrated the known empirical data. Holland and his associates conducted extensive factor analyses to show the commonalities among alternative theories and measures of interests (see Holland, 1976b; Cole, Whitney, & Holland, 1971). J. L. Holland's theory (summarized and elaborated in Holland, 1963a, 1963b, 1963c, 1966, 1968, 1976b, 1985a; Holland & Nichols, 1964a; Weinrach, 1984), which continues to dominate the contemporary measurement of vocational interests and enjoys widespread clinical utilization, is conceptually elegant and easy to comprehend.

Integrating Theory and Empirical Data: The Six-Factor Solution

Holland's model holds that there are six basic occupational personality types: Realistic, Investigative, Artistic, Social, Enterprising, and Conventional. Each type is associated with a particular set of personality characteristics and abilities (see Holland, 1985a, 1987, and Lowman, 1987, for a complete description of the various types). I now briefly define these types (see also Figure 2.1).

1. *Realistic*: People with this type of vocational interest like the outdoors and like to work with manual activities. They are asocial, have difficulty in interpersonally demanding situations, and prefer to work alone or with other realistic persons. Physically robust, the Realistic type is thought to be non- or anti-intellectual. A listing of the jobs associated with the Realistic type (see Holland, 1985b; G. D. Gottfredson & Holland, 1989) shows mostly blue-collar positions along with a few technical jobs such as engineers and pilots. The average educational level, as computed from Holland's (1985b) *Occupations Finder*, was

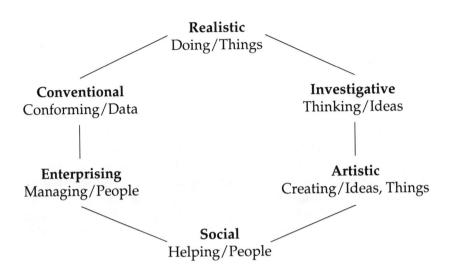

Figure 2.1.   *The Holland hexagonal model. (Source: after Holland, 1985a.)*

reported to be 4.03 on a 6-point scale (1 = *elementary school*, 6 = *college*; see Lowman, 1987), a finding consistent with L. Gottfredson's (1980) summary of a broader sample of occupations. L. Gottfredson found the Realistic type to have the lowest prestige level and the lowest average educational level among the six occupational interest types.

Military settings typify many aspects of the Realistic environment. Essentially thing-oriented rather than person- or idea-oriented, work in the military focuses on equipment-intensive activities: flying airplanes, fighting with weapons, and helping to make machines run. Rarely described as warm or supportive, military personnel are characteristically viewed as "input" needed to get the work done. Prized in such settings are mechanical skills in flying and weaponry as well as control and technical expertise. In everything from wearing uniforms to following behavioral etiquette (e.g., saluting), obedience to authority and adherence to well-defined rules are positively regarded. Positions are defined by rank and, lest role implications otherwise be missed, are clearly displayed by insignia worn on the uniform. For both tactical and strategic reasons, predictability is highly prized, and military bases are known for their similarity, even in layout and physical appearance, from one to the next. Functionality rather than creativity is viewed as desirable. Because these characteristics are in many ways antithetical to the environment needed for raising children, it is probably not surprising that military families are characterized by much conflict and maladjustment in their youth. (Of course, other factors are also relevant in explaining these phenomena, including the absence of fathers and frequent moves.) Overall, then, Realistic types are expected to be asocial, thing oriented, concrete, practical, and inclined toward functional, predictable, and orderly views of the world.

The asocial nature (perhaps more accurately labeled social discomfiture) of the Realistic type is well illustrated by Melville's (1851/1977) description of a presumably Realistic population of whalers:

> After we were all seated at the table, and I was preparing to hear some good stories about whaling; to my no small surprise nearly every man maintained a profound silence. And not only that, but they looked embarrassed. Yes, here were a set of seadogs, many of whom without the slightest bashfulness had boarded great whales on the high seas. . .and duelled them dead without winking; and yet, here they sat at a social breakfast table—all of the same calling, all of kindred tastes—looking round as sheepishly at each other as though they had never been out of sight of some sheepfold among the Green Mountains. A curious sight; these bashful bears, these timid warrior whalemen! (p. 33)

2. *Investigative*: Most of the scientific professions, which are intellectually oriented, fall in this category. The Investigative type emphasizes ideas rather than people, is characterized by high and generally abstract intelligence, is indifferent to social relationships, is troubled by highly emotional situations, and is likely to be perceived by others as being somewhat cold and distant. The educational level of Investigative jobs is the highest of the six types (5.48 on the 6-point scale noted earlier); therefore, high general intellectual ability tends to characterize the group as a whole. Investigative occupations also have the highest prestige levels of all of the six types (L. Gottfredson, 1980).

Just as the military setting is home to many Realistic types, the modern hospital is an institution heavily populated by Investigative types (physicians, researchers, various technicians). Although consumers of medical services do not generally complain that the care they receive is technically inappropriate, they do complain that medical staff are cool and distant and are seemingly unconcerned about patients' personal needs. To the extent that medical facilities are dominated by Investigative types, the values they emphasize would indeed tend to be focused objectively on the dispassionate analysis of data (diseases, treatments, etc.). In the Investigative environment, empathy and the warm, nurturing acceptance of the feelings and needs of patients are seldom rewarded. (Of course, individual Investigative types may be exceptions.)

3. *Artistic*: Creative in orientation, Artistic individuals typically work with ideas and material to express themselves in new ways. G. D. Gottfredson, Holland, and Gottfredson (1975) reported that relatively few artistic occupations exist compared with the distribution of artistic interests. The prestige level of the artistic occupations was noted by L. Gottfredson (1980) to be moderate to high and the educational level to be the second highest among the six types.

Stereotypically, Artistic types tend to flout custom and convention and to live lives that exceed the limits of normally accepted behavior. They are generally regarded as being highly sensitive and emotional and may experience affective disturbances at a higher rate than the general population (see Goodwin & Jamison, 1990; Jamison, 1989). There is some suggestion that the nature of artistic work may encourage the experience of neurotic conditions (see D. E. Schneider, 1979; Wittkower & Wittkower, 1963), for many of the professions in this group. For example,

Had [Tennessee] Williams been perfectly well-adjusted, he might have grown up to spend his life as the manager of a St. Louis shoe company, playing golf on weekends and writing bad novels published by vanity presses. Possibly he would have written even better plays.

One doesn't have to be neurotic to create, though it seems to help in our world. Psychological dysfunctions, if that's what they are, as well as repressive political systems, don't produce art, and truly can hobble an artist; but they also sharpen the interests and channel enormous energies. (Canby, 1990, p. 19)

Or again, Leonard Bernstein, who himself was not known for emotional quiescence, wrote in a letter to the widow of Vladimir Horowitz,

I just heard that [Horowitz] is dead. I send you loving sympathy, but let me add my admiration for you and your long years of devotion to this amazing man. He was not only a super-pianist but a super-musician with all the mental fallibilities such geniuses have. You cared for him and guarded him through a series of neurotic crises the world may never know nor understand; and you returned him to us time and again, refreshed, renewed and even greater. (B. Holland, 1989, p. 13)

More interpretatively, D. E. Schneider expressed the psychoanalytical perspective on the creative artist:

The artist is easily threatened with castration from *external* sources; the threat goes deeper, induces infantile regression and its aggressions more violently, and more often leads to neurotic conflict and perversion than in others not so sensitive. . . .The tendency to wrap himself in a cloak of narcissistic self-love—because his art *in its content* is in greater or lesser degree a transformation of *himself*—in the event of outer rejection is a very powerful one. This is one of the sources of that excessive self-love which destroys art and artists. (1979, p. 140)

The stereotype of the eccentric, starving artist living in a hovel and dedicated to art for its own sake despite personal hardships captures an important aspect of the Artistic type: single-mindedness in devotion to artistic endeavor and willingness to abandon traditional economic values in the pursuit of artistry. Getzels

Drawing by Shanahan; © 1989 by The New Yorker Magazine, Inc.

and Csikszentmihalyi's (1976) important longitudinal study of creative visual Artists found that economic values did not characterize the most serious and successful of their sample. This does not suggest that Artistic types have no interest in extrinsic rewards. Note the enormous wealth of the tiny fraction of highly successful artists. However, most members of the artistic profession as a group have low incomes from their professional artistic activities. Thus something other than monetary reward is presumably needed to sustain productive effort over time.

In purest form, the artist interprets or reinterprets external reality and creates things that did not exist before. Certainly there are differences between practitioners of different types of artistry (see the discussion of artistic abilities in chap. 3). Yet, as a group, artists are not known for conforming to societal norms and expectations, either in their professional or their personal lives. The task of artistic creation demands concentrated energy (Getzels & Csikszentmihalyi, 1976; Roe, 1946) and, for many of the arts, demands self-absorption and an element of narcissism. Moreover, because artistic talent appears to be narrowly distributed in any population (L. Gottfredson, 1980), artists may hold an honored position that enhances the perception of separateness from others.

Artistic settings are less easily described because artistic endeavors are typically practiced alone or in small groups. Artistic work is not generally team work. When artists work collaboratively, conflict can result when such highly independent, narcissistic individuals attempt to work together. Aloneness in the performance of one's work is the characteristic occupational condition of writers, painters, and, to some extent, musicians (especially in their extensive practice demands), along with many other artistic groups. Even among those artists who work with others as part of their job (e.g., actors and actresses), there may be less interdependence than individualized performance in a group. The intensity of internal concentration needed to focus deeply may have as its cost personal narcissism and estrangement from others in the realm of conventional social relationships.

4. *Social*: Oriented toward working through and with other people, Social types tend to be helping in their orientation. They enjoy nurturing and developing others. They work to assist others in need, particularly the less advantaged. They are generally not overly intellectual, at least in the sense of being concerned with intellectual abstractions (for evidence on the separability of social intellectual abilities, see Lowman & Leeman, 1988; Lowman, Williams, & Leeman, 1985), and prefer roles that involve working with people, especially people in distress or otherwise in need of help. Because of their preference for interpersonal work, Social types tend to have excellent interpersonal skills but also tend to be more likely to be psychologically dependent. Nurturance and support, not leadership, are prototypical characteristics, and a certain passivity (or "softness") is expected.

Social types are generally called on by society to perform important but often underrewarded tasks (the Social occupations nearly tied for second place in the prestige ratings of the six interest types (L. Gottfredson, 1980). Although there are certainly exceptions, most Social occupations are richly praised for their societal importance but are poorly rewarded financially. Obviously, many factors influence this paradox, including power issues associated with societal control and the characteristic female composition of many social occupations (see Holland, 1985a; Lowman, 1988). However, another important factor is that Social types do not appear to be motivated primarily by extrinsic rewards. The ability to nurture and support others, to help shape future generations, and to transmit cultural norms and expectations are of inherent value, interest, and importance to Social types. These skills have obvious societal importance in the survival of the culture. Material rewards, although not unimportant to any occupational group, are not the dominant motivating force for Social types.

By their nature, the settings in which Social occupations are practiced tend to be perceived as warm and nurturing, where help and assistance are valued if not always achieved. In addition, the subordination of personal goals to those of others is typical. Even if the modern helping institution is overly bureaucratic, often stultifying, cynical in the face of perceived helplessness, rigid, and overly concerned with legal issues, the underlying values are still those of nurturance, support, and commitment to constructive change. Because much helping is done in one-on-one relationships or in small groups such as classrooms, the social setting is often one of closed doors and behind-the-scenes activities. Because those in need of help are often persons who are economically or psychologically distressed, these clientele predominate in many social institutions. Schools, prisons, and hospitals tend to embody underlying, if not always immediately apparent, values of nurturance and support.

5. *Enterprising*: Also oriented toward people rather than toward things or ideas, people strongest in Enterprising interests seek to control and dominate others (generally in the achievement of specific goals) rather than to assist or nurture them. The Enterprising group ranked fourth in average educational level and in attributed prestige (see L. Gottfredson, 1980).

Enterprising types are good at coordinating the work of others to accomplish a task. They define themselves in terms of their position vis-à-vis others and seek to move ahead and have responsibility for others in a hierarchical work structure. They are somewhat interpersonally distant in the sense that power and control are emphasized. Relationships are usually defined among Enterprising types by determining who has the right or obligation to control or influence the other. When control issues are clearly defined and accepted, there may be less friction than when a relationship is being created and control and dominance issues are unresolved. Emotional intimacy and introspection are usually absent or are expressed only among persons of equal power levels. Although Enterprising behavior can create a less than ideal basis for interpersonal relationships outside of work, the ability to accomplish goals with and through other people in the workplace is an instrumental, task-oriented ability that is both functional and adaptive. The Enterprising type would be expected to fit in well in large, somewhat insensitive and impersonal organizations in which the emphasis is on goal-directed behavior and coordination of the work of others. Extrinsic rewards are important, especially to the extent that they connote power relationships.

Concern with tasks to be accomplished is an essential characteristic of Enterprising types, who generally prefer well-defined, unambiguous goals (Howard & Bray, 1988; Zaleznik, 1977) to grand but impossible to achieve ideals. Neither very simple ambitions nor hopeless ambitions are motivating to the prototypical Enterprising type. On the other hand, Enterprising types typically prefer ambiguity in the *accomplishment* of goals, so that they are free from external influence and control in deciding how a particular goal (say, increasing the profitability of a division by 5%) will be reached.

Finally, the issue of control in enterprising settings is important. It is illustrated by Caro's (1989) biography of Lyndon Johnson. Quoting a cousin of Johnson's, Caro wrote, "Winning had always been so terribly important to him; as a boy, recalls his favorite cousin, Ava Johnson Cox, 'He had to be the leader in everything he did, just *had* to, just could not *stand* not be be' " (Caro, 1989, p. 62). All Enterprising types are obviously not this extreme, but the extremes can sometimes clarify the type.

Enterprising types are generally comfortable working within well-structured hierarchies of power and authority in which each person's status and position are clear. Although Howard and Bray's (1988) important longitudinal studies of managers at American Telephone and Telegraph Co. (AT&T) point to an apparently generalized tendency of the need for autonomy (i.e., escape from rigid control) to increase with age regardless of the organizational level attained, Enterprising types tend to function effectively (in a manner that Artistic types, for example, would actively resist) in settings in which one both controls and is controlled. From a psychological perspective, however, control issues may mask a counterdependency dynamic in which the surface orientation toward power and authority hide more deeply experienced dependency needs. Such needs could help to explain the seemingly contradictory orientation toward control and authority, both in seeking out authority over subordinates and in accepting the authority of superiors.

6. *Conventional*: This type generally functions best in a well-established structure and is skilled at working with detail. The Conventional group ranked next to last (slightly ahead of the Realistic group) in average educational level and in attributed prestige (L. Gottfredson, 1980).

Conventional types tend to prefer working with numbers and performing clerical tasks to working with ideas or people. Although most statements about sex differences in the Holland typology have raised considerable controversy (see Hanson & Raymon, 1976; Holland, Gottfredson, & Gottfredson, 1975; Prediger & Hanson, 1974, 1976a, 1976b), a sex difference does appear to exist in the Conventional area, with more women than men endorsing Conventional vocational interests (Holland, 1985a, 1987).

Conventional types generally do not aspire to high-level positions within the organization and may do best in organized situations in which there is little ambiguity about goals or about the means to accomplish goals. Lowman and Schurman (1982) administered an abbreviated form of the Vocational Preference Inventory to employees in six diverse federal government settings: a hospital, a defense establishment, two units of a social service agency, the national headquarters of a large regulatory agency, and a forms-processing unit of the same agency. They found that the modal employee in the forms-processing unit strongly endorsed Conventional interests.

The Conventional type is generally found in clerical positions or in positions involving the manipulation of numbers (e.g., accounting). Although some people (including, one presumes, most psychologists) might regard adherence to authority and a need to function according to clearly defined rules and structures as undesirable traits, much of the world's work needs precisely this attention to detail. A creative accountant or bookkeeper (*creative* in the sense of being imaginative, with high needs for change and variety) could concoct novel work methods that could very well lead to a tax audit or imprisonment. The important issue is not whether some jobs need to be structured in a rigid, well-defined manner but whether persons with high needs for structure and authority (e.g., Conventional types) end up in those positions.

Table 2.1 shows the major characteristics of the six vocational interest types.

Existence of the Six Types

Do these occupational types exist? Are there six? Eight? Four? When large, diverse populations with many interests are sampled, measured vocational interests tend to be reduced to a small number of factors (see Cole & Hanson, 1971; Cole, Whitney, & Holland, 1971; K. J. Edwards & Whitney, 1972; Holland, 1976b; Lowman & Schurman, 1982; Rachman, Amernic, & Aranya, 1981; Utz & Korben, 1976). Consistent evidence has shown that four to seven factors are found when most vocational interest measures are factor-analyzed. However, although not all studies (e.g., Lowman & Schurman, 1982; Tuck & Keeling, 1980) have supported the precise existence of the six-factor Holland model or the exact hexagonal arrangement hypothesized by Holland (1985a), the basic structure of the model is not generally challenged. Even among samples of psychologically disturbed patients, some of the predicted relationships hold up. Kirkcaldy (1986), for example, found that among a group of psychiatric patients, extraverts were more interested in Enterprising occupations and introverts were more interested in

Table 2.1
Characteristics of the Six Holland Vocational Interest Types

Type	Intelligence	Predominant affect	Orientation toward people	Typical jobs	Cognitive style
Realistic	Low to average	Constrained	Avoidant	Engineer, plumber	Concrete
Investigative	High	Suppressed	Rational, cautious	Scientist	Rational, scientific
Artistic	Variable	Labile	Narcissistic, self-centered	Artist, musician	Divergent thinking
Social	Moderately high	Warm, nurturing	Supportive, dependent	Teacher, therapist	Inductive reasoning
Enterprising	Moderately high	Aggressive	Controlling, counterdependent	Manager	Logical, rational
Conventional	Low to average	Constrained	Withdrawn, avoidant	Clerk, accountant	Rigid

Realistic occupations. (Also of note, those with low scores on the Lie scale in the Eysenck Personality Questionnaire were the least likely to express interest in commercially oriented occupations.)

Relationships Among the Six Interest Types

Holland's (1985a) theory maintains not only that there are six distinct types of occupational personalities but also that the types are related to each other in a hexagonal model as shown in Figure 2.1. In this model, adjacent types are said to be the most similar to each other and distant types the least similar to each other. *Consistency* refers to the degree of internal agreement between a person's scores on the major types and is typically assessed by the degree of agreement among the individual's most highly endorsed scores on instruments such as the Self-Directed Search (SDS), the Vocational Preference Inventory (VPI; Holland 1985c, 1987), or the Strong Vocational Interest Blank (SVIB; Campbell & Hansen, 1981). For example, the Enterprising–Social–Conventional type is thought to differ from the Enterprising–Investigative–Artistic type, with the former being more internally consistent. There has been much research on the basic structure of Holland's model; although there is some quibbling over whether there are five or six distinct factors (some suggest more), the research literature generally supports the basic constructs and typology and the notion of consistency. However, the clinical application of the model is sometimes more difficult, as Case 2.1 illustrates.

Case 2.1: Incongruency Between Measured Interests and Occupation

Craig was 25 years old when he sought help for career counseling due to his uncertainty about his present career goals. He had graduated with a degree in economics from a moderate-sized private university in New England but found that his interests in his present job as an institutional investment advisor were somewhat unsatisfying after a few years. Craig had actually been very successful in this position, and he hesitated to make a major move that might disrupt his present income level. However, he could not help wondering whether he was somehow missing something of importance to him in his work.

Three measures of vocational interest were used: the SVIB, the SDS, and the VPI. There was some discrepancy in his scores across these three measures, but there were also notable consistencies, particularly the major incongruity between the themes of his measured vocational interests and his present occupational pursuits.

SDS		VPI		SVIB	
Enterprising	(37)	Realistic	(8)	Realistic	(53)
Realistic	(33)	Enterprising	(7)	Investigative	(50)
Social	(23)	Investigative	(5)	Social	(49)
Investigative	(22)	Conventional	(2)	Artistic	(44)
Artistic	(15)	Artistic	(2)	Conventional	(37)
Conventional	(15)	Social	(0)	Enterprising	(34)

Code: E–R–S	Code: R–E–I	Code: R–I–S

Most troublesome in this client's profile was the strong presence of Realistic interests while he was working in an occupation in which "R" would be expected to have little outlet. Although the Investigative components of his interests could conceivably be expressed in the research aspects of his current position, the strong presence of Realistic interests was far removed from his current day-to-day activities. Interestingly the client's avocational interests were highly Realistic: restoring old houses, horticulture, machine repair, and athletics. Yet, for this individual, these are somehow not enough. In his work, he was uncomfortable and restless.

How Vocational Interests Relate to Occupational Outcomes

An implicit thesis of this book is that people well matched with their occupations and with the organizations in which they work are more apt to be satisfied, to remain in their jobs, and to be productive employees. Unfortunately, *fit* can be defined in a variety of ways, even within a single domain such as vocational interests. Within this domain, the problem of assessing fit between person and job is well illustrated.

Congruence refers to the degree of fit between a person and a job or organization. It is determined by assessing the degree of match between the person and the job using quantitative methods such as the Zener–Schunelle index (Holland, 1985a) or the Iachon Index (Iachon, 1984). Congruity theorists argue, in brief, that the greater the degree of similarity between the person's vocational interests and the interests called for in the job, the more likely it is that there will be a successful match and that the person will perform the job well and stay with it. In general terms, congruity theory is also the basis of personnel psychology, in which personal characteristics (usually abilities) are matched to job demands.

In assessing the degree to which the congruity argument is supported by research findings, two major types of studies have predominated the literature concerning the population of employed adult workers. The first type examined the concurrent validity of one or more of the Holland vocational preference instruments—usually the SDS (Holland, 1979, 1987), the SVIB (formerly called the Strong-Campbell Interest Inventory; Campbell & Hansen, 1981), or the VPI (Holland, 1985c)—to determine whether relevant criterion groups such as bus drivers, nurses, physicians, or engineers have the vocational interest profiles that would be predicted by the theory. The results of such studies have been mixed, with some concluding that the SDS is a better measure to use with lower level workers than the VPI and some raising questions about the usefulness of the instruments for certain occupational groups or for women. Others have been highly supportive of the usefulness of the instrument for defined occupational groups (e.g., Benninger & Walsh, 1980; Bingham & Walsh, 1978; Fabry, 1975; Fishburne & Walsh, 1976; Gaffey & Walsh, 1974; Harvey & Whinfield, 1973; Horton & Walsh, 1976; Lacey, 1971; Matthews & Walsh, 1978; Mount & Muchinsky, 1978a; Salomone & Slaney, 1978; Schuldt & Stahmann, 1971; Slaney, 1980; Spokane & Walsh, 1978; Walsh, Bingham, Horton, & Spokane, 1979; Walsh, Horton, & Gaffey, 1977; Wolfe & Betz, 1981).

In the second, more rigorous approach, the person–position congruence hypotheses have been tested by either correlating the Holland interest scores with work outcome measures or by comparing ratings on congruence and incongruence (variously defined) with such variables as job satisfaction, desire to leave or remain in a profession, or work motivation. These two methodologies have also resulted in varying degrees of support for Holland's hypotheses and have yielded somewhat less support, overall, than the more extensive literature on similar issues with students and their majors or school environments (e.g., Andrews, 1975; Elton, 1971; Holland, 1962, 1963a; Holland & Nichols, 1964a; J. M. Morrow, 1971; Nafzinger, Holland, & Gottfredson, 1975; Osipow, Ashby, & Wall, 1977; Posthuma & Navran, 1979; Reutefors, Schneider, & Overton, 1979; Spokane & Derby, 1979).

In the workplace, a variety of methods for studying congruence issues have been used. Smart (1975), in a study of departmental chairpersons at 32 moderate-sized universities, assigned departments to one of the six Holland types (e.g., business management departments were categorized as Enterprising). Although the departmental chairpersons' occupational interests were not measured independently, overall job satisfaction levels were differentially predicted by the characteristics of the category to which the chairpersons had been assigned. For example, having a varied and challenging job predicted overall satisfaction for Investigative chairpersons (also for Conventional), whereas receiving recognition for effort predicted satisfaction for Social chairpersons. The variable *guiding departmental growth* emerged as a significant factor for many of the occupational environments, which points to a possible difficulty with this methodology. Smart assumed that chairpersons are similar to the disciplinary group that they oversee, whereas the position of chairperson, presumably managerial, may well be more similar than different across diverse areas of academic specialization, presumably with high Enterprising or Conventional components. To my knowledge, a similar study measuring actual rather than assumed personality types of academic department chairpersons has not yet been reported in the literature.

The correlations between job satisfaction (along with a few other job-outcome variables) and Holland's (1985a) interest scores have been explored by several investigators. Werner (1969), in a study of employed women from each of Holland's six categories, found the vast majority of the sample to be job congruent. Congruence or incongruence generally related only mildly to job satisfaction or achievement. Wiggins (1976) studied the effects on job satisfaction of Holland's six VPI-measured scales, among other variables, for 110 teachers of the educable mentally retarded, presumably a position requiring Social, Artistic, Investigative, or Enterprising elements (Holland, 1985a). Scores on the Social and Artistic scales were significantly and positively correlated with job satisfaction, whereas Realistic scale scores were strongly and negatively associated with job satisfaction. Hughes (1972) reported that consistent and inconsistent Holland types were not differentially satisfied with their employment, nor were inconsistent types more prone to unstable work histories. Doty and Betz (1979) also examined correlations between Holland scores and job satisfaction for a heterogeneous sample of sales managers (an Enterprising–Social occupation). Enterprising scale scores on the SDS were significantly correlated with job satisfaction for men, whereas Social scale scores on both the SDS and the SVIB were significantly correlated with job satisfaction for women. However, there was relatively little variance on the job satisfaction measure used, which may explain why more of the correlations were not statistically significant. Finally, Aranya, Barak, and Amernic (1981) found moderate correlations between high-point Conventional, Enterprising, and Social (C–E–S) Holland scale scores and measures of organizational and professional commitment in samples of accountants from California and Canada. Job satisfaction data were also collected for the California sample. Groups scoring highest on the C–E–S combinations exceeded the other groups on the commitment variables (except for a French Canadian subsample) and on the job satisfaction measure. Although the correlations generally followed the predicted patterns, their magnitudes were not very high; all correlations with the dependent variables were $\leq .26$, with a mean correlation (absolute value) of only .02.

The relation between person–environment congruence and job satisfaction was studied in a more complex manner by Mount and Muchinsky (1978b). These researchers used five scales of the Job Description Inventory (P.C. Smith, Kendall, & Hulin, 1969) that measure satisfaction with work supervision, pay, promotions, and coworkers as well as an overall measure of satisfaction. Mount and Muchinsky expected overall Job Satisfaction and the Satisfaction with Work scale scores to be highest for workers in environments congruent with their Holland personality types. Although several interaction effects occurred between environmental types and congruence–incongruence, the results generally supported the congruence hypotheses. There were demonstrably different patterns for the various interest types on the job satisfaction subscales, with Conventional, Enterprising, and (to a lesser extent) Investigative groups generally differing most dramatically from their incongruent counterparts on the dependent measures. The Social and Realistic personality types showed the least discrepancy on the outcome measures between congruent and incongruent types.

In two studies diverse methodologies have been used for studying the relevance of Holland's (1985a) constructs for the transition from school settings to work. In the first study, Andrews (1975) examined whether adult students who were presently employed in full-time positions and who were attending community college for "self-improvement" or "to find a better job" desired to move to positions more compatible with their Holland personality types. Using a two-point Holland personality coding and a complex methodology, Andrews demonstrated that students were most likely to desire either a move to an occupation that involved no change in its consistency with their Holland type (46% of the sample) or a move to a profession that would be more consistent (37%). Only 17% of the sample were planning to enter a new occupation less congruent with their Holland personality type. In addition to this finding, Andrews presented a method for studying congruence with greater complexity than the simple comparison of two high-point scores on the Holland measures.

In the second study, Schmitt, White, Coyle, Rauschenberger, and Shumway (1978) reported that the Holland interest variables needed to be combined with other variables to predict successfully the occupational choices of high school students. The best single set of predictor variables were those related to high school experiences (e.g., high school grades or athletic activities) rather than to interest scores, but the Holland variables did add unique variance in predicting vocational choices. Schmitt and White (1978), in another study using the same sample as Schmitt et al. (1978) used, found that Holland scores did not relate to variables such as job motivation or the preference for work autonomy in the expected ways. Moreover, the common variance between Holland interest scores and organizationally relevant variables was low. That study was limited, however, by its sample and approach, which measured the work and interest preferences of young people only 3 months out of high school, who described a hypothetically desired job rather than one actually held.

Still another methodology for studying Holland's concepts is the investigation of those who remain in and those who leave an occupation. Gilbride (1973) found no differences in congruence levels between Holland types for persons leaving and those remaining in the clergy. Wiener and Vaitenas (1977) found that persons moving out of Enterprising careers were less ascendant and less dominant (among other differences) than members of a control group who did not make career shifts out of Enterprising occupations. Because dominance and ascendancy are personality traits hypothesized to be important characteristics of the Enterprising types, Holland's theory of congruence–incongruence received indirect support. Another study of midcareer changers was conducted by Robbins, Thomas, Harvey, and Kandefer (1978). They investigated the congruence between old and new occupations for 62 primarily middle-aged male career changers. Less than half of the respondents moved to new careers more congruent with their Holland codes. However, Robbins et al. noted that their method of coding positions was imprecise. Curiously, those moving to more congruent occupations were, on average, no more satisfied with their new career choices than were those who moved to less congruent choices (Thomas & Robbins, 1979). Those studies may also indicate more about career changers than about the role of incongruity because persons who actively change their careers in middle age may be responding to pressures that have little to do with vocational interests.

Results more supportive of Holland's (1985a) congruence theories have come from an interesting series of studies. Meir and Erez (1981) examined congruence ideas in a sample of engineers, and Heiner and Meir (1981) examined congruence ideas in a group of (apparently Israeli) nurses. Although Meir and Erez's study was limited by the use of a one-item measure of job satisfaction, they reported high correlations between satisfaction with work and the congruence of preferred and actual job tasks (e.g., planning, designing, training). Similarly, Heiner and Meir found that working in an area of nursing congruent with one's preferences for various clinical specialties resulted in higher mean satisfaction scores. These studies are significant because they move beyond a simple matching of person and occupation as a criterion of congruence to examine the specific tasks or specialties in the person's job. Each of these studies provided evidence that there is considerable variation within the same profession in types of work performed and in occupational preferences, thus challenging methodologies for assessing congruence that rely on a single Holland high-point coding.

A similar study by Peiser and Meir (1978) integrated Holland's theories with Roe's (1956) instrumentation to define four levels of person–environment congruence. Peiser and Meir also used a one-item measure of job satisfaction. This time the employee group was more diverse (presumably Israeli). They found that job satisfaction increased in small increments across levels, moving from the least to the most congruent. There were significantly more positive correlations between congruence and stability of occupational choice, although usually this factor accounted for only a small percentage of the variable. Finally, Melamed and Meir (1981) studied the relation between vocations and avocations for Australian and Israeli samples representing all six of Holland's occupational groupings. They concluded that subjects tend to select leisure activities consistent with their personality patterns. For persons congruent in personality and occupational choice, leisure activities appear to provide compensatory opportunities. About one third of each sample, however, reported leisure activities simply as a means to release tension or to keep busy. Melamed and Meir also reported that the 13% of the sample who had neither congruent vocations nor congruent avocations had the lowest vocational satisfaction scores. They noted the role of leisure activities in a person's overall life and concluded that nonwork, as well as work activities, should be considered in the study of occupational fit.

Summary

In general, Holland's vocational interest constructs are associated with predictable occupational outcomes when they are defined by matching the person's vocational interests with the demands or characteristics of the job. The appropriate way to measure congruency has not yet been agreed on, nor has congruence always been associated with outcomes in the predicted direction. Generally, the more the job is defined operationally (i.e., by specific tasks rather than a simple Holland coding), the more likely that mismatch will show a result in the predicted direction.

Choosing Appropriate Interest Measures

Currently, there is no single "best" instrument for assessing vocational interests. However, some excellent measures are available, and more measures are regularly published (sometimes without clear need or purpose). Three of the most commonly used vocational preference measures in contemporary clinical use are the SDS (Holland, 1979, 1985c, 1987), the VPI (Holland, 1985c, 1987), and the SVIB (Campbell & Hansen, 1981). These measures also have the largest research base, although much work remains to be done. Another emerging measure for which less research support currently exists includes the Career Assessment Inventory (Johansson, 1986). Because the measurement of vocational interests has become a lucrative industry, new measures emerge with regularity. The psychologist is advised to proceed with caution with new measures until sufficient validity and reliability literature exists to show that the measures are compatible with existing ones.

In any clinical application, one must determine the purpose of the assessment before deciding on which vocational interest instrument is the most appropriate. For example, if vocational interest measures are being used for personnel selection, the psychologist should consider that some measures are more easily faked than others. For example, if the SDS is administered in conjunction with the *Occupations Finder* (Holland, 1985b), people can easily respond to it in the desired direction. However, if the test is administered without the *Occupations Finder* to a relatively test-unsophisticated audience, it can still have utility, especially because it includes an occupational aspirations section that can provide very useful clinical results.

Principles for Interpreting Interest Measures

Determine the Validity of the Profile

Unfortunately, existing vocational interest measures have not been adequately tested for validity to reveal test-taking orientation. Therefore, the validity of an interest profile must currently be assessed at least partly by comparing multiple measures of the same constructs (intertest reliability) and by examining the consistency of the vocational interests derived from the formal measures with the expressed choices to date and with the ability and personality profile. Given the current state of instrumentation, it is generally desirable to administer at least two measures of occupational interests in career assessment as a check for consistency. Of course, the clinician should also note any instrument-specific internal validity indicators, such as the Infrequent Responses Index (IR) and the Like, Indifferent, and Dislike indexes on the SVIB. Although there are obvious incentives for a particular manner of presentation when a person is a job candidate, the possibility for biased presentation of interests when a client (or a client's family) aspires to a particular occupation should not be underestimated.

When there are gross discrepancies among alternative measures of vocational interests, it is important to determine why. The assessor should attempt to determine whether the assessee had a particular test-taking "set" (e.g., by wanting to obtain a job for which psychological assessment is being done) or was motivated by other factors, that needed to be taken into account in the interpretation. Of course, the results of the ability assessment will also provide an important aid in interpreting vocational interests. Thus, someone who adamantly maintains a desire to be a physician or lawyer whose cognitive abilities are grossly inconsistent with the goal may need to explore the origins of the interest in the occupation and be assisted in reevaluating true vocational interests.

Review the Most Highly Endorsed Vocational Interests

What characteristics are known or hypothesized to be associated with the most highly endorsed interest scales? Are the most highly endorsed interest types consistent with each other? Are they consistent with the client's past history and with contemplated career directions? If not, are the areas of divergence consistent with known characteristics of the type? For example, Artistic types are more likely to have highly fluctuating career courses and, consistent with their creativity and divergent thinking, may tend to attempt a variety of occupational pursuits before settling on one that is a good match.

Issues in Comparing Individual With Group Profiles

A common analytical and interpretative technique in working with vocational profile data involves the comparison of individual profiles with those obtained by people in defined occupational groups. The premise is that the closer the match between the individual and the occupational group, the more likely it is that the person will be well suited to that occupational group. This is the approach used, for example, by the SVIB (Campbell & Hansen, 1981) and the Career Assessment Inventory (Johansson, 1986) in their computerized test interpretation program; it is also used by Holland's (1985b) *Occupations Finder*, a listing of the Holland vocational interest profiles thought to be associated with various occupational groups.

The comparison of individual and group profiles can be very effective in helping individuals to identify occupational groups that are of interest and in confirming prior occupational choices. On the other hand, averages can be problematic, as the following research example indicates. Table 2.2 displays the average vocational preference scores of a group of successful managers who were being assessed as candidates for a high-level, publicly visible position. As can be seen, the average profile as a group is Enterprising–Social–Conventional (E–S–C), the coding that the *Occupations Finder* would presumably allocate to the occupation. On the other hand, of the managers assessed, only one actually had the E–S–C profile; the remainder had codes that were not exact matches and, in some cases, were highly discrepant. When it is considered that all of these individuals were functioning effectively in high-level managerial positions, it must be concluded that being misfit on vocational preferences does not mean that a given occupational choice is necessarily inappropriate. It is likely, however, that the role will be implemented differently depending on the vocational preferences of the individuals involved.

This can be illustrated further by considering some of the characteristics of the assessed individuals. Candidate A was a very successful manager of a small company on the West Coast. He prided himself on being creative, innovative, and unusual in his approach to administration. Candidate C, in contrast, had an engineer's vocational preference code. As the chief administrator of a technologically sophisticated company in the Midwest, his interests were well suited to the technology of his firm. However, he was regarded by many as being cold and impersonal, with little feel for or appreciation of the politics of the job. Candidate D was an extremely bright man with a reputation for innovation in creative solutions to problems in factory design. His projective test responses suggested high creativity and imagination. To the untrained ear, his stated goals sounded somewhat grandiose, for he was concerned with such issues as world peace and creating elegant solutions to complex urban problems. At the time of his assessment, he was seriously considering leaving his position to start his own firm.

When to measure vocational interests. Research has generally demonstrated that interests do not crystallize or become stable until 18–21 years of age (an issue discussed well by Super & Crites, 1962). This suggests that vocational interests measured in early youth must be cautiously interpreted in a manner consistent with the person's overall life patterns. In measuring vocational interests using standardized measures, the career assessor should also look at the consistency between the measured vocational interests and the life history, including occupational pursuits as well as avocational and recreational interests. To the extent that there is a discrepancy, especially in dealing with younger clients, the assessor should attempt to understand the reasons for the difference and should determine which informational source is the most descriptive of the client.

There is evidence that test–retest reliability tends to be quite high once interests have stabilized. Strong (1931), for example, in a classic study of the change of vocational interests as a function of age found that intraoccupational differences in vocational interest profiles were significantly weaker than interest differences between the occupational groups. In this cross-sectional study, 2,340 members of eight diverse occupational groups (including engineers, lawyers, insurance salespeople, physicians, writers, and YMCA administrators) showed substantial between-groups differences at all age levels in endorsed preferences for various occupationally related activities; most of the small amount of differences within occupational groups was observed between ages 25–35 but, for the most part, what was liked by young members of an occupational group was also liked by older members of the same occupation. The exception was that interest in cultural activities, in reading, and in desire for autonomy tended to increase with the age of the respondents. Of course, this was not a longitudinal study, so differences in the same respondents over time

Table 2.2

Average Vocational Interest Profile Scores of a Managerial
Assessment Group

Group profile	Candidate A	Candidate B
Enterprising (37.5)	Artistic (43)	Enterprising (35)
Social (34.5)	Enterprising (38)	Social (31)
Conventional (28.4)	Social (37)	Artistic (21)
Investigative (28.1)	Realistic (32)	Conventional (14)
Artistic (27.8)	Investigative (35)	Investigative (12)
Realistic (26.5)	Conventional (26)	Realistic (8)
Code: E–S–C	Code: A–E–S	Code: E–S–A

Candidate C	Candidate D	Candidate E
Realistic (43)	Realistic (43)	Enterprising (38)
Enterprising (35)	Enterprising (35)	Conventional (36)
Investigative (34)	Investigative (35)	Artistic (30)
Conventional (33)	Artistic (29)	Social (27)
Realistic (18)	Conventional (24)	Realistic (24)
Artistic (11)	Social (23)	Investigative (24)
Code: S–E–I	Codes: R–E–I, R–I–E	Code: E–C–A

Candidate F	Candidate G	Candidate H
Enterprising (41)	Social (35)	Social (47)
Social (37)	Enterprising (35)	Enterprising (43)
Conventional (30)	Artistic (32)	Conventional (40)
Realistic (29)	Investigative (30)	Artistic (39)
Investigative (22)	Realistic (25)	Investigative (34)
Artistic (17)	Conventional (24)	Realistic (33)
Code: E–S–C	Codes: S–E–A, E–S–A	Code: S–E–C

Note. E = Enterprising, S = Social, C = Conventional, A = Artistic,
I = Investigative, and R = Realistic.

could not be measured. Nevertheless, the portrait of interests as being stable over time is noteworthy.

Inconsistencies in expressed vocational interests. It is not common for people to seek out career counseling, particularly after young adulthood, because of a pattern of inconsistency or incongruity. Therefore, the career assessor must understand the nature of incongruity or inconsistency and must be prepared to work with a client to increase understanding and to integrate differences.

Discrepancies in apparent vocational interests are not necessarily the counselor's responsibility to resolve. The apparent conflict may need to be explained to the client, along with the best evidence for the discrepancies. Once clients understand Holland's interest typology, they may be able to continue the self-exploration process on their own to better integrate the apparently conflicting aspects of the self.

Sex differences in vocational interests. A large and contentious body of literature addresses whether existing measures of vocational interest are sex biased in the sense that women are erroneously led to express traditional female occupational preferences on the various interest measures. One group (e.g., Hanson & Raymon, 1976; Prediger & Cole, 1975; Prediger & Hanson, 1974, 1976a, 1976b) has argued that interest measures should be scored in such a manner that they are sex neutral, that is, with no mean differences between men and women on the occupational themes. Holland, in contrast, has argued (Holland et al., 1975) that there are real sex differences between men and women and that any vocational interest inventory that does not measure these differences is itself sex biased. Other researchers have found sex differences in vocational interest factor structures (see Tuck & Keeling, 1980). The present practice with computerized vocational interest measures is generally to provide same- and opposite-sex normative data so that a person can know the extent to which she or he is like others in a particular occupational group and can avoid prematurely eliminating occupations from consideration simply because he or she is perceived to be dominated by the opposite sex and therefore inappropriate.

On the other hand, the persistent findings of sex role differences in vocational interests should not be dismissed readily.

Although many women have chosen traditionally male-dominated occupations (e.g., Yogev, 1983), women continue to express vocational interests that are somewhat different from those of men, which suggests that women may avoid particular occupations for reasons other than sex-based barriers to entry. Moreover, it is possible that the manner of role implementation is different among men and women, so that vocational interests and preferred styles and abilities may cause differences in role implementation.

How vocational interests relate to personality and ability. Holland's (1985a) theory maintains that the six vocational interest types are really composites not only of specific interest patterns but of personality and ability types that are implicitly assumed in the typology. Unfortunately, few studies have examined the consequences in job-related outcomes of a misfit between abilities, interests, and personality characteristics. This may be because the Holland model is conceptually well defined and easily translates to a congruence test, whereas there is far less agreement on the abilities and personality traits that characterize a successful fit between the individual and the job.

There is surprisingly little research on the relation between vocational interests and abilities. Most existing studies have measured the few ability areas analogous to interests or have relied on self-report measures of ability (see Baird, 1969; Holland, 1963b; 1968; Holland & Nichols, 1964b; Kelso, Holland, & Gottfredson, 1977; Schaefer, 1976; Sharf, 1970). More recently, Lowman et al. (1985) applied a comprehensive battery of ability measures in a sample of university college women and found considerable similarity in the factor structure of interests and abilities but little common variance between the two domains. This work, which needs to be expanded to men and to non-college-level populations, was recently extended by Randahl (1990) using interest measures and GATB ability scores in a large vocational counseling sample.

Case Examples

The following cases illustrate various congruence and consistency issues in vocational interest assessment.

Case 2.2: Internally Consistent Codes, Consistent Across Measures

Martin F. was in his late 30s at the time of career assessment. External circumstances demanded a family move and so Mr. F. was forced to consider employment alternatives. He had worked successfully and happily in a variety of defense-related jobs in computer technology. In school he had majored in engineering and had left his PhD program without his dissertation completed (ABD) when he married and had to move to a new city. With the new move, he wondered whether he should finally complete his PhD or start a new job similar to what he had already done.

SDS		VPI		SVIB	
Investigative	(48)	Investigative	(10)	Investigative	(65)
Realistic	(45)	Realistic	(9)	Realistic	(63)
Conventional	(22)	Conventional	(1)	Conventional	(54)
Social	(18)	Enterprising	(1)	Enterprising	(42)
Artistic	(16)	Social	(1)	Artistic	(40)
Enterprising	(16)	Artistic	(0)	Social	(38)

| Code: I–R–C | Code: I–R–C | Code: I–R–C |

In this case, the three most highly endorsed vocational interest codes on the three vocational interest measures were the same across the three measures. All three measures of interests demonstrated strong endorsements of the Investigative and Realistic categories. The SDS and the SVIB both had Conventional interests endorsed third most highly, whereas there was less clarity on tertiary endorsements on the VPI scores. This combination of interests, especially Investigative and Realistic in combination, would typically point to science or engineering as the most likely vocational outlet. The presence of Conventional rather than Enterprising as the third most highly endorsed vocational interest code made computer applications more likely than mechanical engineering occupational pursuits (because the latter is more commonly coded as I–R–E or R–I–E). Thus, research applications of mechanical or mathematical and computer sciences would be expected to be compatible. According to Holland's model, the three most highly endorsed codes were highly consistent with each other, being adjacent to one another in the Holland hexagon.

Case 2.3: Internally Consistent Codes, Inconsistent Across Measures

Marissa M. was in her 20s at the time of her career assessment. As an undergraduate at a prestigious university, she had been a promising student in mathematics. However, as she neared the end of her junior year, she became preoccupied with the possibility that there would be few jobs available after graduation and so decided to attend law school to have a safe, "practical" career option. She was accepted by a highly prestigious law school but, as the first year of school went by, she became very unhappy with her choice of professions and especially with her negative perceptions of lawyers. Her own mild and withdrawn manner masked a genuine sociability, but she was certainly not aggressive or forceful, as she found her fellow students to be. She left a summer internship at a prominent law firm after only a few weeks and, following completion of law school, made the decision not to practice law. She was assessed in the context of her trying to decide what to do next with her occupational choices.

Her vocational interests were as follows:

SDS		VPI		SVIB	
Social	(42)	Artistic	(11)	Investigative	(54)
Investigative	(41)	Investigative	(3)	Artistic	(48)
Artistic	(33)	Social	(3)	Social	(38)
Realistic	(14)	Enterprising	(2)	Conventional	(35)
Conventional	(11)	Conventional	(1)	Realistic	(35)
Enterprising	(5)	Realistic	(0)	Enterprising	(32)

Code: S–I–A	Code: A–I–S	Code: I–A–S

The client's codes in this case differed in their order, although not in the most highly endorsed scales, across the three measures of vocational interests. The codes themselves were reasonably consistent with one another, with the Investigative–Artistic combination suggesting preference for an intellectually demanding occupation but one in which there is considerable room for flexibility and creativity. The also-endorsed Social interests may suggest some application to teaching or possibly a helping-oriented profession. Psychology, sociology, or a more abstract field such as philosophy might be suggested.

The virtual absence of any Enterprising interests helps to explain the client's distaste for the law. In this case the apparent incongruity across the three measures was mild, and the two most highly endorsed codes on the SDS and the SVIB were sufficiently close in magnitude of endorsement that the order could be easily reversed.

Case 2.4: Consistent Codes, Inconsistent Across Measures

When vocational interest codes are internally inconsistent, there is a danger that dissatisfaction will result from the inherently contradictory nature of the interests striving to be expressed. This was the case with Strom C., who came for career assessment in his late 20s because he was uncertain about how long his current job—internal training coordinator for a large corporation—would last and was considering some options such as setting up a consulting business. His search was proceeding somewhat haphazardly.

Mr. C. had the following vocational interest scores:

SDS		VPI		SVIB	
Enterprising	(29)	Social	(9)	Enterprising	(55)
Realistic	(23)	Conventional	(7)	Conventional	(54)
Conventional	(22)	Enterprising	(6)	Social	(52)
Social	(21)	Investigative	(1)	Investigative	(47)
Investigative	(14)	Realistic	(0)	Realistic	(40)
Artistic	(13)	Artistic	(0)	Artistic	(32)

| Code: E–R–C | Code: S–C–E | Code: E–C–S |

Although the VPI and the SVIB were reasonably alike in the three most highly endorsed scores, which were generally consistent internally, the high endorsement of Realistic scale scores on the SDS raised doubts as to the appropriate classification of vocational interests. Although the Social–Conventional–Enterprising (or Enterprising–Conventional–Social) combinations were reasonably consistent, the Enterprising–Realistic–Conventional would not appear to be a very easy code to match with occupations. Further clarification of the client's vocational interest scores would be needed.

Case 2.5: Inconsistent Codes, Inconsistent Across Measures

A particularly complicated case occurs when multiple measures yield highly inconsistent vocational interest codes. In such an instance, the career counselor is left with the difficult task of attempting to sort out which of the various alternatives is most descriptive of the client and, even if successful in doing so, still has the problem of codes not being consistent with one another. The following case is illustrative:

SDS		VPI		SVIB	
Social	(32)	Investigative	(5)	Artistic	(50)
Artistic	(26)	Realistic	(4)	Enterprising	(43)
Enterprising	(21)	Enterprising	(4)	Realistic	(39)
Realistic	(19)	Artistic	(3)	Investigative	(34)
Investigative	(14)	Social	(1)	Social	(32)
Conventional	(6)	Conventional	(1)	Conventional	(28)

Code: S–A–E	Code: I–R–E	Code: A–E–R

In this case, except for the low Conventional scale scores, there was wide variability across the three measures. One profile (the SDS) made the client seem compatible with her occupation (high school counselor) at the time of the evaluation, the second (the VPI) suggested engineering or science, and the third was a highly atypical combination that was quite inconsistent internally. With such a profile, it is very difficult to counsel a client properly because there is no assurance that any of the three measures is the "best" description of interests. Assessment of abilities, and of personality characteristics, can be examined in such cases in the attempt to help clarify the discrepancies in the measured interests. Reasons for inconsistency might also be explored. For example, the counselor can examine the separate sections of the SDS to determine whether there was consistency across the subparts. Possibly the client was rating self-estimates of ability, which constitute 40% of the overall score (see Lowman & Williams, 1987) on the SDS.

As these cases illustrate, matching individuals and their jobs is far more complex than present clinical practices or research findings generally acknowledge. There is evidence that a mismatch of person and job will result in lower job outcomes such as productivity and satisfaction. The interest–job outcome relation thus far has been examined primarily as it relates to vocational interests rather than to abilities or personality. The case studies demonstrate the clinical complexity of combining results across multiple measures of interests.

Summary

Occupational interests are well-established individual difference variables that are important in career assessment. The career assessor needs to be familiar both with the structured theories of interest and with the practical realities of interest measurement. The assessor must also exercise considerable caution in drawing conclusions in light of the limitations of current methodologies for assessing interests. Nonetheless, the measurement of occupational interests provides an excellent starting point in career assessment for orienting the assessor to the client and to the abilities and personality characteristics that may need exploration.

3

Abilities

The scientific measurement of abilities exemplifies one of the ways in which psychology has defined its identity and contributed to the study of human behavior. By combining psychometric sophistication with the measurement of real-world problems (such as the appropriate placement of children with mental retardation), psychologists have made much progress both in advancing knowledge and in addressing practical problems. Tools have been created that have improved the placement, remediation, and development of people with varied psychological needs (McClelland, Baldwin, Bronfenbrenner, & Strodtbeck, 1958). At the same time, work on applied problems such as job and school placement has helped to clarify the nature of abilities.

Perhaps because the measurement of abilities has had obvious practical applications, it was developed early and extensively. In many respects, however, important early developments (including the formulation of ability taxonomies and of what, at the time, were sophisticated measuring devices) have not been matched as the field has progressed over time. For example, many ability measures actively marketed today are decades old. Although their test publishers continue to achieve enviable profits without the considerable expense of updating or improving the measures, the current utility of such tests remains undemonstrated.

Partly, this situation may reflect the normal developmental curve of a new field. Rapid early progress often slows as stubborn problems of conceptualization and measurement emerge and persist. In addition, the conceptually constant nature of many abilities makes it difficult to create genuinely useful new instruments (e.g., there are only so many ways to measure verbal or mechanical reasoning ability). Unfortunately, "new" measures of the constructs often seem created to profit the test makers and publishers more than to contribute significant new theories or instruments. However, even if spatial or musical abilities today are conceptually identical to the constructs measured in the 1940s, norms and validity coefficients must still be updated and instruments must frequently be revised to reflect cultural and societal changes. With far too many ability measures, this has not happened. Instead, commercial slothfulness has often led to the promulgation of psychometric antiquities.

Of equal concern for the practitioner is the substantial divergence between new theoretical developments and applied measuring devices. Not all abilities have been theoretically quiescent. Some of the important recent developments in conceptualizing intelligence (e.g., Gardner's, 1983, theory of multiple intelligence; Sternberg's, 1988, work with such constructs as social and "managerial" intelligence) have not yet been translated into tests suitable for routine clinical practice. Despite recent impressive advances in theorizing about the structure of the intellect (e.g., R. B. Cattell, 1987; Gardner, 1983; Hakstian & Cattell, 1978a; Horn & Cattell, 1966; Pawlik, 1966; Sternberg, 1982a, 1982b, 1988) and despite empirical findings on the neuropsychology of abilities and aptitudes (see Obler & Fein, 1988), few researchers have adequately developed or tested the occupational and career counseling implications of their work. At the other extreme, psychologists concerned with applied problems (e.g., industrial psychologists measuring executive talent) have often accepted empirical validity paradigms that, although sometimes improving the quality of selection, have not forced the development of theory.

The net result is that for many career assessors, extensive study is needed to learn about the measurement of abilities. Clinical practice requires an understanding of conceptually complex theoretical models of abilities as well as practical measurement techniques. Without specialized training, assessors must select tests without proper understanding of the theoretical rationale and purpose of assessing each variable.

Although this chapter, therefore, adopts a structural and theoretical approach rather than a superficial "which test to use" approach, it necessarily must eschew detailed review or analysis of current theories of intelligence or of the structure of intellect lest that become the only emphasis (see, however, Sternberg, 1982b, for a summary of recent advances in this area). Nor will I review or integrate all of the recent neuropsychological findings relevant to the academic study of abilities. Research identifying the neurological situs of a particular ability (e.g., whether a patient with a right posterior lesion is unable to navigate around a room) or the consequences of neurological *dis*abilities generally does not directly assist the career assessor, who must instead be concerned with things such as the minimal aptitude level needed for successful performance as a surgeon, an artist, or an engineer.

In this chapter, then, I discuss a number of basic human abilities that are important for the career assessor to understand conceptually and to know how to measure. For convenience of discussion, I present abilities in an order that roughly corresponds to Holland's structure of vocational interests (see chap. 2). Of course, an exact, one-to-one match is not possible, and many abilities (e.g., spatial and intellectual) are applicable not just to one but to several of Holland's interest categories.

Notes on the Selection of Ability Measures

Although some attention is directed in this chapter toward specific tests, this review of abilities emphasizes more the nature of the construct than specific measuring instruments. Too often, training for clinical and counseling psychologists has been test driven rather than construct guided such that their methodologies have been intrinsically tied to the instruments of their training. Psychologists so oriented may experience frustration with the necessarily detailed conceptual review of abilities in this chapter. However, given the continually changing nature of the scientific study and measurement of abilities, I believe it will be better preparation for the career assessor to understand the construct being measured and thus to make an informed selection from the available instruments (which, it is fervently hoped, will change and improve with time) than to learn only about the interpretation of specific tests. Moreover, the same measures of ability will not be best suited for all career assessment tasks.

Skill in evaluating tests will also protect the clinician from the exaggerated claims of validity made by many test publishers. Unfortunately, published measures of ability often have far more limited construct validity for career and occupational applications than test publishers and authors assert. Test publishers often tout a particular test as being suitable for "industrial" purposes or predictive of success in some applied undertaking when the claim is based less on validated evidence than on the creativity of the marketing. The new emphasis on the *practice* of psychology has resulted in a rapid expansion of tests on the market, many of which do not meet even minimal standards of reliability and validity. For too many measures, adequate normative data for career assessment purposes do not exist. Certainly, it is rare to find a clear pattern of validity studies for a particular test demonstrating that the measured trait is necessary or desired for the successful performance of a particular occupation. Making a bad situation worse, the test manuals of many currently published ability measures have set a very low standard, with some still being sold in versions developed 30 or 40 years ago. The practicing psychologist is left to determine whether a particular ability test will predict successful performance in a particular occupation, unfortunately with limited and often outdated data.

How then should the career assessor determine whether a particular measure is appropriate for a given evaluation task? I suggest the following criteria. Of course, the reader will also want to read standard texts (e.g., Anastasi, 1982) for additional guidance.

1. *Validity*. Does the instrument's technical manual and the subsequent research literature show convincing support for the validity of the construct and the predictive validity of the ability? Do sufficient validity studies using relevant populations demonstrate that the measure is appropriate for the present assessment need? This generally requires careful, tedious review of highly imperfect, outdated studies that may not even be cited in the test manual. When available, test reviews in such compendia as the *Mental Measurements Yearbook* series (e.g., Conoley & Kramer, 1989), *Test Critiques* (Keyser & Sweetland, 1983 and subsequent years) and the *Test Validity Yearbook* series (Landy, 1989) can help.

2. *Reliability*. Does the test measure the construct consistently? If not, do known changes account for the apparent unreliability?

3. *Norms*. How recent and how extensive are the normative data for the measure? Test norms for career assessment instruments are frequently inadequate. Norms must be specific to relevant occupational groups and must also be organized by adult age groupings (preferably covering the entire working age range). Because many ability measures have been normed using high school or college populations, the absence of other age-specific norms can make it difficult to interpret adult test results. This is especially true for abilities that show a pattern of decline with age. Moreover, normative data that are decades old (as with many popular, commercially published instruments) have obvious limitations for current applications, especially as the distribution of the variable has changes over time (e.g., American women's spatial abilities).

4. *Commercial availability*. The potential user will want to know whether the test is readily available to the practitioner. Unfortunately, a number of promising measures cited in the research literature, which have been used in studies as standards of particular ability constructs, are not readily available for clinical application (e.g., the Kit of Factor Referenced Cognitive Tests [Ekstrom, French, & Harman, 1976] and the General Aptitude Test Battery [GATB; U.S. Department of Labor, 1970, 1979]). Although such tests may have excellent psychometric characteristics, they typically have not been normed, or the researcher

or publisher may for other reasons prohibit nonresearch applications. This is unfortunate in cases when such measures are superior to commercially available measures.

5. *Clarity of what is being measured.* Is it clear which ability constructs or subconstructs the test is measuring? Simply calling a test a measure of one ability or another does not make it so. Because many abilities are multidimensional, clinicians need to know which dimension a particular test is measuring and whether occupational relevance has been demonstrated for this dimension.

6. *Occupational applications.* Are the occupational applications claimed by the measure's author or publisher clear and compelling? Does the test show a differential pattern of validity for various occupational groups, consistent with what is known about how the groups differ? Is there a clear tendency for those who score well on the test to perform well in relevant occupations or, at a minimum, in training programs? Is the measure assessing something other than general intellectual ability? Has the measure generated studies in the professional literature by a variety of researchers, or have the characteristics of the test been examined only by its authors and by those who stand to gain commercially by positive outcomes?

No test will meet all of these criteria equally well; nonetheless, psychologists choosing tests for career assessment will be well advised to insist that as many are met as possible, especially when there is a choice among competing measures. Currently, *caveat emptor* (let the buyer beware) is the guiding principle in test selection. I know of no test publisher who will defend the practitioner in a malpractice suit generated by inappropriate conclusions derived from an outmoded but still marketed measure.

Characteristics of Selected Career-Relevant Abilities

In the remainder of this chapter, I consider a variety of ability variables, each with occupational relevance. When there is a relevant literature base to help explain the ability measured, I integrate this into the review. Finally, I briefly mention relevant, commercially available measures of the construct, especially if there are preferred instruments.

Primary Abilities

For ease of discussion and organization, I use Holland's (1985a) vocational interest framework to organize the primary abilities presented here. Although Lowman et al. (1985) showed a factor structure of primary abilities in a sample of college women to be analogous to Holland's interest structure, there were areas of inconsistency, and the work still needs to be replicated with other groups, especially men. In the following discussion, I group primary abilities according to Holland type in which there is either a theoretical or an empirical reason to believe that a relationship exists.

Realistic Abilities

Theoretical and conceptual issues. Abilities in working with things rather than with people or ideas is the presumed major area of competence for those whose primary abilities are found in the Realistic domain. A review of the Realistic occupations associated with Holland's classification system (see Campbell & Hansen, 1981; G. D. Gottfredson, Holland, & Ogawa, 1982; Holland, 1985b) shows that most Realistic occupations are blue-collar jobs requiring manual skills or, for those few at the white-collar level, are occupations in fields such as engineering (for some but not all subspecialties) and navigation. An orientation toward things rather than toward people appears to be a meaningful distinction in ability structures, one that affects not only occupational choice but also other life activities, such as preferred child-rearing methods (Ispa, Gray, & Thornburg, 1984). The most prominent abilities expected to be important for success in Realistic occupations would therefore be physical, mechanical, and possibly spatial (because spatial and mechanical abilities are closely linked). Of course, each of these abilities (especially spatial) may also relate to non-Realistic occupations (e.g., spatial ability relates to artistic performance); I note these relationships in discussing the ability.

Mechanical and Physical Abilities

The ability to think mechanically requires understanding principles about the physical world and about how machines work and operate. Practical applications of mechanical ability also require the ability to work with one's hands and to translate knowledge about things to specific applications.

The major research work on mechanical abilities and aptitudes was completed between the 1920s and the 1940s. Perhaps the most significant treatise on mechanical abilities is that of Paterson, Elliott, Anderson, Toops, and Heidbreder (1930), which summarized work on an impressive mechanical test battery validated in the 1920s. The United States at the time was transforming from an agricultural to an industrial base, and the valid selection of people with mechanical abilities was of great societal importance. Paterson et al. (1930) defined mechanical ability as

> the ability to succeed in work of a mechanical nature . . .
> that which enables a person to work with tools and machinery and the materials of the physical world . . . that which
> enables a person to succeed in a . . . restricted range of vocational and trade school courses. (pp. 6–7)

Additional work was completed in the 1940s, and special attention was directed during World War II toward developing efficient selection batteries for such war-related occupations as pilot. Since then, there have been few studies in the professional literature on mechanical abilities, and no significant or "revolutionary" tests have been published in the ensuing years to measure mechanical abilities or strengths. Unlike spatial abilities, in which controversy over sex differences has generated a cascade of research in the last two decades, work on the measurement and application of mechanical abilities has been quiescent. Few substantively different conclusions can be drawn today than were put forth in the early days of mechanical ability test development.

As a practical matter, the measurement of mechanical abilities for the type of career assessment emphasized in this book is probably most appropriately directed toward higher level occupations requiring mechanical skills. People whose skills are most appropriate for unskilled labor or lower level mechanical applications are unlikely to seek out the type of expensive individualized assessment and counseling that is presented here. Employers may use mechanical or physical ability measures to screen large applicant groups, but typically the emphasis is on measuring only one or, at most, a few abilities rather than a combination of ability, interest, and personality data. Therefore, in this book, tests that measure mechanically relevant abilities but also make use of intellectual or spatial abilities are the most relevant.

There has been some controversy about whether mechanical abilities represent a distinct category of ability or a combination and integration of other primary abilities (Super & Crites, 1962). Whether distinct or integrated, the ability to function successfully in occupations calling for mechanical skills generally assumes a competency in real-world, thing-oriented activities. At the higher levels (skilled mechanics, engineers, and certain types of scientists), this involves understanding principles about the physical world and about how machines work and operate. In lower level Realistic occupations, *physical* abilities assume greater emphasis. Thus, an engineer may examine a structure and, using mechanical principles, determine a method to improve structural stability, whereas a riveter may put the structural repairs into place. Realistic vocational interests may figure prominently in the interest patterns of both, but the engineer may have conceptual and mathematical skills without skills in manual dexterity, the presumed province of the skilled laborer.

Notes on physical abilities. Realistic-related abilities, especially among blue-collar workers, include the ability to work effectively with one's hands, limbs, and body. Fleischman's important and life-long work (e.g., Fleishman, 1954, 1957, 1982, 1984) of developing a taxonomy of physical abilities as well as an index of effort (Fleishman, Gebhardt, & Hogan, 1984) included identifying several types of physical ability. In one study of 38 tests of various aspects of psychomotor ability (Fleishman, 1954), multiple factors were identified, including Wrist–Finger Speed, Finger Dexterity, Rate of Arm Movement (speed with which gross rapid arm movements can be made), Aiming (ability to perform quick and precise movements requiring eye–hand coordination), Arm–Hand Steadiness, Reaction Time, Manual Dexterity (arm–hand movement skill), Psychomotor Speed, Psychomotor Coordination, and factors labeled Spatial Relations and Postural Discrimination. In subsequent work, Fleishman (e.g., Fleishman, 1957, 1964, 1984; Fleishman & Hempel, 1956; Fleishman & Quaintance, 1984; Howell & Fleishman, 1981) has examined gross motor abilities associated with physically demanding jobs and has developed methods for categorizing the physical characteristics or demands of jobs (e.g., Fleishman, 1984; Schneider & Schmitt, 1986).

Unfortunately, much of Fleishman's work and that of other researchers in this area (e.g., Rahimi & Malzahn, 1984) has relied on specially devised mechanical measures that have not yet been standardized so that psychologists in small practices can easily make use of them. Measures of physical ability that are more accessible (but lack adequate validity and norms for career assessment) include the Purdue Pegboard, the Minnesota Rate of Manipulation Test, the O'Connor Finger and Tweezer Dexterity Tests, and various hand dynamometer measures (for hand strength).

The cost and time investment of administering a lengthy battery of physical ability measures makes it unlikely that career assessment clients will routinely be tested for physical abilities. Moreover, because physical abilities do not seem to generalize readily from one area of strength to another (e.g., fine motor skill and trunk strength show low correlations), it is probably best not to routinely administer a comprehensive physical ability battery unless the client has a special interest in a job that is primarily physical (e.g., many blue-collar jobs) or unless a preliminary screening suggests that physical aptitude is the area of greatest strength. Physical abilities may also be more relevant when there are large applicant pools and a well-defined job for which specific physical abilities can be determined and an appropriate screening battery can be selected. For these reasons (and due to space limitations) I do not discuss physical abilities further.

Dimensionality of the construct. Insufficient factorial data are reported in the literature to establish the dimensionality of mechanical abilities as they apply to contemporary career assessment. However, some important early studies have been reported. Harrell (1940) factor-analyzed 37 variables (including the Minnesota Mechanical Ability Tests, the MacQuarrie tests, Stenquist's Picture Matching Test, and scores on O'Connor's Wiggly Blocks) and reported five factors. These included a Perceptual factor, a Manual Agility factor, a Spatial factor, and a Verbal factor. Harrell noted that mechanical ability variables loaded primarily or spatial and perceptual factors. Harrell's (1937) earlier study of the mechanical abilities of cotton mill machine fixers (aged 19–51) showed that two primary factors resulted from mechanical tests administered in a 7-hour test battery: perceptual and spatial. Super and Crites (1962) concluded that mechanical ability has factors of spatial ability, perceptual ability, and mechanical knowledge (the latter, presumably trainable). R. B. Cattell (1987) identified mechanical aptitude (a_{mk}) as a separate primary mental ability and included a measure of it in the Comprehensive Ability Battery (Hakstian, Cattell, & IPAT Staff, 1982). The Kit of Factor Referenced Cognitive Tests (Ekstrom et al., 1987), however, does not include a measure of mechanical ability.

Conceptually, at least two types of job-related mechanical abilities can be differentiated: (a) understanding the principles of how mechanical objects function and (b) translating that understanding into practical, concrete action (e.g., repairing objects or using tools to get some task accomplished). In actuality, many Realistic jobs require the use of one's hands without demanding specialized knowledge of mechanical issues (e.g., a line worker who assembles car parts day after day, performing the same motions over and over again). If the job is so fractionated that it requires either no special skills or skills at such a low level that virtually anyone could accomplish the task, then it is probably Realistic *interests* rather than abilities that make it possible for someone to function successfully in such a setting. Low levels of intelligence and ambition and a personality style that is oriented toward predictability rather than change may also help an incumbent function effectively in such a position over the long term.

Relation to other aptitudes. Mechanical abilities have been consistently shown to relate more to spatial and to practical abilities than to verbal skills. Although it is possible to have spatial abilities and not direct them toward mechanical aptitudes (see Borg, 1950; Lowman et al., 1985), if one does have mechanical abilities, it is likely that good spatial abilities will also be present.

Paterson et al. (1930) identified two aspects of mechanical abilities: the manipulation of tools and materials and the ability to secure information about tools, materials, and their uses. Super and Crites (1962) noted that mechanical abilities generally load on three major factors: spatial, perceptual, and mechanical information. Although some argue that mechanical abilities are merely an amalgam of these abilities rather than a separate ability domain in its own right, the measurement of mechanical abilities (or at least the understanding of mechanical principles) is fairly easy and can contribute unique variance to a career ability profile.

Occupational applications. Scores on many of the tests of mechanical ability have been validated against relevant job criteria. Most commonly, measures tapping mechanical abilities have been validated in populations of youth against such criteria as grades in shop courses. Because scores on measures of mechanical ability appear to increase with age and experience (and particularly with exposure to mechanical tasks), many of the validity studies are of limited usefulness in assessing adult populations unless adult normative data are available or occupation specific.

Research needs. For occupations in which mechanical abilities are relevant, profiles still need to be developed that distinguish the relative importance of mechanical, spatial, perceptual, and intellectual abilities. New, updated norms are needed for virtually all present measures of mechanical ability. Age distributions across the adult span as well as expanded occupational norms are also sorely needed.

Measurement issues. A sex difference in mechanical abilities in favor of men has been reported, although component parts of mechanical ability, especially perceptual skills, have shown a sex difference in favor of women (Anastasi, 1982). Accordingly, scores on measures of mechanical ability should be compared with same-sex as well as opposite-sex norms when sex-specific norms are available. Scores on measures of mechanical ability, especially assembly tasks, appear to increase with age and experience; scores on mechanical ability tests by older subjects who have worked in mechanical jobs may therefore be elevated compared with scores of those without such experience (Super & Crites, 1962).

Mechanical aptitudes have typically been measured by paper-and-pencil measures such as the Bennett Mechanical Comprehension Test or the Mechanical Ability subtest of the Comprehensive Ability Battery (Hakstian, Cattell, & IPAT Staff, 1982) or the Differential Aptitude Tests. Such tests typically require the assessee to use mechanical or physical principles to solve problems (e.g., Which of two helicopter designs could lift off from the surface of an atmosphere-free planet? Which of two pulleys would enable a load to be lifted more easily?). Omnibus ability measures such as the Differential Aptitude Test (Bennett, Seashore, & Wesman, 1982, 1989), the GATB (U.S. Department of Labor, 1970, 1979), and the Comprehensive Ability Battery (CAB; Hakstian, Cattell, & IPAT Staff, 1982) all include separate measures of mechanical aptitudes. Most have pictures depicting various mechanical or physical principles and ask the respondent to make judgments involving mechanical reasoning. Although the tests are presumed to measure aptitude for mechanical reasoning more than specific knowledge, it is likely that clients will score higher if they have studied scientific courses. Alternatively, J. O'Connor (1927, 1943), whose work still influences the field of vocational assessment many years after his death, developed a multipart, three-dimensional cube, the rapid assembly of which was thought to measure an aptitude indicative of success in mechanical occupations. Unfortunately, comparisons of the O'Connor Wiggly Blocks with alternative measures of mechanical and spatial ability have not been favorable for this method of measurement (see Harrell, 1940). MacQuarrie (1927) developed a series of measures of mechanical ability that encompassed many of the physical factors of Fleishman (1964, 1984; e.g., tracing, tapping, and pursuit subtests).

Spatial Abilities

Conceptual issues. Virtually all factor theorists of human abilities include a spatial or spatial visualization factor that is separable from general intellectual ability and can be distinguished from other primary abilities (R. B. Cattell, 1987; El Koussy, 1935; Gardner, 1983; Michael, Guilford, Fruchter, & Zimmerman, 1957; Pawlik, 1966; Thurstone, 1938; Vernon, 1950; Wallbrown, Mcloughlin, Elliott, & Blaha, 1984). Vernon and El Koussy referred to spatial abilities as the K factor, whereas R. B. Cattell (1987) referred to such abilities as Universal Index (UI) Number 3 (also designated by the subscript index letter "s" and more generally as S). Although the construct has been defined (when formally defined at all) in a fairly similar way from one ability structure to the next (usually as the ability to visualize or mentally manipulate two- or three-dimensional objects), the early theorists did not determine exactly what is included and excluded in the construct and did not evaluate the multidimensionality of spatial abilities to occupational preferences or settings. Moreover, marker variables (specific measures) that have been used to assess spatial abilities have varied widely from one researcher to another, and surprisingly few studies have examined the correlations between the alternative measures of spatial ability to determine both the factorial structure of spatial ability and the extent to which the alternative measures in fact assess similar abilities or constructs.

Of the primary mental abilities (with the possible exception of verbal abilities), spatial ability has been studied the most extensively, with much research directed toward the persistent question of whether there are indeed sex differences in favor of men (see, e.g., Harris, 1981); toward the neuropsychology of spatial abilities and dysfunctions (Benton, 1982; Portegal, 1982; Ratcliffe, 1982; Sheehan & Smith, 1986); and, more recently, toward the genetic and hormonal mechanisms that lead to spatial and other ability differences (Christiansen & Knussmann, 1987; Diamond, Carey, & Back, 1983; Geschwind & Galaburda, 1985b; Jacklin, Wilcox, & Maccoby, 1988; Resnick, Berenbaum, Gottesman, & Bouchard, 1986).

Although the finding is controversial (see, e.g., Berfield, Ray, & Newcombe, 1986), researchers have generally found a consistent difference between men *on average* and women *on average* on tasks that are typically used to measure spatial ability (Maccoby & Jacklin, 1974; Vandenberg & Kuse, 1979). The *mechanism* to explain this difference appears to have both genetic and early hormonal influences (Geschwind & Galaburda, 1985a; Harris, 1981; Jacklin et al., 1988). It is thought that men *on average* have earlier and ultimately more specialized right-hemisphere development, resulting, in comparative spatial and other right-hemisphere strengths. Men and women whose brains are less lateralized (e.g., in whom language functions are strongly represented in the nondominant hemisphere) typically show superiority of verbal over spatial and other nonverbal ability functions (e.g., Geschwind & Galaburda, 1985a; Resnick et al., 1986). Fluctuations in hormonal levels may also affect differences in such abilities as spatial thinking so that time of measurement is significant (see Christiansen & Knussman, 1987).

Lynn and Hampson (1987) found that Japanese children (aged 4–6 years) were superior to other racial groups on measures of spatial and number ability. Nagoshi and Johnson (1987) reported that a racial difference between subjects of White and Japanese ancestry remained when general intelligence was partialed out of the cognitive ability factors. After partialing, subjects of Japanese ancestry scored higher than those of White ancestry on Spatial and Perceptual Speed factors. Sanders, Wilson, and Vandenberg (1982) found that sex interacted with handedness and ethnicity in predicting spatial abilities: Strongly left-handed men had higher spatial abilities than did strongly right-handed men, whereas women had the opposite pattern.

Although the question of sex differences in spatial ability is very important for the psychology of individual differences, for cognitive science, and for understanding possible patterns of sex differences in ability and interest, it is somewhat less important in conducting individualized career assessments. Here, the issue is not just whether there are *average* group differences (a controversial approach even in the research literature; see e.g., Stanley & Benbow, 1982) but whether the individual assessee possesses sufficiently high spatial ability to encourage particular vocational pursuits.

Spatial abilities are apparently affected by practice and by sustained attention to spatial tasks (Eliot, 1987; Embretson, 1987; Stericker & LeVesconte, 1982). Moreover, different patterns of spatial ability may require an instructioned set to improve performance (see, e.g., Casey, Brabeck, & Ludlow, 1986).

However, the amount of effort that may be required to obtain even modest increments in the ability may be substantial (Ericsson & Faivre, 1988). Lord (1985), Dorval and Pepin (1986), Embretson, Wolff and Frey (1984), and others have reported the positive effects of training on spatial visualization ability, including video game playing. Even though Embretson (1987) found substantial improvement in test results when spatial aptitude training preceded measurement, a sex difference remained. Unfortunately, such studies usually do not control for interest: It is possible that individuals choose to practice those skills in which they have prior interest and ability. Thus, although spatial ability scores apparently can be affected by practice, it may not be practical for the career assessor to recommend intense practice in spatial skills unless there is convincing evidence that the individual's ability profile is otherwise well suited to a career that requires spatial ability and unless the client shows enough ability to warrant the likelihood of significant improvement.

Dimensionality of the construct. Factor-analytic studies have been conducted for many decades yet remain surprisingly inconclusive about the structure of spatial abilities (McGee, 1979). This is partly accounted for by the diversity of measures that have been used to measure spatial abilities. I. M. Smith (1964), for example, listed 60 spatial measures, the most recent of which was a 1960 publication; new spatial measures have appeared since this volume was published. Not surprisingly, with so many different instruments being used, there are often inconsistent results from one study of spatial abilities to the next.

McGee (1979) reviewed the various factor-analytic studies conducted over the years and concluded that there was convincing evidence for at least two factors of spatial ability. The first factor, perhaps most important in occupational and educational applications, is a Spatial Visualization factor defined by Ekstrom et al. (1976, p. 173) as "the ability to manipulate or transform the image of spatial patterns into other arrangements" and described by McGee as "the ability to mentally manipulate, rotate, twist, or invert a pictorially presented stimulus object" (McGee, 1979, p. 19; see also Marmor, 1976). This typically large factor appears in most factor studies of the structure of spatial abilities (e.g., Poltrock & Brown, 1984). The second factor is a Spatial Orientation factor, defined by Ekstrom et al. (1976, p. 149) as "the ability to perceive spatial patterns or to maintain orientation with respect of objects in space" and described by McGee (1979, p. 19) as "the comprehension of the arrangement of elements within a visual stimulus pattern and the aptitude for remaining unconfused by the changing orientation in which a spatial configuration may be presented." Pawlik (1966) noted that spatial orientation's chief markers are similar to those used in navigating an airplane. Still other researchers have posited the existence of additional factors. Vernon (1950), for example, cited evidence that suggested a possible subfactor of memory for shapes versus imaginative manipulation of objects. Lohman (1979) differentiated between major (Spatial Relations, Spatial Orientation, and Visualization) and minor (Closure Speed, Serial Integration, Visual Memory, etc.) factors in spatial ability.

Relation to other aptitudes. Ample evidence exists that spatial ability can be differentiated from general intellectual ability, even though (depending on how it is measured) it shows positive correlations with it (see, e.g., Hakstian & Cattell, 1974, 1978b; Super & Crites, 1962). The measurement of spatial ability may be more or less dependent on intellectual skills, depending on how the construct is measured. For example, in some studies, the marker for spatial ability has been performance on measures such as the Block Design subtest of the Wechsler Adult Intelligence Scale–Revised (WAIS–R; e.g., Gormly & Gormly, 1986; MacLeod, Jackson, & Palmer, 1986) or the Raven's Progressive Matrices Test (e.g., Lynn & Gault, 1986). Although the Block Design subtest may be an effective measure of nonverbal intellectual ability, it is unclear whether it is also a good measure of spatial ability. In any case, it would be expected to be highly correlated with intellectual ability. Similarly, Raven's test is primarily a measure of nonverbal general intellectual ability or of reasoning ability, not of spatial ability (see Court, 1983). Conclusions about spatial ability drawn on the basis of measures such as these are therefore likely to suggest that spatial and intellectual abilities are more closely related than would conclusions based on other, less intellectually dominated tests.

The mechanical ability domain has been most closely associated with the spatial domain, and some researchers (see Bennett & Cruikshank, 1942) have posited a spatial–mechanical factor. On the other hand, spatial abilities are also important in other areas. Evidence has been presented of a relation between spatial ability and artistic aptitude (Bryan, 1942; Hermelin & O'Connor, 1986; Lowman et al., 1985), architecture aptitude (J. M. Peterson & Lansky, 1980); math aptitude (Benbow, 1988), especially for women (Ethington & Wolfle, 1984; Fennema & Tartre, 1985; Sherman, 1983; Solan, 1987); and physics aptitude (Pallrand & Seeber, 1984).

Occupational applications. From an occupational perspective, many of the proposed taxonomies of spatial ability have few obvious implications for the evaluation of job-relevant or educationally relevant spatial abilities. Regrettably, there has been little research examining how such factors differentially apply to occupational pursuits. Most studies that have claimed that spatial ability is related to successful occupational performance have focused on predictive validity studies (see McGee, 1979, pp. 23–38) using measures of spatial ability whose subfactor loadings have not been adequately examined. Other often-quoted studies are, on close scrutiny, simply presumptions about the need for spatial ability (e.g., perhaps most notoriously, United States Employment Service, 1957). It is therefore difficult to know whether it is spatial orientation, spatial visualization, or some other ability or combination of abilities that accounts for any observed occupational differences.

In the present context, spatial abilities would theoretically be expected to be important in some but not all Realistic occupations, in many Investigative occupations, and in some Artistic occupations. They would be expected to be less important in most Social and Conventional occupations. The role of spatial abilities in Enterprising (managerial) occupations, typically viewed as verbal rather than thing oriented, is debatable.

J. O'Connor, (1941) reported that surgeons, scientists, architects, engineers, draftsmen, and mechanics scored high on measures of structural visualization, whereas people in the more verbally oriented occupations (e.g., law, accounting, teaching) tended not to make use of the trait and to score lower on measures of it. Although O'Connor primarily used a three-dimensional psychomotor assessment device (the O'Connor Wiggly Block [J. O'Connor, 1927]), which required use of the hands and eye–hand coordination in contrast to the more recent paper-and-pencil measures, the occupational differences O'Connor suggested have held up reasonably well in the empirical literature.

A frequently quoted listing of occupations that require scores in the top 10% on measures of spatial ability was published by the United States Employment Service (1957). Although most of the occupations listed have received at least some support from other literature, it is often overlooked that the list was composed largely without empirical data (I. M. Smith, 1964). However, it is interesting that the overwhelming majority of the occupations listed fall into Holland's (1985a) Realistic, Investigative, and Artistic categories (in that order).

Many engineering students (a Realistic or Investigative occupation) do well on measures of spatial ability (Bingham, 1937; Likert & Quasha, 1970). I. M. Smith's (1964) review of the early literature on how spatial ability relates to school performance showed that spatial aptitude predicted higher performance in shop and industrial design courses, in math (especially geometry), and in university-level engineering courses. Higher science grades were also correlated with spatial ability. Spatial ability has also shown good power for predicting dental school success (Thompson, 1942). W. V. Bingham (1937) also argued that spatial ability was important to both medicine and dentistry.

Airplane pilots generally score highly on measures of spatial ability. Guilford (1948) identified three spatial factors relevant for flying ability: Perceptual Speed, Visualization, and Length Estimation. However, there were high correlations among the three dimensions. More recently, H. W. Gordon and Leighty's (1988) study of tests used to predict training success in a sample of 600 naval student aviators found that two aspects of spatial skills (mental rotation and locating points in space) were especially discriminating of those aviators who graduated and those who dropped out of flight training. In another study, H. W. Gordon, Silverberg-Shalev, and Czernilas (1982) found that fighter pilots were more likely than bomber pilots, navigators, and helicopter pilots to score highly on a measure of spatial ability and to show a pattern of right-brain lateralization.

Right-sided abilities were measured by three tests in Gordon's Cognitive Laterality Battery (see H. W. Gordon, 1986): Orientation (determining whether a rotated three-dimensional figure is the same as that originally presented); Localization (reproducing on an answer sheet the location of an X projected in a black frame on a slide); and Form Completion (identifying a picture whose parts were partially erased). Fighter pilots performed in a superior manner on these abilities and scored significantly higher than both other occupational groups and a normal comparison group. Performance on those measures was positively associated with success in the pilot training program. Among other findings of this study is the need to examine occupational subgroup differences: All flying personnel, for example, may not require spatial ability to the same degree. Perhaps career assessors can use spatial ability test results to help clients in professional training programs for pilots or engineers, among others, to select an appropriate area of specialization.

The differential influence of spatial ability in other occupational subspecialities has not been adequately studied empirically. Diverse occupations with many areas of specialization (e.g., medicine, engineering, law, psychology) may require separate ability and interest profiles for each area of specialization. Note, for example, that industrial psychologists are included in the U.S. Employment Service's (1957) list of occupations requiring a high degree of spatial ability, whereas other applied psychology specialities do not appear on the list.

Although Realistic (technical and engineering) and Investigative (medical, dental, and scientific) occupations are especially likely to show an association between spatial ability and occupational success, they are not the only areas in which spatial abilities are relevant. Spatial ability has also been found in many of the Artistic professions. Although some of the artistic professions have an obvious need for spatial ability (e.g., sculptors), reproductive and visual artists also require spatial ability (D. W. Barrett, 1945; Bryan, 1942). Architecture, which combines engineering and art (see MacKinnon, 1962, 1970), also appears to require spatial ability (see J. M. Peterson & Lansky, 1980). Gardner (1983) argued that music also requires a kind of spatial ability, an idea that has been supported by others (Lynn

& Gault, 1986; see also the music ability section that follows later). Gordon, Charns, and Sherman (1987) presented evidence arguing that right-hemisphere skills, including spatial ability, are associated with success in managerial positions, especially in more complex jobs. However, their findings have not been replicated, and others (e.g., J. O'Connor, 1943) have argued (with limited evidence) that spatial ability can be dysfunctional in management. Because the sample sizes were small and the findings were somewhat inconsistent in the Gordon et al. (1987) study, additional studies on the relation between spatial skills and managerial performance are certainly needed. It is possible that managers in particular types of business (e.g., manufacturing, transportation, or technical engineering) would benefit from spatial skills more than managers in other types of business. Finally, H. W. Gordon (1988) provided suggestive evidence that visuospatial skills are more likely to be associated with defects in reading and language achievement, at least among school children. However, children with verbosequential skills show a relative deficit in arithmetic skills. This finding may predispose students with spatial ability into object-related studies while discouraging the development of social and interpersonal skills.

To summarize, three somewhat distinct occupational clusters appear most consistently to make use of spatial ability: engineering and technical (Holland's, 1985b, Realistic and Investigative groupings), scientific (Investigative), and artistic (especially the visual arts). It is presently unclear whether the same type or quantity of spatial ability is called for in all three occupational clusters or whether spatial subfactors better account for a pattern of occupational or educational success. Interests presumably interact with abilities to determine whether the same spatial aptitude would be directed toward art, music, engineering, or science (note, e.g., the Lowman et al., 1985, finding that spatial and artistic abilities clustered together in a sample of college women. Whether interests precede and direct abilities or are directed by them cannot be answered by the existing literature.

Research needs. For career assessment and counseling purposes, the greatest research need is for measures of spatial ability to be updated (at least in the last decade) with adult normative data for the general population, grouped by age (as with IQ tests) and by occupation. In addition, there is a need for multidimensional aspects of spatial ability to be examined in occupational settings. Such studies will help to determine whether spatial dimensions such as orientation, visualization, and mental manipulation relate differentially to career and occupational outcomes. Finally, more work is needed on the interactions between spatial ability, other types of ability, (e.g., general intelligence) and personality constructs.

Measurement issues. High spatial ability (although there are no exact rules for determining what level of elevation constitutes "high") is probably related to interest in and greater likelihood of success with a variety of occupations primarily related to science, engineering, and the visual arts. Conversely, low levels of spatial ability (say, below the 25th percentile on general population norms) probably point to higher verbal abilities, and success in a field requiring spatial ability would be less probable. There is inadequate data for interpreting midrange scores and for determining whether, given particular interest patterns or strong motivation, the individual intent on a particular career for which spatial ability is presumed important should be discouraged from its pursuit.

What are the best tests of spatial ability? Spatial ability has been measured in a wide variety of ways (e.g., Estes, 1942). No single test meets all of the criteria recommended for use in career assessment. The spatial subtests of the Differential Aptitude Test (Bennett et al., 1982, 1989) and the GATB have some utility, but occupational norms may not be available to the individual practitioner, and the GATB (U.S. Department of Labor, 1970, 1979) is still unavailable outside of the government, except to nonprofit institutions. Although its norms are now badly (if not inexcusably) outdated, the Minnesota Paper Form Board (Likert & Quasha, 1970), among currently published measures, still presents one of the broadest ranges of occupational normative data in a commercially available test and therefore holds a slight advantage over many of its competitors in the paper-and-pencil measures of spatial ability. Individually administered apparatus measures, such as the O'Connor Wiggly Block Test (J. O'Connor, 1927), appear to offer no particular advantage over the paper-and-pencil measures to justify their time and expense. Other measures (e.g., the Kit of Factor Referenced Cognitive Test's spatial measures; Eliot, Medoff, & Kimmel, 1987) offer valuable tests of spatial subfactors but lack norms and are not recommended for clinical use or for counseling applications by their authors (Ekstrom et al., 1976).

Because of its persistent predictive power for success in selected occupations, a measure of spatial ability should be included in any comprehensive test battery measuring career-relevant abilities. However, for reasons already discussed, career assessors must be cautious about drawing sweeping conclusions about the occupational implicatons of a single test. If a career assessee unambiguously scores low or very low on a good measure of spatial ability, and if the person has no special interests or other aptitudes necessary for spatially related occupations, then a single measure will probably be sufficient. However, if an individual scores marginally high on a spatial measure and aspires to an occupation that presumably requires the ability, then the assessor may need to administer additional tests to assess consistency of performance or ability in spatial subareas.

Other measurement factors must also be considered. Embretson (1987) advocated a dynamic testing approach in which spatial test-taking skills are first trained and then measured. The speed factor (e.g., Dziurawiec & Deregowski, 1986; Embretson, 1987) must also be taken into account in interpreting the results of spatial tests. Evidence has been reported in the literature indicating a tendency for spatial ability to decline with age (Flicker, Bartus, Crook, & Ferris, 1984; Meudell & Greenhalgh, 1987; Moore, Richards, & Hood, 1984; Puglisi & Morrell, 1986; Zagar, Arbit, Stuckey, & Wengel, 1984), but this apparent pattern may be caused more by slowed reaction time than by deterioration of the ability. Because most standard measures of spatial ability do have a signficant speeded component (indeed, some researchers believe that the ability to solve spatial problems rapidly and correctly defines the ability) it may be necessary in testing older clients to consider both a "speeded" and a "power" (no significant time limit) score. In such cases, it may be necessary to allow clients to finish a timed measure to determine if low or marginal scores are primarily due to the time factor (Tinker, 1944, described a methodology for this type of administration).

Because handedness may affect performance on spatial tasks (Burnett, Lane, & Dratt, 1982; Schachter & Galaburda, 1986; Sheehan & Smith, 1986), the assessor should routinely collect information on preferred handedness, perhaps using a measure such as the Edinburgh Handedness Inventory (Oldfield, 1971). However, there is conflicting evidence in the literature on the relation between spatial ability, hand preference, and the extent of hand preference (see Burnett, Lane, & Dratt, 1982; Casey et al., 1986; Shettel-Neuber & O'Reilly, 1983).

Sex differences should also be considered in intrepreting test results. Because women as a group characteristically score lower than men on spatial ability measures, a woman who scores high compared with both own-sex and opposite-sex norms on spatial ability measures should probably be encouraged to consider professions for which the ability is needed. For women, the assessor should determine whether the assessee's age (e.g., early pubertal status) would be expected to have an impact on the results obtained and also whether the assessee is experiencing menstruation at the time of the assessment because this may lower test scores on measures of spatial ability. Retesting may need to be conducted in such cases.

Other factors important for interpreting test results include a history of alcohol abuse, which has been demonstrated to lower spatial ability (Clifford, 1986). The examiner should also inquire whether the client is taking medications at the time of assessment because performance on many cognitive ability measures can be lowered or otherwise affected by medication (Helmes & Fekken, 1986; J. Taylor, Hunt, & Coggan, 1987). Occupational history (e.g., exposure to toxic fumes) may also lower performance on spatial tasks (Arlien-Soborg, 1984).

Investigative Abilities

Theory and conceptual issues. The Investigative occupational group contains most of the scientific professions. Although a specific scientific interest pattern or set of patterns has long been demonstrated (e.g., Roe, 1951), intellectual skills (Wolman, 1985; verbal and nonverbal reasoning and general intelligence) are most predictive of success for Investigative occupations. Both L. Gottfredson (1980) and Lowman (1987) have noted that the Investigative occupations on average require the highest educational level (and presumably the highest average level of intelligence) of all of the Holland interest types. However, one must remember that general intelligence is perhaps the single most important factor for determining job success in a variety of occupational pursuits (a point made exuberantly by Hunter, 1986).

Because clinicians are usually well trained in intellectual assessment, at least using standard measuring devices such as the WAIS–R, a thorough review of the measurement of intellectual abilities is not made in this section (see Wolman, 1985). However, Pawlik (1966, p. 552) appropriately cautioned: "For too many practicing psychologists . . . important issues begin and end with the king of abilities—intelligence." Intelligence is certainly an extremely important ability for career assessment, but by no means is it exclusively important.

The concept of intelligence itself has been under significant revision in the last decade or so. Efforts by a variety of researchers are moving concepts of intellectual functioning in new directions. Sternberg (1982a), for example, proposed a "triarchic" theory of intelligence (not without critics, see Neisser, 1983) and noted the importance of incorporating *process* in the measurement of intellectual abilities. Of special importance in Sternberg's componential approach to intellectual development (Sternberg, 1982a) is a meta-construct: the ability to recognize the nature of the problem to be solved (a construct akin to Pawlik's, 1966, Sensitivity to Problems factor) and to then select a strategy and methodology for solving it. Some problems provide lower level, routine components to solve, whereas others demand higher level organization and strategizing. Sternberg also explored the intelligence required to solve practical, real-world problems and noted that, because solutions are often culturally specific, the context in which the problem is presented must be considered (see Sternberg, 1988; Sternberg & Wagner, 1986).

*"I'm a social scientist, Michael. That means I can't explain
electricity or anything like that, but if you ever want to know
about people I'm your man."*

Drawing by Handelsman; © 1986 The New Yorker Magazine, Inc.

Virtually all intelligence theorists and analysts include factors
for verbal comprehension, verbal reasoning, and numerical reasoning in their models and factor structures of primary human
abilities (e.g., Hakstian & Bennet, 1977; Irvine & Berry, 1988;
Pawlik, 1966; Thurstone, 1938) for levels of intellect at least at
the average level or above (e.g., Benbow, Stanley, Kirk, & Zonderman, 1983). Greeno (1989) defined critical thinking as the
ability to think reflectively, rather than by rote, in the evaluation
of constructs. Gardner's (e.g., 1982a, 1983) theory of multiple
intelligence included linguistic intelligence and mathematical–
logical intelligence as separate intelligence domains. Krutetskii
(1976) found in school-age populations a number of components of math ability, including logical thinking; rapid, broad
generalization ability; flexibility of thinking; and generalized
math memory, among others. This finding may help to explain

why math is grouped by tests such as the WAIS–R as a verbal rather than as a performance (nonverbal) measure.

It is reported that reasoning abilities can be improved with systematic intervention (e.g., Stankov, 1986; Wood & Stewart, 1987). Verbal reasoning abilities appear to show a slight increase and nonverbal reasoning abilities to show a slight decrease with age (e.g., Zeidner, 1988; see also Ruth & Birren, 1985). Greeno (1989) noted that social environments can facilitate or impede the development of critical thinking skills.

Dimensionality of the construct. Broad cognitive ability tests generally find a verbal ability factor or factors (e.g., Beck et al., 1989; R. C. Johnson & Nagoshi, 1985) and often find a related but separable numerical ability factor (e.g., Hakstian & Cattell, 1974). Pawlik (1966) noted that "the two factors . . . . [of] Verbal Comprehension (V) and Numerical Facility (N) are best confirmed of all aptitude factors known." (Pawlik, 1966, pp. 546–547). Pawlik also noted that a Verbal Comprehension factor had been found in virtually all factor-analytic studies (over 50 to that point) in which verbal tests were included. Among primary abilities, R. B. Cattell (1987) identified verbal ability and numerical ability (the ability to manipulate numbers) as well as deductive (logical evaluation) reasoning and inductive reasoning.

The Kit of Factor Referenced Cognitive Tests (Ekstrom et al., 1976) includes several cognitive aptitude factors in a model of primary abilities. These include (with the number of marker variables in parentheses following each aptitude): Verbal Comprehension (5), Logical Reasoning (4), General Reasoning (3),[1] and Number (4), as well as several fluency measures, which include cognitive abilities.

Verbal abilities have generally shown high intertest correlations, so that a single factor or a small number of verbal ability factors are typically found (for an alternate view, see Sincoff & Sternberg, 1987). Verbal factors generally assess understanding of words and ideas (verbal comprehension) and logical

---

[1]All variables in this factor were mathematical, which may make this analogous to the nonverbal factors of other researchers.

reasoning with words (verbal reasoning) and are typically measured by reading comprehension, vocabulary, synonyms, proverb, and analogy tests. In the verbal reasoning area, Pawlik (1966) tentatively identified three verbal reasoning factors in addition to the verbal comprehension factors: Deduction, applying a rule or a general principle to a specific case; Induction, discovering a rule or a principle from case examples; and General Reasoning, whose exact meaning is somewhat ambiguous. He noted that several theories have posited a single logical reasoning factor. As have other factor theorists, R. B. Cattell (1987) differentiated these factors from those associated with more "creative" abilities, such as word and ideational fluency. A factor analysis of both convergent and divergent higher order thinking ability measures revealed three major factors: judgment, verbal–spatial reasoning, and an inferential/deductive factor (Fontana, Lotwick, Simon, & Ward, 1983). Taking a different approach, Gardner (1983) identified four aspects of "linguistic intelligence." Three of these seem especially relevent for career assessment: the persuasive aspects of language, its use in remembering information, and its use in educating others. The fourth has to do with the metalinguistic aspects of language.

Pawlik (1966) found numerical fluency in 40 studies. Numerical fluency, which appears to be as ubiquitous as the verbal ability factor (Pawlik, 1966), generally encompasses skill in manipulating numbers and is to be distinguished from arithmetic or higher level mathematical reasoning, which requires more complex reasoning ability. Gardner (1983) similarly differentiated isolated hyperability in numerical calculations (e.g., autistic savants with great computational skills but below normal intelligence; see P. A. White, 1988) from abstract mathematical ability. At its highest levels, the mathematical reasoning ability is removed from real-world pragmatic concerns.

Kass, Mitchell, Grafton, and Wing (1983) reported on the results of nearly 100,000 U.S. Army applicants who took the Armed Services Vocational Ability Battery, which is typical of the broadbrush ability measures. Factor analysis showed Verbal Ability and Quantitative Ability factors. Hammond's (1984) factor analysis of the 12-test GATB examined results in a sample of 1,084 Irish workers from 151 companies (about two thirds of whom were men). Hammond found not nine factors (as the GATB publishers claim) but four. The first factor encompassed the traditional verbal and numerical tests and was interpreted as being "symbolic." Other factor studies using still other measures have generally reported nonverbal ability factors (e.g., Naglieri & Insko, 1986).

Relation to other aptitudes. When multiple batteries of reasoning and general intellectual abilities are administered, verbal and numerical ability factors generally show fairly high correlations with each other (see Hakstian & Cattell, 1974; Pawlik, 1966). A high correlation between overall intelligence and verbal and numerical abilities has also been reported (Horn & Cattell, 1966), possibly enhanced by the tendency to measure general intelligence in ways that emphasize these components of the ability. However, verbal ability must be differentiated from verbal fluency, which refers to the rapid and sometimes creative production of words or selected words rather than the convergent type of verbal ability measured by most verbal comprehension tests (e.g., Richardson, 1986). Gardner (1983) noted, as have other investigators, a relation between logical–mathematical talent and musical ability. Whittington (1988) reported, on the basis of a large sample, that large differences in verbal and nonverbal intelligence were often associated with patterns of underachievement.

Occupational applications. Some recent work examining the applicability of general intelligence to occupational performance has suggested that intelligence is the best, if not the only, variable for discriminating among differing levels of performance on the same occupation (L. Gottfredson, 1986a, 1986b; Hunter, 1986). This position has often been supported by large-scale studies using measures such as the GATB, an instrument not without problems.[2]

The argument that all job performance differences are accounted for by intellectual factors has some limitations. This idea is often based on evidence that has *only* measured

---

[2]Hammond (1984), for example, found that the GATB measured not the factors it claimed but rather a smaller number of more general factors.

intellectual or closely related cognitive abilities. Although intellectual abilities may subsume a number of other career-related variables (e.g., high IQ scores are often associated with Investigative vocational interests), nonintellectual factors may certainly influence occupational choice. Moreover, meta-analyses of the relation between academic performance (highly correlated with intelligence test scores) and occupational achievement have generally shown low correlations. Samson, Graue, Weinstein, and Walberg (1984), for example, reviewed 35 studies of the relation between academic performance and occupational performance (measured by means such as income, job satisfaction, and effectiveness ratings) and concluded that only 2.4% of the variance in occupational performance was accounted for by academic achievement or intelligence test scores. Although disputed by some (e.g., Hunter, 1986; R. L. Thorndike, 1985), this finding has been echoed by others (e.g., Baird, 1985; C. W. Taylor, Albo, Holland, & Brandt, 1985; see also Arvey, 1986). Baird (1985) noted that academic performance more accurately predicts accomplishment in adult professional life if the measured academic skills are occupationally relevant.

Although the data are not as extensive as folklore and enthusiasts might suggest, evidence is reasonably clear that occupations do differ in the average intellectual performance of their members, generally in a manner reflecting the average educational level associated with the occupation (R. B. Cattell, 1987; Matarazzo, 1972; for a balanced discussion of the association between education and worker quality, see L. Gottfredson, 1980). The professions (medicine, law, accounting, etc.), for example, attract and require, on average, a higher level of intelligence and persistence than do nonprofessional, white-collar occupations. On the other hand, the same caveats that apply to averaged vocational interest data also apply to averaged ability data: Averages disguise significant differences among members of the same profession. Furthermore, an analogy between public and private schools can also be applied to occupational groupings. Students attending private schools average much higher intellectual abilities than do those attending public schools, but the range of scores is generally greater in the public schools. In like manner, the range of intellectual ability in blue-collar occupations is generally higher than in white-collar jobs. Thus, employees can be found in large manufacturing organizations who have very high levels of intelligence (abilities often effectively used by neither the possessor nor the employer), whereas few members of the professions would be expected to have low levels of intelligence. Nevertheless, minimal levels of verbal skills and reasoning ability are important even at low organizational levels (see Junge, Daniels, & Karmos, 1984).

Although intellectual abilities are important in individual career assessment, they are only one type of ability that must be examined to reveal the overall career profile. Sheer intelligence in the general intellectual sense may help to explain underachievement or boredom, but alone it is insufficient to explain many aspects of career behavior. Occupations differ systematically on abilities other than intelligence. It seems unlikely, for example, that intellectual abilities predict differential success among professional athletes, garbage collectors, artists, and musicians.

Gardner (1983) identified linguistic intelligence as a crucial ability for writers and poets. Logical–mathematical intelligence and, to some extent, verbal reasoning ability is judged to be important in math and science (e.g., McCammon, Golden, & Wuensch, 1988).

Verbal and numerical ability tests have shown predictive validity even for relatively low-level positions (e.g., Dong, Sung, & Goldman, 1985; Ghiselli, 1966; Hakstian, Woolsey, & Schroeder, 1986). Verbal abilities also appear to predict successful training outcomes (e.g., Ghiselli, 1966). For a discussion of the relation of intelligence to managerial and executive abilities, see the Enterprising Abilities section.

Research needs. Although occupational differences in intelligence have been widely assumed, the number of studies on which such conclusions have been drawn is surprisingly small. Research examining the accomplishments of those who score average or below average on traditional measures of intelligence yet who are at least minimally successful in Investigative-type occupations is needed. Verbal and nonverbal intelligence factors must be studied in relation to various occupational achievements. The relation between numerical reasoning and higher order mathematical abilities needs further study, particularly as they relate to Conventional skills in computation versus Investigative use of nonverbal reasoning abilities.

Measurement issues. The administration of standardized tests of intelligence does have a place in career assessment, especially because so many career choices are influenced by intellectual ability levels. From the career standpoint, any standard measure of intelligence with adequate reliabilities and validities can be used to determine the degree of intellectual ability possessed by the client. Short, sometimes dated, measures of verbal comprehension and numerical fluency are occasionally used in career assessment as the sole measures of intellect, but this approach has obvious limitations.

In the verbal area, most broadbrush ability measures (e.g., the Differential Aptitude Test, GATB, and Comprehensive Ability Battery) include subtests measuring verbal comprehension and verbal reasoning skills, generally measuring the latter by various analytical reasoning tasks (e.g., x is to y as a is to ___) or by other abilities related to the use of words. Most measures also include subtests measuring numerical fluency or computational ability. The Wide Range Achievement Test–Revised (Jastak & Wilkinson, 1984) provides age-specific norms for adult populations. New methodologies for the measurement of verbal reasoning skills in personnel selection have also been suggested (Colberg, 1985).

At higher levels of abstraction, more suitable for the testing of college-level individuals and above, are tests such as the Watson-Glaser Critical Thinking Appraisal (Watson & Glaser, 1980), which requires close reasoning and the drawing of conclusions from complex verbal passages.[3] In the nonverbal reasoning area, Raven's series of tests (Raven, Court, & Raven, 1977a, 1977b) continues to provide good measures of nonverbal reasoning, although the norms provided by the test manual leave much to be desired (see also Burke, 1985; Paul, 1985–1986; see also Dash & Rath, 1986). In addition, the usefulness

---

[3]This test has been criticized, however, for several of its features (e.g., Modjeski & Michael, 1983; Norris, 1988).

of the test with Hispanic populations has been reported (Powers, Barkan, & Jones, 1986).

Artistic Abilities

The Artistic group of occupations encompasses considerable diversity. Although J. L. Holland's (1985a) scheme groups all of the artistic professions into a single category, there are important differences among the talents associated with such pursuits as art, music, and writing. Even within a single Artistic occupation, such as music, types of talent can diverge considerably. Composers, musicians, and music critics all have musical talent, but each occupational subgroup has a unique constellation of abilities.

Although Holland (1985a) maintained that Artistic types are generally "creative," a person may have Artistic vocational interests and score well on artistic-related tests yet not be particularly creative in the sense of creating something that did not previously exist. Illustrative at one extreme is the musical talent expressed by autistic savants (Gardner, 1983; Minogue, 1923; Viscott, 1970), individuals of otherwise limited cognitive abilities who have a distinctive capacity to memorize and repeat music, yet whose "creativity" may be minimal.[4] At the other extreme is the specialist in musical composition who literally creates music that did not previously exist. Similarly, Helson (1978) identified distinctive personality characteristics that differentiate writers and critics of children's books, and Getzels and Csikszentmihalyi (1976) found that among artists-in-training, important differences in personality and ability differentiated those who specialized in fine arts, graphic arts, and art education. Therefore, to attribute common characteristics to all members of a large family of occupations is a risky venture.

Conceptual issues in musical ability. Theorists and factor analysts of intelligence have generally included musical ability among the primary mental abilities (R. B. Cattell, 1987; Vernon,

---

[4]However, McLeish and Higgs (1982) noted that most people with intellectual impairment are also musically impaired, so that autistic savants are not the norm among those who are intellectually limited.

1950). Gardner (1983; Walters & Gardner, 1986) included music as one of seven major "intelligences," noted that musical talent has evolutionary value, and described a neuropsychological situs for musical ability. However, possibly because of the expense of testing and the relatively narrow distribution of the talent, many standard ability batteries such as the Differential Aptitude Test and the GATB do not include measures of musical talent.

Age affects the development and expression of musical talent, which is thought to mature early (Shuter, 1968; Shuter-Dyson & Gabriel, 1981), although not in all areas (see Farnsworth, 1958, pp. 216–217). Moreover, people whose musical talent develops early may not be consistently high performers over time. For example, musical prodigies may experience a breakdown in performance as they move from adolescence to adulthood (Bamberger, 1982). Psychoacoustical perceptual discrimination abilities are believed to increase with age as short-term memory skills improve (Zenatti, 1985).

The distribution of musical talent in the general population is surprisingly unstudied. Wing's (1968) opportunity samples of persons with musical talent imply that the ability normally appears in distribution curves that are similar to those for intelligence. Favoring this view, Halpern (1984) demonstrated that nonmusicians approach new musical material in a way similar to that of musicians and obtain considerable information from new music. However, in the United States, a small percentage of the workforce will find careers in the musical area (see L. Gottfredson, 1980, 1986b); therefore, extreme talent may be needed for occupational relevance, in contrast to intelligence, in which moderate levels can be applied to a variety of occupational pursuits. A musician is highly unlikely to be successful professionally unless his or her talent is at the extreme end of the musical ability distribution. Nonetheless, much more research is needed on the distribution of music talents and on their correlation with success in music before definitive conclusions can be drawn.

Finally, there is some indication that handedness may affect musical talent. Deutsch (1978) and others (e.g., Quinan, 1922) have noted that left-handedness is associated with increased auditory or musical processing ability, especially in pitch memory. However, sinistrality is certainly not a prerequisite for musical talent, nor is dextrality a contraindication to performance ability.

Dimensionality of the construct. Seashore's (1939) well-known and still used (although not without controversy; Henson & Wyke, 1982) measures of musical talent assess six dimensions. The three best validated of these are Rhythm, Pitch, and Tonal Memory, and the remaining three are Loudness, Timbre, and Time. Although the Seashore Measures of Musical Talents are still marketed (with no updating in decades), they have not been subjected to extensive factor analyses or compared with other measures of musical talent to clearly establish what is being measured psychometrically. I now discuss those studies that have been reported in the literature.

Another well-known measure of musical aptitude is Wing's (1960) Standardised Tests of Musical Intelligence. Factorial study of Wing's (1941) musical ability battery revealed three major factors: a large general factor, a factor related to the perception and discrimination of sound qualities, and a factor related to judgment of the quality or goodness of music (see also Vernon, 1950). E. E. Gordon (1986) performed factor analyses on the Musical Aptitude Profile, still another measure of music ability. His factors differentiated between stabilized and developmental (accomplished versus potential) music ability. Teplov (cited in Shuter, 1968, pp. 237–238) hypothesized three basic musical aptitudes, including *tonality*, the ability "to sense the tonal relationships of the notes of a melody and the emotions expressed by melodic movement . . . closely connected with pitch discrimination"; the ability to *reproduce a tune when heard by ear*, which is presumably related to tonal memory; and the ability to *feel and reproduce rhythmic movement*.

Naoumenko (1982), a Russian, postulated a hierarchical system comprising both general musical talents (emotional-imaginative, rational, reproductive) and specific musical talents (rhythm, creative imagination, and "sense of closure"). Karma (1985) also suggested a way of conceptualizing musical talent that differs from the psychoacoustical approaches such as that of the Seashore tests. Karma instead proposed a cognitive-processes model of musical ability, which encompasses such musical abilities as recognizing patterns, understanding timing, and analyzing internal structures.

In contrast to other areas of ability, the factor-analytic study of musical talents remains mostly undeveloped. Drake (1939) factor-analyzed all then-published musical measures that had reliabilities greater than .31 (!) and found one general factor and three specific factors of musical ability. Farnsworth (1958) reviewed the early factor studies and noted anywhere from one general musical factor to eight highly specific factors (e.g., pitch, memory, etc.). Interestingly, in a Swedish study by Franklin (cited in Farnsworth, 1958) in which the Wing, the Seashore, and other, nonmusical tests were administered to the same subjects, two factors emerged, a mechanical–acoustic factor (on which loaded such measures as pitch, timbre, time, and loudness) and a "judicious-musical factor" (or an aesthetic factor), which pertains to the ability to make judgments about the quality of music. Because different aspects of musical ability are measured by tests such as the Seashore and the Wing, factorial studies that include multiple measures of musical ability probably provide a clearer understanding of the factor structure underlying musical talent.[5]

The use of the voice, rather than the ability to play a musical instrument, calls for still other factors. Lundin's (1967, p. 272) review of the factors that make for singing ability identified the following as relevant: *pitch intonation and control; vibrato* ("a rapid series of pulsations in the tonal stimulus, most commonly in its pitch, but . . . frequently also accompanied by pulsations in loudness and timbre"); *tonal intensity* (greater intensity is more desirable, and it is often associated with the physiological characteristics of the throat); *resonance* (at both low and high points); and *stability of tone intensity.*

Relation to other aptitudes. Although some theorists have argued that music is primarily a right-brained activity, and differences do seem to exist at least for men in how musicians

---

[5]The various music tests tend to have poor intercorrelations with each other (see Farnsworth, 1958; Shuter-Dyson & Gabriel, 1981).

and nonmusicians process information (see Hassler & Birbaumer, 1986), more recent theorizing demonstrates that a number of abilities associated both with the dominant and the nondominant hemispheres govern the expression of musical talent (Judd, 1988; Karma, 1983). Nonmusical factors also appear to be important in musical talent. Depending at least partially on the specific musical ability (e.g., composing vs. performing) and on the instrument played, these abilities may include finger dexterity, access to emotions (presumably Gardner's [1983] social intelligences), and linguistic skills (Judd, 1988; Karma, 1983; Super & Crites, 1962). Memory factors captured partially by tonal memory measures are also relevant.

Relations between musical talent and other abilities have been examined and have shown generally negative results. R. S. Morrow (1938) found little relation between musical talents (as measured by the problematic Kwalwasser–Dykema Music Tests) and mechanical and aesthetic judgment abilities. Wing (1941) found a slight relation between musical abilities and scores on intelligence measures, a result confirmed by others reviewing this literature (see Hobbs, 1985; Lundin, 1967) that may be partially artifactual to the specific measures used. For example, little relation has been shown between the Seashore measures and intelligence, whereas a stronger relation with intelligence has been shown when other criteria of musical ability are used (Mursell, 1939; see also Shuter, 1968, pp. 308–311; Shuter-Dyson & Gabriel, 1981, pp. 295–301). Lynn and Gault (1986) found a positive relation between intelligence as measured by the Raven's Standard Progressive Matrices and the Wing music measures, especially pitch change and pitch memory. Moreover, as Anastasi (1982) noted, the absence of a relation between scores on measures of music and intelligence does not mean that intelligence is not needed for success as a musician because different research paradigms may be needed to establish the connection.

A relation has been reported between scientific (especially mathematical) aptitudes and musical talents (Arenson, 1983; Revesz, 1953; Shuter, 1968; Vernon, 1951, cited in Shuter, 1968). Gardner (1983) noted a correlation between music (especially rhythm) and mathematical talents and postulated that a correlation may also exist with spatial abilities. Karma (1982) examined the relationships among acoustic ability, spatial ability, and verbal abilities in a cross-age sample of music students. Among the youngest children (9–10 years old), there was a relation between verbal and acoustic but not spatial abilities, and the girls in the sample did better on the music tests, consistent with their generally superior verbal abilities. However, the sex difference dropped out with the older music students, and a possible relation between spatial ability and acoustical ability was then found. Hassler and Birbaumer (1984) and Hassler, Birbaumer, and Feil, (1985) also reported a relation between musical talent and spatial ability but, interestingly, did not find that men and women in their sample differed on spatial abilities (possibly suggesting an atypical, preselected, or self-selected sample). In a 1-year follow-up, creative musical ability was significantly related to spatial orientation in both sexes and to spatial visualization ability for men. This study again suggests a difference between those who perform music and those create it, with spatial ability possibly being more important in the latter activity.

N. O'Connor and Hermelin (1983) compared a group of young music and art students (all identified as being exceptionally talented in their respective fields). They found that the musically gifted students, independent of intelligence, demonstrated higher language-processing abilities than did the artistically gifted students, who were better at comparing and recognizing visually presented shapes.

Finally, artistic interests (or lack thereof) probably play an important role in determining whether latent talent will be developed. That interest may be needed to make music ability functional is widely accepted (see Shuter, 1968). Moreover, for young men, music may be regarded by some as being a feminine activity (Shuter, 1968), so that the ability may go undeveloped.

Occupational applications. Commonly used measures of musical ability (e.g., the Seashore Measures of Musical Talent, the Wing, and Gordon's Musical Aptitude Profile) have had a mixed pattern of predicting occupational success. Most studies (e.g., Drake, 1933; Harrison, 1987a, 1987b) validating musical ability measures have been instructor ratings or grades in music courses as criteria rather than criteria related to ultimate success as musicians. Highsmith (1929) reported high correlations between scores on the Seashore measures and course grades (although intelligence was a better predictor of academic music courses); however, the reliability of the Seashore measures was low. When professional musicians have been the subject of investigation, questions have been raised about their performance on measures such as the Seashore because they do not always perform in an excellent manner on this test (Henson & Wyke, 1982).

Research needs. More studies are needed examining the factor structure of musical talents utilizing both measures of psychoacoustical ability (such as the Seashore) and measures of aesthetic judgment (such as those included in the Wing and the Gordon). An evaluation is also needed comparing psychological instruments not only with teacher ratings but also with long-term success in the field of music. Finally, there is a need for more careful analysis of the relationships between musical talent and other areas of ability, such as social and interpersonal abilities (particularly, orientation to one's own feelings and to others' feelings), physical abilities (when psychomotor performance is important, as in stringed instruments), and scientific talent.

Measurement issues. A variety of measures of musical ability have been developed over the years, many no longer commercially available and many with serious problems of poor reliability or technical inadequacy (e.g., Mills, 1984). Excellent early reviews of tests have been provided by Drake (1933), Farnsworth (1958), Lehman (1968), Shuter (1968), and Wing (1968). As was the case when these reviews were published, there is still no universally accepted measure of musical ability, and problems remain with all of the commercially available measures of musical talent. The career assessor must be very clear about the goal of measuring musical ability. Identifying the presence of musical ability is a different task from differentiating among the gradations of talent for those already identified as musically gifted. Different instruments have value for these separate purposes.

Three measures of musical ability continue to dominate the literature despite significant problems with each and despite their dated vintage. These are the Seashore Measures of Musical Talents (Seashore, Lewis, & Saetveit, 1960), the Wing Standardised Tests of Musical Intelligence (Wing, 1968), and the Musical Aptitude Profile (E. E. Gordon, 1965). Each measure takes a somewhat different approach to assessing musical ability. These tests are compared in Table 3.1.

The Seashore tests were developed as a measure of acoustical perception on the premise that the constructs measured should be relatively independent of training influences and should reflect basic, fundamental aspects of musical talent. Critics (well summarized by Lehman, 1968; Wing, 1968) have put forth a variety of arguments against the Seashore and have challenged its reliability and mixed pattern of validity as well as its basic premise. Moreover, Wing (1968) noted that the degree of precision imbedded in the Seashore measures exceeds that which may be needed even by exceptionally accomplished musicians. Also, the subtests may differentially apply to success with different instruments and in different cultures. Stringed instruments, for example, require a great deal of sensitivity to pitch (Shuter, 1968). Farnsworth (1931) also noted that different cultures place more and less emphasis on varying pitches, stating, for example, that music from Eastern cultures is less pitch sensitive than that of Western cultures. Moreover, the unusually fine gradations of psychoacoustical characteristics on the Seashore may require discriminatory power exceeding that needed to be a successful musician. Shuter therefore argued that searching for cutoff scores when using the Seashore may be more promising than accepting the assumption that more is better. Nonetheless, the Seashore measures are actively used and are also used in some neuropsychological testing batteries because at least some aspects of musical ability are centered in specific parts of the brain. Three subtests seem to have the best reliability and validity: Rhythm, Tonal Memory, and Pitch. Drake (1933), for example, found the Pitch subtest to be the best of the Seashore measures in predicting musical academic criteria (exam and principal ratings. Similarly, Highsmith (1929) found the best reliabilities on an earlier version of the Seashore for the Pitch and Tonal Memory subtests.

The interpretation of performance on the Seashore measures is not uncomplicated. What is desired is not that the person being evaluated score at the top of the various Seashore scales but that some minimally acceptable level of basic psycho-acoustical skills be demonstrated. Seashore himself, according to Brennan (1926), believed that scoring at the 50th percentile demonstrated sufficient musical skills (as measured by his tests) for musical performance. Unfortunately, no reliable cutoff scores are available that would provide validated minimal cutoff scores, and the test manual is unhelpful in this regard.

The Wing measures use only piano music and consist of subtests somewhat similar to Seashore's, including chord analysis (requiring the subject to identify the number of pitches present in various chords), a memory test (judging whether notes in two series are the same or different), and pitch change (judging whether chords are the same or different), along with rhythmic accent, harmony, intensity, and phrasing (measuring musical acuity and preferences for different types of music). Shuter's (1968) review of the Wing tests noted that the Chord Analysis test successfully discriminated among a carefully selected group of music students (Eastman School of Music) with presumably high musical talent, although the Pitch Change and Memory tests, which are highly associated with a general musical factor, were not as differentiating of overall music student competency. On the other hand, these two subtests may be good at identifying less talented musical students. Shuter (1968) noted that the appreciation subtests of the Wing measures were not useful with very young children but discriminated between average and weak music students. Other evidence suggests that the Appreciation of Phrasing test, which requires judgment as well as perception, may be useful for differentiating between groups with and without musical ability.

The Wing measures, if used as a whole, are long (60 minutes). They are not readily accessible in the United States and may have limited usefulness in non-British cultures (Lehman, 1968; Rudocy & Boyle, 1979).

Table 3.1

Comparison of the Seashore, Wing, and Gordon Musical Tests

Component	Seashore	Wing	Gordon
Rhythm	Rhythm Are two series of notes the same or different?	Rhythmic Accent Are two series of notes the same? If different, which is preferred?	Rhythm Imagery: Tempo Is the tempo in two passages of music the same or different? Rhythm Imagery: Meter Are the accents the same or different in two passages of music?
Tone	Tonal Memory Which note in a second set has been changed?	Memory Test Are 30 pairs of melodies the same or different? If different, which note was changed?	Tonal Imagery: Melody Is a second passage with added notes the same or different from the first if the added notes were removed? Tonal Imagery: Harmony Similar to Tonal Imagery: Melody except that bass and melody are present. If added notes in a second playing were removed, would lower voice be the same?
Pitch	Pitch Is a second note higher or lower in pitch than the first?	Pitch Change Are two chords the same or is the second pitched higher or lower?	

(table continues)

Table 3.1   (*continued*)

Component	Seashore	Wing	Gordon
Chord Analysis		Chord Analysis How many notes are present in a series of chords?	
Loudness	Loudness Which of two notes is loudest?	Intensity Are two series of notes equally loud? If not, which is preferred?	
Timbre	Timbre Are two tones the same or different in tonal quality?	Harmony Are two series of notes harmonized the same? If not, which is preferred?	
Timing	Time Is the second tone longer or shorter than the first?		
Phrasing		Phrasing Rhythmic Accent, Harmony, Intensity, and Phrasing all have an evaluative and aesthetic component.	Musical Sensitivity Style: Which of two tempos is best? Phrasing: Which of two phrasing patterns is more desirable? Balance: Which of two endings to a passage is more desirable?

E. E. Gordon's (1965) Musical Aptitude Profile (MAP) is a long (3 sessions of 50 minutes each) but potentially valuable measure of musical abilities, especially for use with students of identified musical talent. The subtests on this measure include Tonal Imagery (Melody and Harmony), Rhythm Imagery (Tempo and Meter), and Musical Sensitivity (Phrasing, Balance, and Style). Like the Wing, Gordon's MAP uses actual musical instruments rather than specially generated sounds; however, it uses several stringed instruments, not just the piano, and also makes use of professionally trained musicians. Reported reliabilities for the combined scores are good, and the measure has shown reasonably good validity (Lehman, 1968). Harrison (1987a) recently published a 5-year follow-up study of 135 college freshmen who had completed musical measures on the MAP. With grades in music theory and applied theory as a criterion, the best validity coefficients were obtained by the Tonal Imagery, Rhythm Imagery, and Composite scores.

As a tool for differentiating between musical talent and nonmusical career-related abilities, the Seashore appears to be helpful, especially because of brevity. The three subtests of Pitch, Tonal Memory, and Rhythm appear to have the best validity and are probably sufficient for differential screening in a comprehensive career battery. However, when musical talent is indicated (either by a screening test such as the Seashore or by avocational or educational history), the lengthier measures of musical talent should be considered, especially the MAP. The Wing measures may have limited utility in the United States.

Other measures have been developed for screening musical talent, but many of these were validated for use with elementary schools, and few have adult norms (see Mitchell, 1985). The Australian Test for Advanced Music Studies has been favorably reviewed (Colwell, 1985; Wehner, 1985) but may be difficult to obtain in the United States. Reviews of other measures are available in the literature (Lehman, 1968).

It remains true, however, that subtle differentiation of musical talent is best evaluated by expert judges. Therefore, if the career assessor determines that musical talent is the assessee's special talent and interest, trained professionals will be needed to review samples of the person's performance. However, people with musical or other artistic talents often seek out career counseling not so much to determine whether they have the talent but because they need to know what other options they might have, given the intensely competitive nature of the performing arts and the limited number of musicians and artists who are able to support themselves through their artistic efforts.

Conceptual issues in art. Gardner (1983), one of the major researchers on the development of artistic abilities (see Gardner, 1973, 1982a) did not identify artistic ability as a separate "intelligence," although he did review artistic talents in discussing his concept of "spatial intelligence." Vernon (1950) grouped artistic abilities under the category of aesthetic discrimination. R. B. Cattell (1987; Hakstian & Cattell, 1978b; Hakstian et al., 1982) identified both aesthetic judgment ability (the ability to "detect examples of adherence to basic principles of good art or designing"; Hakstian et al., 1982, p. 7) and representational drawing ability ("the ability to draw accurate reproductions of stimulus figures"; Hakstian et al., 1982, p.8) as separable primary abilities. Interestingly, the representational drawing ability loaded on a Visualization Capacity factor, whereas aesthetic judgment ability had its highest loading on a factor labeled General Retrieval Capacity and was described as the "capacity for the retrieval of concepts or items from long-term memory storage" (Hakstian & Cattell, 1978b, p. 663). Pawlik (1966) did not specifically identify art abilities in his model of cognition and aptitudes but did identify a "visual thinking" cluster of aptitude variables that were associated with speed of perception, spatial visualization, and gestalt perception. Similarly, R. B. Cattell's constructs refer to the capacity for re-creative art or drawing, not necessarily the ability to create new works of art that will be recognized as substantial or significant. Getzels and Csikszenthmihalyi's (1976) noteworthy study of art students identified the importance of differentiating between those able to do well with a presented problem (e.g., creating a graphic illustration for marketing a product) and those able to devise a new solution to an artistic task. For the latter, they noted the importance of "problem finding," which requires the artist to define the problem to be worked on as well as its

solution. This approach appears to be critical to successful performance in art and may differentiate those who are able to
draw or re-create from those who have the capacity to create
important works of art.

N.C. Meier (1942) noted that in his study of 40 artists "of
significance," all had been producing art at an early age. The
role of parental encouragement and family background in the
successful development of both artistic and musical talent has
been noted by many researchers, including Freeman (1984).
J. M. Peterson (1979) reported a tendency for students in design,
art, and architecture (and, to a lesser extent, engineering) to
exceed the expected rate of left-handedness and (J. M. Peterson
& Lansky, 1980) for left-handed architecture students to be
overrepresented among highly rated students. Left-handedness appeared in this study to be associated with greater "visual
thinking" ability, contrasted with those students whose approach was more "cognitive/conceptual." Although current
thinking about the laterality of brain functioning is rapidly
changing (see Geschwind & Galaburda, 1985b), success in art
may be associated with relatively superior visual thinking ability (normally associated with right-brain functions).

Artistic and aesthetic abilities are also relevant in a variety of
occupations other than art. Musicians, writers, artists, actors,
and poets are obvious examples of artistic professional groups,
whereas advertising executives, graphic artists, and managers
of creative groups represent less obvious applications of artistic
talent. Whether there is a generally "creative" trait common to
a number of different occupations, including art, remains un-
settled. J. P. Guilford (1957) believed that fluency, originality,
and evaluative factors were especially important in the arts but
also argued for the presence of specific factors depending on
the type of creative work.

Dimensionality of the construct. Dewar's (1938) early analysis of the factor structure associated with a number of art ability
measures (e.g., the Meier–Seashore, the McAdory Art Test,
and the Bulley and Burt "postcards" of art judgment) reported
only a single artistic factor in a sample of high school girls.
However, N. C. Meier (1939, 1942) and most subsequent
investigators have reported a number of dimensions believed

to be important in artistic production. These included aesthetic judgment ("probably the most important single factor," N. C. Meier, 1942, p. 156), creative imagination, perceptual facility (sensitivity to the visual world), greater absorption and retention of visual materials, drawing skills, manual and motor skills, at least average intelligence, perseverance, and high levels of energy and persistence. N. C. Meier's "aesthetic judgment" (or aesthetic sensitivity) has been identified by several researchers as being important (see, for example, Dreps, 1933). N. C. Meier (1928) defined the construct as the

> ability to recognize compositional excellence in representative art-situations, or the ability to sense quality (beauty?) in an aesthetic organization. It is the ability which are the artists manifest, to arrange, to re-arrange, and to select, the arrangement superior in organization; also to know when a composition has in it too much or too little, when the light and shade relations are correct, and when its elements are in conformity with the principles of aesthetic structure. (p. 185)

Getzels and Csikszenthmihalyi's (1976) work suggests that artistic ability encompasses a number of dimensions including aesthetics, problem finding and solution, as well as spatial skill in perceiving and manipulating objects. Getzels and Csikszenthmihalyi's work also confirms that there are differences among those who specialize in one aspect of art or another (e.g., graphics art v. fine arts).

Hermelin and O'Connor (1986), in a small-sample study, found that 12–14-year-old subjects gifted in art and mathematics had superior visual recognition memory compared with IQ-matched subjects and that the artistic youth were especially good at constructive imagination, given very few cues, whereas the mathematical youth exceeded all groups in solving verbally presented spatial problems. Rosenblatt and Winner (1988) also examined the importance of visual memory for artists and non-artists. They found that artistically able students had better incidental visual memory (i.e., the capacity to recall visual information when that was not part of the instructional task) for two-dimensional (although not for three-dimensional) tasks. They also noted that visually gifted children (for whom art would be one manner of directing the ability) possess a variety of skills, including focused attention, visual–motor mastery allowing for representational accuracy, aesthetic abilities, and creativity allowing unusual compositions to be produced.

Relation to other aptitudes. Artistic ability has been demonstrated to be related to spatial abilities (Gardner, 1983; Lowman et al., 1985). However, Bryan (1942) found that students at the highly competitive Pratt Institute scored only in the average range (compared with general population norms) on the Revised Minnesota Paper Form Board. Interestingly, no sex difference was found on the spatial ability test, suggesting the possibility of an atypical sample. There was, however, a difference by major, with art education students (mostly women) earning the highest scores on this measure. R. S. Morrow (1938) examined the relation between musical, mechanical, and artistic (aesthetic) ability using several measures, including the Kwalwasser–Dykema Music Tests, the Meier–Seashore Art Judgment Test, and the Stenquist Assembly Test. Factor analysis showed that art test scores were more strongly associated with mechanical ability than were scores on music measures. Because mechanical abilities are strongly associated with spatial abilities (which were not measured in the Morrow study), it is possible that the results actually demonstrated the predictable relation between art and spatial ability rather than a theoretically unexpected interaction between mechanical and artistic abilities.

The relation between artistic talent and other abilities has been examined by other researchers. Dreps (1933) found a negative relation between art abilities (measured by several different tests) and motoric abilities. The relation between artistic ability and general intelligence has been the object of much attention and speculation. Bryan's (1942) study of highly selected art students found that her overall sample scored about average for college students on an intellectual measure, although the men were inferior to the women on this dimension. Among youth, an association has been found between drawing ability and intelligence (see, e.g., Parvathi & Natarajan, 1985).

Indeed, among the very young, picture drawing may be used to assess intellectual ability, as in the Goodenough–Harris procedure for assessing intellectual development on the basis of a count of the number of body parts included in the picture of a person (Goodenough & Harris, 1963). Farnsworth and Issei (1931) found little relation between the Meier–Seashore Art Judgment Test and intelligence. Tiebout and Meier (1936) studied an elementary school sample from Des Moines, a high school (Grades 7–12) sample from Milwaukee selected for their artistic ability, and a group of 50 artists of national prominence. Using the Kuhlman–Anderson measure of intelligence, these researchers found little relation between intelligence and rated artistic production, although both artistic groups exceeded the average scores on intelligence, with the professional artists scoring on average in the superior to very superior range.[6] That artistic ability *can* be separable from general intellectual abilities is illustrated by the finding of artistic autistic savants, that is those with highly developed artistic ability but seriously impaired intellectual abilities (e.g., N. O'Connor & Hermelin, 1987).

N. O'Connor and Hermelin (1983) reported that students gifted in the visual arts were superior to those gifted in musical ability on recognizing and storing nonverbal material. These researchers also reported that artistically gifted youth appear to process visual material in a different manner (simultaneously rather than sequentially) than do other gifted students.

Perhaps the most comprehensive study of art students' abilities and personality characteristics was conducted by Getzels and Csikszenthmihalyi (1976). Students from the Art Institute of Chicago, a prestigious art training center, constituted the sample. Complete data were obtained from 179 students, or 56% of all second and third-year students in the school. Four major fields were represented: fine art, industrial art, advertising art, and art education. A number of psychological measures were used in addition to extensive evaluations of actual art products. Cognitive ability tests included the Wonderlic

---

[6]This study was flawed in that the intelligence measure was collected through the mail and only about 25% of the targeted sample of 200 participated.

Personnel Test I, Unusual Uses subtest of the Torrance Tests of Creative Thinking, Brick Uses, Things Categories, Object-Question Test, Word-Associate Test, Hidden Shapes, Match Problems III, Spatial Visualization subtest of the Guilford–Zimmerman Aptitude Survey, Perceptual Memory, and Welsh Figure Preference Test. On the intelligence measures, the art students scored at the college average, except on a speeded test of intelligence (the Wonderlic) that yielded scores, especially for men, that were lower.[7] All subjects exceeded the college norms on the Spatial Visualization. This difference was especially strong for women. Similarly, the art students exceeded college norms on the Welsh Figure Preference Test. Although normative data were not reported for the creative ability measures (Brick Uses, etc.), scores revealed substantial differences in the expected direction between high- and low-performing art students.

G. Clark and Zimmerman's (1983) review of 70 years of studies on the identification of artistic talent concluded that no single ability factor is associated with artistic talent and that measurement of diverse characteristics must therefore be made.

Occupational applications. Because people with artistic skills are often selected for jobs or assignments on the basis of work samples, psychological screening measures may best be used as a preliminary screen of artistic talents and to assess artistic vocational interests. Predictive validity studies of the major measures of art ability are somewhat inadequate.

Carroll (1933) found reasonably good correlations between the Meier Art Judgment Test (MAJT; then called the Meier–Seashore Art Judgment test) and art teacher ratings and found that this measure was superior to the McAdory Art Test on this criterion. H. O. Barrett (1949) found the Meier to have some value in predicting to the criterion of expert evaluation of actual art work but to have less value in this prediction than school grades. N. C. Meier's (1928) original research on the measure revealed that it differentiated appropriately among criterion groups, with art faculty scoring the highest. D. W. Barrett (1945)

---

[7]However, neither of the two measures can be regarded as an adequate measure of intellectual ability. The second measure used the right–wrong cognitive items on the 16PF.

found the MAJT to show good discriminating power for differentiating between art majors and control populations (although the means of both art majors and control groups were high compared with typically reported norms). A weighted battery of tests was recommended for testing aesthetic judgment, values, spatial ability, and interests.

Research needs. More sophisticated measures of artistic talent and better understanding of the dimensions of artistic ability are sorely needed. Research is needed to differentiate the ability patterns of various types of artistic professionals (e.g., graphic designers v. painters). Relations among existing measures of artistic ability need to be better understood.

Measurement issues. Although several measures of artistic ability have been generated over the years (see Kintner, 1933, for a review of early measures), many are no longer commercially available (e.g., McAdory's [Carroll, 1933]; J. P. Guilford & Guilford's [1931] line-drawing measure). Dewar (1938) compared several tests of artistic ability in a sample of 338 high school girls. Measures included the MAJT, the McAdory Art Test, and Bulley and Burt's measure of artistic appreciation (Bulley, 1933). High correlations among some but not all of the measures were reported, and the author noted a single general artistic factor. The best predictor (using teacher ratings as the criterion) came from the Bulley–Burt "postcard" measures, although the MAJT also had generally high correlations. The MAJT (Meier, 1940) was until recently still available commercially and has some utility (those still having access to the measure, however, may be able to obtain permission from the publisher to reproduce it). Scores on the MAJT have been reported to be relatively unaffected by training in art (Carroll, 1933). Prothro and Perry (1950) reported no sex differences in a sample of college and high school students but did find a racial difference (Blacks scored lower on the measure). Dreps (1933) found relatively high correlations among the MAJT, the McAdory Art Test, and Lewerenz's (1927) art tests, although the sample sizes were small and there was unique variance associated with each measure.

The Comprehensive Ability Battery (CAB; Hakstian & Bennet, 1977, 1978; Hakstian et al., 1982) includes both an aesthetic measure and a measure of reproductive drawing ability, for which normative data are available for high school and college students and for a few "convenience samples." The validity data for this measure are minimal (Nichols, 1985; K. R. White, 1985). The Horn Art Aptitude Inventory is still published and includes a sketching as well as an imagery exercise. However, validity studies for the Horn are limited. Some of the early tests of artistic measurement, such as the McAdory Art Test, are no longer commercially available.

In addition to a measure of aesthetic appreciation, the career assessee who has strong artistic interests might also be administered a measure of color vision such as the Dvorine Color Vision Test (also called the Dvorine Pseudo-Isochromatic Plates) or, when extreme sensitivity to subtle color changes is important, a measure such as the Farnsworth–Munsell 100-Hue Test for the Examination of Color Discrimination.

Other artistic abilities. Few primary abilities are uniquely relevant to nonmusical and nonartistic areas of creative performance. Although Mumford and Gustafson (1988) made a valuable effort to identify a "creativity syndrome" that would cut across multiple types of creativity, their emphasis was more on characteristics of personality that influenced creativity than on ability structures per se.

In activities such as writing, acting, and dance, with the latter two being illustrative of the performing arts, there are probably unique abilities that are necessary for successful performance in each profession. Such abilities have been largely unidentified and unexamined, however, and certainly popular and widely studied primary abilities (such as spatial, verbal reasoning, and so on) have yet to be applied systematically to these areas. Thus, dance may well require, on the ability side, several physical and kinesthetic primary abilities, but whatever the requisite physical abilities may be, they have not been carefully examined by researchers specializing in the psychology of abilities.

There are many factors that might explain the paucity of study of artistic ability profiles. Not the least of these is the fact that creative occupations are generally perceived to be tangential to society's quotidian efforts, interesting and alluring perhaps, but a low-base-rate phenomenon perhaps not viewed as worthy of extensive exploration, particularly when such drastic external selection criteria apply. For most artistic occupations, the reality is that few who aspire to such fields will succeed (see, e.g., Kogan, 1990). Additionally, compared with other occupational groups, it is more difficult to obtain representative samples because there are relatively fewer individuals in the performing artist domain (see L. Gottfredson, 1980) and they often live in large metropolitan areas, particularly New York and Los Angeles. Moreover, as with architecture, performing arts professions may combine at least two major and divergent types of abilities, as well as personality and interest factors. Thus, what may differentiate a dancer from a professional athlete may not so much be the exact physical abilities required (which may not be, at least for certain types of athletics, that dissimilar) but the artistic interests and a pattern of what will be termed here, for lack of clarifying literature, a personality characteristic. The differentiating personality characteristic may be the self-centered, somewhat narcissistic capacity to rely on one's *self* as the medium to translate a creative "problem" into an artistic expression or solution (see Csikszentmihalyi & Csikszentmihalyi, 1988).

This "self" centeredness in many Artistic occupations is identified by MacKinnon (1962) in his differentiation of *scientific* and *artistic* creativity. The former involves the scientist as a translator between externally defined reality, whereas the artistic creativity necessitates the creator to externalize one's own self to the public arena. Thus, a quasi-ability (in fact, a hybrid ability–personality construct) potentially differentiating many performing artistic ability patterns and, say, scientific ones is the intense focus on self as the means for creating. Partly related is Csikszentimhalyi and Csikszentimhalyi's (1988) construct of "optimal" or "flow" experiences, which may be crucial components of many types of artistic and creative achievement and which identify a type of intrinsic motivational pattern by which the work itself provides one's primary source of reward. Other characteristics (again posited in the interspace between abilities and personality characteristics to be discussed in more detail in chap. 5) include (a) tolerance of ambiguity; (b) psychological openness to new experience (often appearing, for men, as elevations on measures of psychological femininity; see chap. 4);

(c) independence; (d) nonsociability; and (e) the aforementioned intrinsic motivation pattern (Arieti, 1976; Barron, 1972; J. P. Guilford, 1950, 1959; Roe, 1946, 1952; C. W. Taylor, 1964; Torrance, 1965; Vernon, 1970).

Although obviously not an ability pattern per se, the presence of psychopathology, especially of affective disturbances (most notably manic-depressive or cyclothymic disorders) is a concomitant of extreme artistic talent at a level far exceeding population-expected levels (see Andreason & Canter, 1974; Andreason & Powers, 1975; Goodwin & Jamison, 1990). To this list of common characteristics or working conditions of creative individuals for performing artist one might also add persistence in the face of a known early demise to one's career, or in the case of actors, to known conditions of unemployment throughout what is likely to be a very brief career (see Kogan, 1990).

Space does not permit extensive explorations of each type of artistic talent. A few suggestive factors can be noted, however.

Writing. As a group, writers are often rated near the top of various lists of the average intelligence scores found among members of various occupational groups (R. B. Cattell, 1987; Matarazzo, 1972; see also Wallace & Walberg, 1987; Williams, Winter, & Woods, 1938). However, although general intelligence would be an expected characteristic of writers, the studies supporting such conclusions are inevitably small and flawed. Moreover, one would expect to find within-groups occupational differences among writers. Groups of writers, for example, whose job involves both extensive social contact *and* writing (e.g., journalists), would not be expected to be as intellectually talented as writers whose job involves highly independent, solitary activities. Other ability factors expected to relate to writing would include (a) verbal fluency and (b) planning and goal-directedness (Ackerman & Smith, 1988; Hayes & Flower, 1986; Wallace & Walberg, 1987). Expert writers incorporate both ease with the creation of words and an internal "critic" that enables them to shape and direct what is written (Townsend, 1986). For nonfiction writers at least, so-called domain knowledge (i.e., content knowledge) is also relevant and can be differentiated from a discourse component (McCutchen, 1986); the latter implicitly makes use of knowledge of writing or textual structure (see

Englert, Stewart, & Hiebert, 1988). This factor and its complexity are noted by writer Annie Dillard (1989):

> Every book has an intrinsic impossibility, which its writer discovers as soon as his first excitement dwindles. The problem is structural; it is insoluble. . . .Complex stories, essays and poems have this problem, too—the prohibitive structural defect the writer wishes he had never noticed. He writes it in spite of that. He finds ways to minimize the difficulty; he strengthens other virtues; he cantilevers the whole narrative out of this air and it holds. (p. 23)

Nonability factors associated with writing include the capacity to work alone, which would be associated with commonly encountered personality characteristics of writers. These include introversion, neuroticism (especially manic-depression; see Goodwin & Jamison, 1990), sensitivity to moods (Powell & Brand, 1987), and independence (Mohan & Tiwana, 1987). An unusually high rate of substance abuse has also been described (Dardis, 1989; Goodwin, 1988; Hayter, 1988). Subtypes of writers must be examined and become better researched because, for example, in Jamison's (1989) work, although affective disorders were much more commonly encountered among eminent British writers than in the general population (a finding mirrored in samples of American writers by the research of Andreason; see Andreason & Canter, 1974; Andreason & Powers, 1975), poets, playwrights, and biographers differed in the extent of their experience of the disorder, with biographers being the least affected. Similarly, Helson (1978) found several differences in the psychological makeup of a group of writers and a group of critics. Similarly, Barron (1972) described many "nonrational" experiences in creative writers that might not be expected in writers of nonfiction.

Professional dance. In addition to kinesthetic and physical abilities, dancers have been reported to be unusually sensitive to the perception of movement and oriented toward feeling and intuition (Kincel & Murray, 1984). Although their careers are short (Pickman, 1987), they tend to see themselves as participating in an important undertaking with a known early demise (Kogan,

1990). On the negative side, there is a high incidence of preoc-cupation with weight and body condition, with delayed men-arche, amenorrhea, anorexic disturbances, and preoccupation with food commonly reported in the literature (Braisted, Mellin, Gong, & Irwin, 1985; Brooks, Warren, & Hamilton, 1987; Lowenkopf & Vincent, 1982; Weeda & Drop, 1985). Even young dancers may experience problems with poor self-esteem (Bakker, 1988).

Acting. The essence of acting involves assuming the identity of someone else and making that character believable (Barron, 1972). Actors as a group have demonstrated, as indicated in the few available scientific studies, generally high levels of psy-chopathology (e.g., Fisher & Fisher, 1981). It is difficult to know the extent to which the acting process per se attracts those with preexisting psychopathology or whether the forced unemploy-ment and underemployment so commonly found in the profes-sion contributes to the creation of anxiety and other psychological difficulties.

Other performing arts professions. Scant but incipient psycho-logical research attention has been aimed at abilities associated with other performing arts, such as comedians (Fisher & Fisher, 1981) and specialized artistic talents such as sculpting, pottery making, graphics design, and so forth, or of subtypes of artistic talent (e.g., poets versus nonfiction writers). That there are important differences among various subgroups of artistic oc-cupations is suggested by research findings such as those of Helson (1978). She found important personality differences among writers and critics of children's books. The critics were found to be more socially ascendant and conventional, whereas the writers were less conventional and more in touch with alternative states of consciousness. Conclusions about such oc-cupational groups await further research.

Social Abilities

Theory and conceptual issues. Social intelligence has been studied long and extensively (E. L. Thorndike, 1920). Despite a wealth of psychological literature, no tangible product suitable for routine clinical application has resulted. Unfortunately, some of the earliest research in this area resulted in applied measures that turned out to be overly loaded with intellectual abilities, so that a bright person could do well on a measure such as the Social Intelligence Test of the George Washington University Series and still have poorly developed social skills (Walker & Foley, 1973; see also R. L. Thorndike & Stein, 1937).

"Social intelligence" is the term apparently coined by E. L. Thorndike (1920), which is generally used to refer to abilities in the social sphere, especially abilities to understand and relate effectively to others. Thorndike differentiated among three types of intelligence: abstract, cognitive intellectual abilities; practical abilities (especially those abilities relevant in working with mechanical objects); and abilities used in working with other people (the "social intelligence" construct). "Social intelligence" as discussed in this book refers specifically to social and interpersonal abilities, not to the environmentally influenced generic aspects of intelligence labeled "social intelligence" and differentiated from so-called "biological intelligence" by writers such as J. J. Eysenck (1986). Moreover, an important distinction must be made between social abilities with occupational relevance and what Lowman (1988) termed social *dis*abilities, that is, the failure to develop the minimally acceptable social skills needed for basic social intercourse ("social competence"; Hartup, 1989).[8]

In recent years, the work of Gardner (1983), Sternberg and Wagner (1986), and Cantor and Kihlstrom (1987) has rekindled interest in this often-neglected topic. The relative neglect of social intelligence (at least compared with intellectual abilities) in the last 50 years is, of course, a phenomenon of curiosity and interest in and of itself. When thousands of studies on adult cognitive intelligence are compared with a score or so of studies on social intelligence during the same period, the disparity in research attention is striking. Part of the difficulty is associated with the inadequacy of early measures of social

---

[8]Two observations are relevant. First, Cartledge (1987) found that social skills may be important even among people with learning and occupational disabilities. Second, Hartup (1989) noted the ability to form both vertical and horizontal attachments, which is analogous in the workplace to interacting successfully with peers, subordinates, and superiors.

intelligence (see Walker & Foley, 1973), but environmental and political factors may also be a factor (e.g., women rather than men have typically excelled in this ability).

The differentiation of social and general intelligence has been a matter of continued concern because verbal measures of social intelligence are often closely linked with cognitive intellectual abilities. For example, the Social Intelligence Test of the George Washington University Series (Moss, Hunt, Omwake, & Woodward, 1955) was a widely used early measure of social intelligence that fell into disfavor because it was found factorially to be overly associated with intelligence (Chlopan, McCain, Carbonell, & Hagen, 1985; Walker & Foley, 1973). The literature on social intelligence has also been criticized for (a) the failure to consistently define social intelligence across studies, (b) an overreliance on paper-and-pencil measures, and (c) a relative absence of external criteria to demonstrate validity.

On one measure of social intelligence with fairly good supporting data, the Four Factor Tests of Social Intelligence (Behavioral Cognition) by O'Sullivan and Guilford (1976), the test authors reported somewhat more consistent support for external validity than for convergent validity. Those authors concluded that "no 'social-intelligence' measure currently has the status to serve as a calibrator for any other" (O'Sullivan & Guilford, 1976, p. 13). Although this conclusion is as appropriate today as when it was written, it is at odds with the usual tendency to validate measures of social intelligence by correlating them with other tests.

More recent findings suggest that, when social intelligence is measured by appropriate devices, especially behavioral measures, it appears to constitute a dimension of ability separable from other aspects of intelligence (Lowman, 1988). This finding is consistent with J. P. Guilford's (1967) structure of intellect (SOI) model, which long ago identified social intelligence as a separable domain. Hoffman (1981) distinguished between how people understand things and how they understand other people; the latter (which Hoffman considers to be an innate ability) developed on the basis of affect, which, through empathy, allows one to understand what other people are feeling.

Dimensionality of the construct. "Interpersonal skills," or social intelligence, appears not to be a unidimensional construct. Psychotherapists, for example, must be able to relate to disturbed individuals, to probe for unconscious meaning, and so forth, but they do not necessarily need to have good interpersonal relationships with one another or with nonpatient populations. This is illustrated in Gardner's (1983; Walters & Gardner, 1986) differentiation of two types of "personal intelligences": access to one's own feeling life, labeled by Gardner as "intrapersonal intelligence" (presumably important to novelists and to certain types of psychotherapists), and the ability to notice and make distinctions among other individuals, labeled by Gardner as "interpersonal intelligence" (needed by teachers and parents). That these aspects of social intelligence can be differentiated is suggested in a study by Aderman and Berkowitz (1983), which demonstrated that the willingness to be helpful was related to self-concern: Those who were the most preoccupied with themselves were the least likely to be helpful to another in an experimental situation. This may help to explain how an unusually perceptive novelist or salesperson, whose focus is on how observed behavior relates to a personal goal or need (to write books, to make a sale), might be socially perceptive but interpersonally unhelpful to others.

Nor may these be the *only* occupationally important dimensions of social skills. For example, Gardner's (1983; Walters & Gardner, 1986) interpersonal intelligence appears to encompass both cognition (understanding what needs to done) and action (doing it). Although there may be a high correlation between knowing what to do and being able to do it, there is no reason to believe that sensitivity to others' reactions and ability to act on that sensitivity are necessarily related, as exemplified by the splendid psychological perceptions of certain novelists and critics and their notorious socially insensitive personal lives. Unfortunately, the measurement of social intelligence is considerably less developed than other aspects of occupational ability. If no singular measure has been developed to serve as a criterion against which other measures (O'Sullivan & Guilford, 1976) can be evaluated, at least part of the problem in the development of a clinically useful measure of social intelligence lies in the variability with which social intelligence has been defined. J. P. Guilford's (1967) multidimensional model of intelligence, for example, postulated 30 different components of social intelligence, although only four measures were ever published in a form that could be used in practice (O'Sullivan & Guilford, 1976). Interestingly, the four (reduced from six; see Hendricks, Guilford, & Hoepfner, 1969; O'Sullivan & Guilford, 1975) published measures of social intelligence (Expression Grouping, Missing Cartoons, Social Translations, and Cartoon Predictions, which are subtests of the Social Intelligence Test) based on J. P. Guilford's models all relate to the ability "to recognize or understand behavioral units, classes, relations, systems, transformations, and implications" (O'Sullivan & Guilford, 1976, p. 1). Yet, job-related social abilities presumably require more than behavioral cognition; the understanding must also be translated successfully into behavior. The manifestation of social intelligence is not measured by most social intelligence tests.

Riggio (1986) identified a number of social skills, especially in the nonverbal area. These include emotional expressivity (sending nonverbal communications); emotional sensitivity (receiving and decoding nonverbal communications); emotional control (controlling and regulating nonverbal behavior); social expressivity (verbal speaking skill and the ability to engage others in social interaction); social sensitivity (decoding and understanding verbal communication skills and knowledge of the norms governing acceptable social behavior); social control (skills in presenting oneself competently in social situations); and social manipulation (the ability to manipulate social situations to affect the outcome). Unfortunately, the instrument put forth by Riggio has not yet been validated in career and occupational contexts.

More recently, Sternberg and Smith (1985) conducted studies of social intelligence as a cognitive ability. Barnes and Sternberg (1989) identified the importance of being able to decode social information for effective social and interpersonal relations. They theorized that those effective in social and interpersonal relationships are better able to judge the nature of relationships among people on the basis of nonverbal information (e.g., being able to tell whether people in photographs have a relationship with one another). Of course, if validated by additional research, this aspect of social intelligence is only one factor in a larger constellation. Its career and behavioral implications have not been tested.

Relation to other aptitudes. Because early studies used measures of so-called social intelligence that were really surrogate measures of general intellectual ability, the relation between intelligence and social intelligence remains undetermined. Presumably, intellectual factors are most important in the cognitive aspects of social intelligence (i.e., knowing the right thing to do in a social context). However, Marlowe and Bedell (1982) argued for the independence of social and general intelligence, and Tenopyr, Guilford, and Hoepfner (1966) differentiated behavioral cognition from semantic and symbolic activity. However, studies (e.g., Osipow & Walsh, 1973) have persistently reported correlations between social and general intelligence. More complexly, Hoepfner and O'Sullivan (1968) noted that the intelligence–behavioral cognition relation may differ depending on the level of intelligence; behavioral cognition tests may discriminate best with low-intelligence subjects.

A recent study by W. Frederiksen, Carlson, and Ward (1984) suggested that social intelligence needs its own taxonomic system that operates parallel to but separable from general intellectual ability. Those authors argued for the development of a taxonomy of social ability situations to facilitate the study of the skills needed in interactions calling for social intelligence. They provided one such taxonomy for measuring the interpersonal aspects of the physician–patient relationship.

Occupational applications. Suppose that nothing had been published on social intelligence as it applies to the workplace and that the researcher or practitioner were confronted with the need to create a taxonomy of work-related social abilities on the basis of characteristics of *job* duties. What would be important to include in such a listing? Clearly, this would vary from one type of work or work setting to another, and different jobs would call for different amounts of social and interpersonal activity and for different types of social interaction. For example, a grouping of occupations requiring social abilities might resemble the listings in Table 3.2.

Table 3.2
Hypothetical Taxonomy of Social Demands of Jobs

Degree of social involvement	Social job dimensions
Very high	Interacts with people more than 50% of time on the job; performs therapeutic, educative, or managing roles (e.g., business manager, nurse, psychotherapist).
High	Interacts with people 25%–50% of time on the job. Although significant time spent with others on the job, the contact may not be primary (e.g., college professor, social science researcher).
Moderate	Interacts with people less than 25% of time on job but in manner requiring social facilitation (e.g., a high-level executive).
Slight	Interacts with people some percentage of time on the job but does so in a manner in which recognition of and manipulation of peoples' feelings and reactions is minimal (e.g., a clerk in discount department store).
Low	Very limited interaction with people on the job; no requirement for therapeutic or influencing roles (e.g., theoretical physicist who does not teach, novelist).
Very low	Adequate social functioning is not only not required, but the work setting or group is anti- or unsociable (e.g., computer technician).

Even with such a taxonomy, occupations might differ in the *type* of social facilitation required. A clerk, for example, who interacts with customers throughout the day but only to greet them and to answer factual questions may require a different set of social skills than a teacher, manager, or minister (Nauss,

1973), who must interact with others to facilitate their work, to make a sale, or to motivate others. Types of social interactions with others might include in order of increasing complexity):

• talking with people face-to-face and exhibiting positive, prosocial behavior (e.g., a pleasant receptionist);

• assessing the reactions of others and attempting to influence those reactions (e.g., a good salesperson);

• matching one's own reactions to the needs manifested by others (e.g., a teacher); and

• creatively influencing others by assessing their behavior, engaging others in "relationships," transforming the behavior of others by one's own actions (e.g., a manager or salesperson).

From a career assessment perspective, at least three *occupationally relevant* aspects of social ability can be identified (O'Sullivan and Guilford, 1976; Riggio, 1986; and others; see also Macher, 1986).

First is the ability to *perceive* that a situation or task requires the involvement of others (or what can be termed *social sensitivity*).

Second is the ability to *understand* the behavior and feelings of others. O'Sullivan and Guilford (1976) called this behavioral cognition and defined it as "the ability to understand the intentions, thoughts, and feelings of others as these are mediated by nonverbal cues and insofar as these can be communicated by static materials such as drawings, cartoons, words, etc." (p. 13).

Third is the ability to *respond appropriately* in a given social situation (social behavior). However, what is "appropriate" in career and work contexts will, of course, vary with the specific demands of the situation. An "appropriate response," as noted in this section, may not always be socially desirable behavior. Manipulation of others, for example, may be needed by a manager or salesperson, whereas nurturance and support are demanded of a psychotherapist or teacher.

A few studies have examined the relations between social abilities and occupational or school outcomes. Tenopyr (1967), for example, noted that in a sample of 10th-grade high school students, behavioral cognition tests added small but statistically predictive power to the relation between cognitive ability tests and grades. She noted, importantly, that grades were also influenced by the student's ability to determine which aspects of the course were considered to be important by the teacher. Ferris, Bergin, and Gilmore (1986) found social skills (along with mental ability, imagination, and flexibility) to predict successful flight attendant performance outcomes. Other, hard-to-locate research studies examining the relation between social cognition and work or school outcomes are summarized in O'Sullivan and Guilford (1976).

From the perspective of careers and occupations, then, it is important to determine the specific nature of the social abilities required in a particular career or occupation and to distinguish between social *dys*function and social skills. For example, many jobs require at least a modicum of interpersonal skill for the employee to get along with coworkers and supervisors even though this may not be a primary factor in predicting to success on the job. A line worker, for example, might be occupationally misfit if perceived by coworkers as obnoxious and bothersome, particularly if the job (although primarily making use of mechanical and physical abilities) involved team assembly. For low-level jobs, it may not be worth the cost and effort of psychological screening in preemployment selection to rule out such social skills deficits. However, for a manager, social incompetence can have devastating effects on the organization. Salespeople, psychotherapists, and teachers, must by definition interact interpersonally with people as a significant if not major component of their work. Poor interpersonal skills would seriously impair their ability to perform the work.

In career assessment, the evaluator will ideally determine the specific social components applicable to the career in question. Then, selection of the relevant social and interpersonal abilities will be matched with the relevant career component. Because there is no empirically validated taxonomy of jobs corresponding to separate components of social intelligence, the assessor will have to exercise judgment to accomplish this task. When social abilities are not primary for a particular occupation but are still relevant predictors of success on the job, the assessor might best direct measurement efforts toward the behavioral rather than the cognitive aspects of social intelligence.

Measurement issues. The ideal measure of social and inter-personal ability would overlap modestly with intelligence and would measure behavioral as well as cognitive aspects of social intelligence. Its validity data would reveal a clear pattern of differentiating between those occupational groups high and low in social skills (e.g., teachers vs. engineers) and, within an occupational group, would differentiate between groups rated by competent evaluators as high and those rated as low on social abilities. A sex difference in favor of women would also be expected (e.g., Bronfenbrenner, Harding, & Gallwey, 1958; Shanley, Walker, & Foley, 1971). The measure would identify these who can act competently in social settings, not just those who can identify the "right" thing to do. Unfortunately, such a measure does not currently exist.

In clinical practice, it is important to differentiate between the occupations for which social skills have clear relevance for performing a job successfully from those for which they may be desirable but not crucial. (There may also be jobs for which the possession of social skills is dysfunctional, at least in the sense that highly skilled individuals may feel decidedly misfit and unstimulated.) For occupations in which social skills are clearly required, the formal assessment of these skills is desirable.

Most of the proposed or published measures of social intelligence and empathy have at best a mixed record of support in the professional literature. Note that clinical assumptions about social intelligence being adequately measured by tests such as the Wechsler intelligence scales (e.g., Sipps, Berry, & Lynch, 1987) are often false. A promising early measure, the Four Factor Tests of Social Intelligence (Behavioral Cognition) [O'Sullivan & Guilford, 1976], has recently been reissued, regrettably with no updating of the instrument or its norms (which are inadequate for career assessment purposes) and with no summarization of studies supporting the instrument's validity (e.g., Reardon, Foley, & Walker, 1979). The subtests of this measure appear to have differential validity (see Osipow & Walsh, 1973). Caution should therefore be used in drawing definitive conclusions about a person's social abilities on the basis of this measure. More recent, promising tests for the behavioral aspects of social intelligence include the Interpersonal Problem Solving Ability Test (Getter & Nowinski, 1981) and, for the measurement of basic social skills, Riggio's (1986) Social Skills Inventory. The assessor may also wish to include what would typically be viewed as personality measures of constructs such as empathy (Clark, 1980), especially using the Hogan Empathy Scale (Hogan, 1969) or the Questionnaire Measure of Emotional Empathy (Mehrabian & Epstein, 1972; see the Chlopan et al., 1985, excellent review of empathy measures) as part of a battery intending to measure social skills. There are limits to such an approach, as Gough's (1987) Empathy scale on the California Psychological Inventory (CPI) suggests. For example, when group means are reviewed, the highest average scores on the CPI Empathy scale were earned, among student groups, by those majoring in education (reasonable) and premedical studies (counterintuitive) and, among occupational groups, by Irish managers and business managers (plausible) and by architects and mathematicians (counterintuitive). It should also be noted that the empathy construct itself may be multidimensional (J. A. Johnson, Cheek, & Smither, 1983) suggesting that some but not all dimensions of empathy have occupational relevance.

Enterprising Abilities

Theory and conceptual issues. Because managerial talents are important in American society, and because industrial–organizational psychologists have largely confined their attention to the abilities, interests, and personalities of executives, a large and relatively rich literature is available. Necessarily, the present summary is abbreviated.

Somewhat surprisingly, ability variables that predict managerial outcomes in complex organizations have been small, although only a small number of variables have been systematically researched, and only in recent years has much sophistication emerged in the measurement of managerial abilities (see Guion, 1987). The modal successful manager fits a pattern suggestive of a relatively narrow distribution of abilities.

Sternberg (Sternberg & Wagner, 1986) suggested the construct of "managerial intelligence" to address the unique ability patterns of people in executive and managerial professions. However, close examination of this idea, and of the measuring devices used so far in his research, suggests that managerial intelligence is not so much a unique or separable entity but an amalgam of primary abilities and other individual difference variables (e.g., personality factors). In many respects, so-called managerial intelligence is mostly an extension of Sternberg's (1982a) metaconstruct of recognizing the nature of the problem to be solved and selecting an appropriate strategy to solve the problem.

For the Enterprising group, perhaps more than any other occupational grouping of the six Holland types, the primary abilities that predict managerial success are not abilities unique to the Enterprising area (although ultimately some may be found) but are a combination of abilities that are shared with other occupational groups. Of course, a major thesis of this book is that cross-domain variables must be examined in each career assessment. Yet, when Artistic ability patterns were discussed, for example, abilities were found that were, if not unique to that area, then certainly concentrated there. Enterprising ability profiles show a common pattern of the successful manager or entrepreneur, but it encompasses few unique primary abilities, at least among dimensions of ability currently accepted as primary abilities. Partly, this situation also reflects the artificiality of separating variables into interests, abilities, and personality characteristics as if there were no overlap among them. When there is overlap, as R. B. Cattell (1987) noted, personality variables act as much like ability variables as personality variables (see also Mayer, Caruso, Zigler, & Dreyden, 1989; Megargee & Carbonell, 1988). This also partly reflects the primitive nature of the categorization of social and interpersonal abilities because the managerial ability pattern certainly requires the ability to work with and through other people.

For these reasons, I deviate from the structure of this chapter and instead present a profile of the typical manager rather than a discussion of primary abilities. I also differentiate between subcategories of Enterprising talent (e.g., managers vs. leaders, managers vs. entrepreneurs). A preliminary note is needed on the apparent masculine bias in this section. Historically, most of the studies examining the characteristics of managers have focused on male rather than female managers. This reflects the reality that managerial ranks, until recently, were largely closed to women. Although men still predominate the managerial occupations, far more women are managers now than were in the past. Studies on female managers (e.g., Hennig & Jardin, 1977; Nieva & Gutek, 1981; Wiley & Eskilson, 1983) are mentioned when relevant, but (as noted later in this section) few sex differences in abilities, interests, or personality characteristics have been noted between successful male and successful female managers.

So many researchers and theorists have examined the duties and personal characteristics of successful managers that it is impossible to adequately review this literature in the space allotted. However, even a casual review results in the striking conclusion of consistency in the dimensions of the manager's job and in the psychological characteristics deemed important for success in the field.

A variety of definitions of the managerial job have been put forth over the years. Campbell, Dunnette, Lawler, and Weick (1970), for example, defined the managerial job as

> any set of managerial actions believed to be optimal for identifying, assimilating, and utilizing both internal and external resources toward sustaining over the long term, the functioning of the organizational unit for which a manager has some degree of responsibility. The effective manager is . . . an optimizer in utilizing all available and potential resources. (p. 105)

Ghiselli (1963), whose writings on human abilities remain valuable long after their original appearance, described the managerial job as requiring (a) the ability to direct the activities of others, (b) intelligence, (c) self-assurance, (d) identification with high occupational levels, and (e) initiative. Ghiselli (1963) elaborated that management perhaps does not represent the very highest levels of abstract thinking, but it does involve the capacity to see and develop novel solutions to problems. While not synonymous with leadership, managerial talent does manifest itself in the effective direction of others . . . it implies a willingness to depend on oneself coupled with a self-generated impetus to activity and a striving for and a willingness to accept the authority and responsibility which goes with high level positions in organizations. (p. 640)

Similarly, Miner (1978, in summarizing 20 years of role prescription theory, noted the following essential characteristics of successful managers: (a) a positive attitude toward authority; (b) a desire to compete; (c) a desire to exercise power; (d) a desire to stand out; and (e) a desire, or at least willingness, to perform routine administrative duties (attend meetings, prepare budgets, etc.; see also Nash, 1965). Note that, taken alone, any of these variables could describe the modal incumbent of many professions. Medical students are competitive, actors like to stand out, and accountants suffer routine cheerfully. It is the constellation of these traits, taken as an aggregate (particularly the attitude toward authority and toward the exercise of power), that appear to differentiate the profile from others.

Similarly, Klemp and McClelland (1986) identified sets of requisite competencies found among senior managers in two broad categories: intellectual and influence. Intellectual generic competencies included (a) planning and causal thinking, (b) diagnostic information seeking, and (c) conceptualization and synthetic thinking. Influencing competencies included (a) need for power (see McClelland & Burnham, 1976); (b) exercising power within groups; and (c) "symbolic influence," essentially, personal power by example. A final competency was self-confidence (Klemp & McClelland, 1986, p. 41). These classifications clearly illustrate the interdomain constructs and the need to examine the interaction between abilities and personality variables.

Probably the most valuable research on managerial talent to appear in the literature are the longitudinal studies conducted on the American Telephone & Telegraph (AT&T; Bray, Campbell, & Grant, 1974; Howard & Bray, 1988; see also Rychlak,

1982) and Sears (Bentz, 1985) executives. A now-outdated but still important book (Campbell et al., 1970) provides a good summary of early research literature on the abilities and personality characteristics of managers, including studies done at Exxon, at the University of Minnesota, and by the American Chamber of Commerce.

Studies such as those of AT&T (Bray et al., 1974; Howard & Bray, 1988) and Sears (Bentz, 1985) managers and executives have examined predictors of the future success of would-be executives using psychological measures of ability, interests, and personality. Of course, there is no assurance that what constitutes success in large bureaucratic organizations such as Sears and AT&T will constitute success in smaller organizations such as small businesses, but these results may at least suggest similarities and dissimilarities.

Careful examination of these studies points to a consistent picture of the successful corporate executive (more qualitative, clinical descriptions of the managerial "type" can be found in Kofodimos, Kaplan, & Drath, 1986; Kotter, 1982; Mintzberg, 1973). Men (more about women managers later) who perform better in managerial positions tend to be bright (in an applied rather than academic sense), generally well-educated, "take charge" individuals who, from an early age, excelled in competitive activities such as sports and grades and who naturally gravitated (and had done so throughout their lives) to roles in which they could be in charge. Successful managers also appeared able to sacrifice individual needs to those of the corporation and able to present themselves and their organizations positively, both in word and in personal appearance (Nykodym & Simonetti, 1987).

The modal executive has moderately high to high general levels of intelligence and education (e.g., Bentz, 1985; Campbell et al., 1970; Gakhar, 1986; Ghiselli, 1963, 1966; Howard & Bray, 1988; Jaskolka, Beyer, & Trice, 1985). There is some evidence that general intellectual ability predicts how far one will rise within a managerial hierarchy (see Korman, 1968). As Klimoski and Brickner (1987, p. 251) put it, "there seems to be no doubt that intelligence is important for managerial effectiveness." The type of intelligence used by managers, however, is applied rather than theoretical (see Wagner & Sternberg, 1985; Klimoski & Brickner, 1987; Virmani & Mathur, 1984). An ability not as well validated that has been discussed as a possible predictor of managerial success is spatial ability (H. W. Gordon et al., 1987). This modal profile appears to have some cross-cultural validity (e.g., Ansari, 1982; Ansari, Baumgarter, & Sullivan, 1982).

Personality factors have also shown relevance for predicting success in managerial occupations (e.g., Ghiselli, 1969; Olson & Bosserman, 1984). The value of positive relationships with others (a personality and ability construct) apparently lessens as one rises in the hierarchy (see Howard & Bray, 1988) but has been noted by many investigators (e.g., Ansari, 1984; Maitra, 1983), although a balance between tough-mindedness and cordiality is apparently in order. Other promising personality variables include need for achievement (McClelland, 1961) and power, especially at lower organizational levels (Erez & Shneorson, 1980; McClelland & Boyatzis, 1982). Stress tolerance, particularly of the role overload variety (too much to do in too little time), is also needed for many managerial jobs (Boyd & Gumpert, 1983). Managers and executives also typically have outgoing personality styles and good interpersonal relations (Deb, 1983) as well as interests and skills in overseeing the activities of others to get a job done (J. S. Brown, Grant, & Patton, 1981; Megargee & Carbonell, 1988). Moderately high levels of what psychologists might term *sociopathy* may also help advance one's career (see Harrell & Harrell, 1973; Lowman, 1989).

To the extent that these summaries do describe a generic managerial profile, it becomes clearer why primary mental abilities alone have not had the best track record in predicting managerial success (e.g., Korman, 1968). Assuming authority over others, interacting with subordinates in a controlling manner, tolerance for routine, competitiveness, needs for power and achievement—these are at least as much characteristics of personality as they are of ability. In addition, as with social intelligence, measurement of the interpersonal skills related to these factors is difficult to achieve in the usual ability test.

Perhaps no other career area has been studied in so much behavioral detail as "leadership" (more accurately, "managership"). Because managership has typically been studied by psychometrically sophisticated psychologists (primarily industrial–organizational psychologists), extensive factor analyses have been reported for over 30 years. No matter how measured, however, these studies have consistently shown that two factors emerge with regularity: a structural variable, typically, (and inappropriately) labeled "initiation of structure," and an interpersonal variable, typically labeled "consideration."

Managers are appropriately known as "doers," and what they characteristically do best is providing order, reaching objectives, and, above all, working with and through other people. Controlling others as a vehicle for getting things done is a central feature of the business management role. Personal needs and objectives must be consistent with and generally subordinated to the needs of the organization. Unlike artistic enterprises, in which the emphasis is on the unique product, in business and industry the typical emphasis is on mass production of the same product or service. With a hamburger chain, for example, the task is assurance that a large number of individual employees will deliver the same burger in thousands of locations. Conformity to prescribed behavioral rules have obvious survival value in such settings; conformity is valued not just as a control mechanism but also as a means of assuring quality control.[9]

Types of managers and leaders have also been discussed in the literature, and it is reasonable to conclude that there are subtypes of assessees whose career paths are appropriate to the Enterprising domain but whose paths will differ within that framework. Managers in public-sector organizations, for example, may differ systematically from those in private-sector organizations (Warrier, 1982).

Managers versus leaders. Since the publication of Zaleznik's (1974, 1977, 1989) important papers differentiating managers from leaders, it has become clear that people who make it to the top in large, complex organizations are frequently different from those who remain in midlevel positions. On Maccoby's

---

[9]This important point is often lost on clinical and counseling psychologists, who may view such behavioral prescriptions as undesirable intrusions into one's personal creativity.

(1976) clinically derived taxonomy of managerial types, leaders, in contrast to managers, emerge as closest to the "gamesman." In contrast to leaders, who are idiosyncratic, high risk takers, keen conceptualizers, and often psychologically conflicted (Kets de Vries, 1985) and complex individuals, managers emerge as "company men," "craftsmen," or "jungle fighters" who strive to get ahead along well-defined tracks. As Katz and Kahn (1978) appropriately noted, much literature on leadership describes a psychology of working within existing structures rather than creating new ones. In Zaleznik's terms, it is a psychology of managers, not leaders.

Zaleznik (1974) also differentiated leaders who manage others on a charismatic versus a consensus basis and noted the psychological characteristics that claimed to differentiate the two groups. Specifically, Zaleznik argued that charismatic leaders are inner directed, heavily influenced by their relationships with their family of origin, and behaviorally complex (mixing passivity and assertiveness), possessing the ability to inspire their followers on an affectively charged basis. In contrast, Zaleznik portrayed consensus leaders as more extraverted managers who *follow* opinion, who emphasize the past rather than the future, and who do not as easily develop an emotional attachment with their followers.

Managers versus entrepreneurs. Much recent attention has been focused, especially in the popular literature, on the psychology of entrepreneurs (those who found and manage their own companies, sometimes within a larger organizational context, e.g., Goleman, 1986; Kiam, 1986). The individual who aspires to self-employment differs from the prototypical manager in a number of ways, primarily on personality dimensions. These include a preference for individuality, an antagonism toward authority, and a willingness to take more extreme risks than is typical of managers. Not all recent research agrees with this profile, however. Hisrich (1990), among others, identified a variety of other variables associated with entrepreneurship, including existence of a family member entrepreneur role model.

Begley and Boyd (1987) compared companies led by founders with those led by managers. The entrepreneurial firms had higher growth rates, showed more competitiveness, and were

less financially successful than the managerially oriented companies. McClelland (1986), in a cross-cultural study of successful versus average entrepreneurs, found the former group to
be characterized by a proactive rather than a reactive style,
higher achievement motivation, and a greater commitment to
others. (These characteristics are hardly distinguishing of entrepreneurs, however, and might equally well describe effective
managers.)

Female managers may differ less from entrepreneurs than do
male managers. Waddell (1983), for example, found a distinction between women business owners and women secretaries,
with the former scoring higher on internal locus of control,
need for achievement, and masculinity, but not between female
managers and business owners. If women perceive fewer opportunities available to them if they perform well in a traditional
corporate hierarchy, they may be more inclined to start their
own firms, whereas men, who continue to dominate the higher
corporate levels, starting their own firms may be more likely
to do so because of a different ability or personality structure
than their corporate counterparts.

Subtypes of entrepreneurs have also been identified, including those who are in business as crafts specialists, often with
high standards, and those who are self-employed because it
represents an opportunity for rapid advancement. In an empirical study, the former group had an Enterprising–Realistic–
Artistic Holland interest coding, and the latter had an Enterprising–Artistic–Investigative interest coding (Scanlan, 1980).
Other differences were also noted.

Managers versus sales personnel. A meta-analysis of the determinants of sales performance by Churchill, Ford, Hartley,
and Walker (1985) showed personal factors, including aptitude,
to be important in predicting sales performance. Mayer and
Greenberg (1964) identified two essential psychological components for success in sales: empathy and complex ego strength
such that failure to make a sale (such failures are common) is
taken personally enough to be an inspiration for new effort but
not enough to devastate the individual or cause renewed efforts
to cease (the ego characteristic is labeled by Mayer and Greenberg as high ego drive). Empathy, or the ability to correctly

identify the psychological orientation of the sales prospect, has been noted by other researchers and writers (e.g., T. V. Rao, 1981; von Bergen & Shealy, 1982). The role of optimism and a positive, dependable approach has also been noted (e.g, Plotkin, 1987; Sprowl & Senk, 1986).

Measurement issues. As this review suggests, within the Enterprising domain, it is important at least to measure general intellectual ability, organizing ability, social and interpersonal abilities and interests, and, within the personality domain, such characteristics as dominance, need for achievement, and tough-mindedness.

Assessment center methodologies, in which multiple candidates are evaluated on a variety of dimensions, including their ability to interact with others in group activities, have shown promising validity (see Hunter & Hunter, 1984; Klimoski & Brickner, 1987; Schmitt, Gooding, Noe, & Kirsch, 1984; Schmitt, Noe, & Fitzgerald, 1984). However, such methods are expensive and may be difficult for the clinician to undertake in a small practice setting (M. R. Edwards, 1983). Most assessment center studies have shown that the overall rating of the candidate (in which data from a variety of sources are assembled clinically into a single or a small number of ratings) indicates superior validity to any single component of the assessment exercise. Components of the typical assessment center include group discussion exercises, paper-and-pencil tests, job simulation exercises such as the in-basket (see Bray et al., 1974; N. Frederiksen, 1962; N. Frederiksen, Saunders, & Wand, 1957; Hakstian et al., 1986), and various specialized measures such as Edwards's (1983) "objective judgment quotient." Many components of the assessment center methodology may not be commercially available or adequately validated. Other managerial assessment methodologies have also been reported (e.g., Childs & Klimoski, 1986; King, 1985; Miner, 1985; Weekley & Gier, 1987), and measures for specific Enterprising occupational groups have also been published (e.g., the Diamond Sales Aptitude Test; Oda, 1982, 1983).

Sex differences in the aptitude pattern associated with successful managerial performance appear to be minimal (e.g., Ritchie & Moses, 1983; Steinberg & Shapiro, 1982), although some researchers have reported selected variables on which men and women differ concerning management and sales (e.g., Anderson & Thacker, 1985; Bartol & Martin, 1987). Women may also still be at a competitive disadvantage compared with men in reaching higher levels of management (Hennig & Jardin, 1977; Kanter, 1977), although this may be changing rapidly (e.g., Keown & Keown, 1982; Tsui & Gutek, 1984; Wiley & Eskilson, 1983). Ambitious and talented Enterprising women may elect to open their own businesses as a way of dealing with perceived roadblocks to their successful performance within a traditional, male-dominated Enterprising environment.

Both age (see especially Howard & Bray, 1988) and level within the hierarchy (e.g., Ansari, et al., 1982; Cornelius & Lane, 1984; McClelland & Boyatzis, 1982) must be taken into account in deciding which variables to measure and in interpreting results. Superior levels of intellectual functioning may be required for higher levels of executive talent but may be problematic for positions in which there is little opportunity for upward mobility.

Characteristics of the organization must also be considered in evaluating personality variables. Companies that reward upward mobility (where much of the selection literature has been conducted) may differ from those that reward status quo. Job analyses should take into account the reward structure of the organization and who it "really" wants to hire; in some companies, this may be discrepant with its espoused desires.

Conventional Abilities

Theory and conceptual issues. The Conventional occupations largely involve clerical and numerical duties that are typically found in lower level positions within an organization. Because these occupations typically require the systematic manipulation of numbers or data, two abilities are expected to be the most prominent: (a) Perceptual Speed and Accuracy (PSA; Cattell's Perceptual Speed of Figural Identification [UI4]) and (b) Numerical Ability, here termed *Numerical Computational Ability* (NCA; R. B. Cattell's, 1987, Number Facilitation [UI2]). Two of Cattell's other factors (Speed of Closure and Visual Cognition) may also be relevant. If Conventional positions also require the use of machines (e.g., typewriters or adding machines), manual dexterity skills may be needed. In the few higher level Conventional occupations that exist (e.g., accountants and computer-related occupations), general intelligence and reasoning abilities may also be necessary.

Hakstian and Cattell (1974, p. 174) defined PSA as the ability "to rapidly [assess] . . . visual stimuli, usually to determine the sameness or difference of the members in pairs of such stimuli." Pawlik (1966, p. 542) identified the essential characteristic of his factor P (Speed of Perception) as being "fast speed in comparing visual configurations." The NCA factor (N, in Cattell's, 1987, scheme) refers to facility with basic mathematical processes, especially addition, subtraction, multiplication, and division, and is to be differentiated from higher level numerical reasoning, which theoretically relates more to the Investigative occupations.

Both PSA and NCA skills have been identified in a variety of research. Pawlik's (1966) Perceptual Speed factor, J. P. Guilford's (1967) Figural Identification component, and the Perceptual Speed factor of the Kit of Factor Referenced Cognitive Tests (Ekstrom et al., 1987) all appear to be referring to something similar. NCA is also well represented in the factor-analytic studies of primary abilities (e.g., the Number Aptitude factor in the Kit). Computational mathematical abilities appear to emerge naturally, independently of schooling (L. B. Resnick, 1989). R. C. Johnson and Nagoshi's (1985) study of abilities in a large, cross-ethnic sample showed that Perceptual Speed and Accuracy were separate factors.

NCA is affected by practice and memorization (see L. B. Resnick, 1989). In practical tasks such as typing, PSA also improves with practice and training (Salthouse, 1986a) but appears to decline with age (e.g., Elias, Elias, Robbins, & Gage, 1987), with older subjects making more errors and taking longer to master such perceptually dependent skills as word processing (although some studies have shown no age difference in overall typing speed despite slower reaction times and tapping rates; see Salthouse, 1984a).

Dimensionality of the construct. The PSA construct is generally not reduced to subfactors in most factor-analytic studies.

However, an early factor analysis of clerical aptitude tests, including 17 clerical aptitude tests and a measure of general intelligence, showed three major factors: perceptual analysis (accuracy), speed, and verbal ability; these factors accounted, respectively, for 17%, 14%, and 11% of the variance, or collectively accounted for less than half of the variance (Blair, 1951). Measures such as the Minnesota Clerical Test (Andrew, Paterson, & Longstaff, 1979) include subtests for verbal material (names) and quantitative material (numbers), but such subtest scores have generally been highly correlated.

NCA is also not reduced to subfactors in most common measures of the ability, although a variety of mathematical processes have been identified (see, e.g., Resnick, 1989). Resnick noted that the preferred adult strategy for solving computational math problems is automaticity or retrieval, which is a low-effort, rapid-response methodology. Osborn (1983) found that a test developed to measure math ability resulted in a four-component factor solution, including a computational factor and a pattern recognition factor.

Relation to other aptitudes. Pawlik (1966) differentiated the Perceptual Speed factor from the Gestalt Perception factor (see also R. B. Cattell, 1987). The Perceptual Speed factor includes measures requiring the comparison of two numbers or names to determine if they are the same or different, and the Gestalt Perception factors include Speed of Closure (UI5) and Flexibility of Closure (UI6). The former, in R. B. Cattell's (1987) scheme, is a Visual Cognition factor, whereas the latter is highly related to personality factors and is akin to the Field Dependence–Independence factors. Although three of these loadings are consistent with theory (and would primarily be associated with Holland's Realistic classification), inclusion of PSA on this factor is somewhat unexpected. However, Riggio and Sotoodeh (1987) found an arithmetic test to correlate with measures of finger dexterity in predicting the performance ratings of microassemblers.

Hakstian and Cattell (1978b), in a study of 20 primary ability variables (all, regrettably, measured solely with tests from the authors' own Comprehensive Ability Battery; see Hakstian et al., 1982; Hakstian & Gale, 1979), found no relation between

PSA (their "P" variable) and verbal ability (r_{xy} = .01) but found sizable correlations between P and NCA (their "C") and spatial ability (correlations of .40 and .42, respectively) in a Canadian high school sample. Their P and C variables loaded on the same ability factor, which was also associated with spatial ability and mechanical ability. Lowman et al. (1985) found, in a sample of 149 college-level women, that PSA, as measured by the Minnesota Clerical Test, loaded on a factor separate from computational abilities, as measured by the Wide Range Achievement Test–Arithmetic (the latter loaded more with the intellectual ability measures). Blair's (1951) finding of a third factor related to verbal abilities in a clerical aptitude test suggested a possible minor intellectual factor in clerical abilities.

McGue, Bouchard, Lykken, and Feuer (1984) reported in a sample of monozygotic and dizygotic twins and triplets that there was a relation between some of the measures of PSA and speed of spatial processing and speed of information processing. More generally, Lindley, Smith, and Thomas (1988) raised important considerations about the relation between timed paper-and-pencil tests and psychometric intelligence. Speed of information processing, they noted, generally shows a high and negative correlation with intelligence when the task to be done is simple and a high and positive correlation with intelligence when mental transformations are required rather than simple tasks such as copying numerics (or, presumably, the Digit Symbol subtest of the Wechsler scales). Thus, perceptual speed may need to be considered in relation to intelligence in evaluating career implications.

Occupational applications. Ghiselli's (1966) work on the ability patterns of occupational groups examined validity coefficients for clerical occupations. Training criteria, not unexpectedly, were generally better predicted by general intelligence measures than by primary abilities. Curiously, however, against job performance criteria, perceptual accuracy tests generally did no better than intellectual abilities in predicting job performance for general and recording clerks. Computing clerks were an exception in that perceptual measures exceeded intelligence and other primary abilities. On the other hand, both perceptual and intellectual factors did predict well for these occupations, at least by the usual standard of validity coefficient magnitude found in personnel selection studies. Arithmetic (i.e., Number Facility) predicted best for most types of clerks, especially against training criteria. Gael, Grant, and Ritchie (1975) have examined predictive validity of minority and nonminority clerks using work sample criteria.

Extensive analyses have been made of the occupational skills utilized in typewriting and word processing (see Glencross & Bluhm, 1986; Grudin, 1983; Salthouse, 1984a, 1984b, 1986a, 1986b; Shaffer, 1986), which are surprisingly complex abilities requiring perceptual, motoric, and cognitive skills in "chunking" together information.

As usual, it is the combination of abilities that will determine specific occupational fit. Those people, for example, who score high on perceptual speed but low on intelligence may be best suited for routine clerical positions, whereas those who combine intelligence with rapid information-processing skills may do best in higher level clerical or computer applications. The higher level Conventional occupations such as accounting and computer technology necessitate high levels of general intelligence and reasoning ability.

Changing environmental conditions must also be noted. With the automation of clerical and simple computational tasks becoming the norm even in small offices, many Conventional occupations have been redefined or eliminated. Presumably, with a lower demand for routine and low-level clerical tasks, those people with predominantly Conventional interests and abilities may have more difficulty finding outlets for these skills unless they are also able to use intelligence and reasoning to make sense of numbers. Analytical abilities that combine a preference for information-processing activities with the ability to determine and make sense of patterns of data will presumably become more important in the emerging workplace.

Research needs. Additional studies are needed comparing PSA and other speeded perceptual abilities (e.g., speed and flexibility of closure). To the extent the latter variable measures something akin to creativity, it would be expected to be negatively associated with PSA in Holland's (1985b) Conventional interest type. On the other hand, a positive correlation would be expected between PSA and speed of closure. More studies are also needed examining the relation between PSA and NCA, particularly using measures of NCA that are minimally "contaminated" with higher level mathematical skills.

Measurement issues. There are many measures of perceptual speed and accuracy and of numerical ability. These include most of the wide-spectrum ability tests such as the DAT and the CAB. An early study (Bair, 1951) reported the Minnesota Clerical Test (Andrew et al., 1979) to be a superior measure of clerical ability. This test appears to predict well computerized performance even though it is a paper-and-pencil measure (Silver & Bennett, 1987).

The Wide Range Achievement Test–Revised (Jastak & Wilkinson, 1984) includes a measure of arithmetic that has good normative data and, in the first half of the adult form, which measures primarily computational skills, Beck et al. (1989) reported that an advanced computational ability factor was found in a factor analysis of 409 psychiatric patients' test scores using the Wechsler Adult Intelligence Scale–Revised. In contrast, the Quantitative Thinking subtest (Test Q) of the Iowa Tests of Educational Development (Ansley, Spratt, & Forsyth, 1989) has been reported to be a relatively pure measure of math problem-solving ability rather than computational skills. Scores on the two might therefore be contrasted when the differentiation of these two factors is important.

The discussions in this chapter are necessarily incomplete. For example, I did not include variables or constellations of variables such as memory, creativity, or speed and flexibility of closure here. These variables certainly deserve further examination, particularly as the literature examining the career implications of these variables and their factorial relation with other ability measures increases. A case study demonstrating the clinical assessment of ability measures is provided in chapter 6.

Chapter

4

Measuring Personality
Characteristics

A s it relates to career assessment and counseling, the measurement of personality constitutes one of the most neglected areas of systematic inquiry (see B. Schneider, 1987).
This apparent neglect is attributable to several factors. First,
early work in applying personality characteristics to problems
of personnel selection led to the belief that these variables were
not very predictive of job performance (e.g., Ghiselli & Barthol,
1953; Guion & Gottier, 1965; Kinslinger, 1966). Yet, later studies
(see, e.g., Bernardin & Bownas, 1985; Miner, 1985) showed that
the conclusions had been far too negative, sweeping, and premature, based as they were on few studies. Even now, the
prejudice manifested by many industrial–organizational psychologists against personality variables continues. For example,
Guion (1987) wrote that the negative Guion and Gottier (1965)
review was not updated "because the reported use of such
measures since the mid-1960s has not been large enough to
merit the summary" (p. 200).

Significantly, several of the measures used in personnel selection studies (many of which are reviewed in Burbeck & Furnham, 1985; Guion & Gottier, 1965; Hargrave & Berner, 1984;
Lowman, 1989) assessed how *psychopathology* rather than normal personality characteristics predicted job performance. An
obvious limitation of such an approach is that psychopathology
per se is often not associated with impaired job performance.

Indeed, in certain jobs, the presence of psychological dysfunction may actually be predictive of success (J. A. Johnson, 1986; Lowman, 1989). Thus, for certain occupations, psychopathology or personality dysfunction appears to be expected, if not desired. For example, this expectation is stereotypically applied to writers and many of the creative professions. As Proust put it (no doubt, too extremely), "without nervous disorder there can be no great artist" (cited in Coles, 1989, p. 30).

Many "normal" personality variables (e.g., achievement motivation, dominance, introversion–extraversion) have remained inadequately tested in their ability to predict career-relevant outcomes, although there have been promising starts (see Bernardin & Bownas, 1985; Ghiselli, 1971; Guilford, Zimmerman, & Guilford, 1976, chap. 17; Howard & Bray, 1988; Miner, 1985; see also R. B. Cattell, 1987, chap. 12).

A second relevant factor accounting for the neglect of personality variables by career researchers concerns their extensive reliance on personality assessment devices that were not designed for occupational choice or personnel selection. Unfortunately, few personality instruments have been designed for this purpose. Again, there are exceptions, including the Miner Sentence Completion Scale (Miner, 1978) and, to some extent, the more recently developed Hogan Personnel Selection Series (Hogan & Hogan, 1986). On the other hand, test catalogues issued by major publishing firms labeled with such inviting but misleading titles as "Test Catalogue for Business and Industry" are generally not exceptions to this rule. Thus, vocational applications have typically come *after* the development of the test rather than before. Typically, broadbrush personality assessment devices designed for personality assessment in clinical contexts have simply been redirected to the purpose of occupational assessment. When variables on such measures have been relevant and appropriately measured, some of these tests have proved useful in career assessment. However, the vast majority of personality measures have been inadequately validated for occupational applications.

The California Psychological Inventory (CPI; Gough, 1987) and the Sixteen Personality Factor Questionnaire (16PF; R. B.

Cattell, Eber, & Tatsuoka, 1970) provide good examples of this dilemma. These measures are widely used in career counseling contexts, and career-oriented literature exists for both instruments. Gough (personal communication, August 7, 1989), for example, has assembled a bibliography of CPI applications in police selection contexts that, as of June 1989, numbered 23 entries.

Both the CPI and the 16PF have assets and limitations for career assessment purposes. Apart from neither measure having been designed for vocational purposes, several of the CPI scales were developed from work with specialized populations. An example is the CPI Socialization (So) scale, which was initially validated against a criterion of juvenile delinquency or inappropriate rebelliousness. It is certainly possible, and perhaps highly likely, that people who score in the same direction as the disturbed-youth sample will be poor employment risks or ill suited for an occupation demanding social conformity. However, it is also possible that they actually will be, in certain occupational settings, an asset to the organization. Studies in career and personnel selection contexts are necessary to reach appropriate conclusions.

It can be argued that both of these measures do provide occupational norm referents. Indeed, the manuals for the 16PF (R. B. Cattell, et al., 1970) and the CPI (Gough, 1987) provide occupational profiles for several groups such as accountants, airline pilots, musicians, and sales personnel. Unfortunately, the sample sizes for the profiled groups are generally small, the samples are highly selective (not representative), and the interpretations are enthusiastic compared with the results, particularly concerning the interoccupational differences, which sometimes do not occur in the predicted direction. Similarly, Gough's (1987) important revision of the CPI presents 13 occupational samples and a number of educational samples grouped by major, but the results do not always conform to expectations about the characteristics associated with the various professions. Illustrative of the problems are two recent CPI scales: Managerial Potential (Mp) and Work Orientation (Wo). For example, if there is a conceptual reason explaining why research scientists (generally not known for managerial prowess) score the highest among the occupational samples on the *Mp* scale, it is not articulated in the test manual.

Similarly, two second-order variable scores (internality–externality and norm favoring–norm questioning) in the revised CPI result in a grouping of each respondent into one of four personality types: *alpha, beta, gamma,* and *delta* (Gough, 1987). When occupational samples are considered, some strange bedfellows occur. Modal female deltas, for example, include mathematicians, prison inmates, and pharmacy students, whereas male mathematicians and pharmacy students are modal betas. Similarly, modal gammas include male MBA graduate students, juvenile delinquents, psychology graduate students, and San Francisco area residents (Gough, 1987), who perhaps share more commonalities than psychologists might like to think. There is a strong need for criterion-based studies examining whether the second-order groupings on scales of this nature differentially predict various work-relevant criteria.

Finally, there is the issue of intraoccupational differences. As several researchers (e.g., Mossholder, Bedeian, Touliatos, & Barkman, 1985; Osipow, 1987; Zytowski & Hay, 1984) have demonstrated, important differences exist in abilities and interests within the same occupation. The global differentiation of occupational groups does not address the more complex question of subgroupings within the same occupation. Members of the same occupational group may include clusters of individuals whose average scores on measures of personality (or interests or abilities) differ significantly. The task of mapping those differences and assessing the implications for work behavior largely remains to be done (see Osipow, 1987).

Thus, the occupational relevance of personality measures that have been developed for other purposes must be established empirically. This requires convincing evidence that a test predicts career issues as well as the original criteria on which it was initially validated. Empirical validation is needed to assure both assessors and their clients that scoring in a particular direction on a scale is associated with predictable occupational consequences. This expectation is articulated in the test validation standards of the American Educational Research

Association, American Psychological Association, and National Council on Measurement in Education (1985):

> *Standard 6.3.* When a test is to be used for a purpose for which it has not been previously validated, or for which there is no supported claim for validity, the user is responsible for providing evidence of validity (p. 42).
> *Standard 7.1.* Clinicians should not imply that interpretations of test data are based on empirical evidence of validity unless such evidence exists for the interpretations given (p. 46).

Perhaps the most important and neglected issue in the validation of personality measures for career assessment is the need to provide a theoretical rationale for observed inter- and intraoccupational personality test differences and to determine empirically whether the predicted differences do hold. Consider, for example, the need for achievement variable. Would differences be expected between a group of physicians and a group of construction workers on this variable? Does scoring highly on a need for achievement measure imply that one is best suited for a particular occupation? Is it possible to experience job satisfaction in a low-status job while scoring consistently high on a need for achievement measure? Might not need for achievement be patterned differently in various occupations? For example, ambitious members of artistic occupations might score low on typical measures of need for achievement because they reject conventional societal norms of advancement and of getting ahead, yet they may be still be highly ambitious.

Another possibility is that certain personality variables such as need for achievement may differentially predict job success only when the "fit" within an occupation has been established on the basis of other measures. Thus, scores on a measure of need for achievement, to continue the example, would be unlikely to determine whether a person would make a good physician or a good engineer. Personality variables alone may not effectively differentiate career choice. Comparison of a person's personality profile to a modal group of occupational incumbents may therefore not be appropriate unless it is first established that the requisite abilities and interest patterns are present. Personality measures may be useful in career assessment only when (a) there is a clearly differentiated, occupation-specific profile on the personality variable (e.g., extraversion and sales); and (b) there is evidence that scoring in a manner different from the modal profile is associated with career dysfunctions or lowered work performance.

This approach implies a sequential model: The assessment of interests and abilities would precede the measurement of personality characteristics. If the person being assessed has both the interest and minimal ability patterns associated with a particular occupational group, then psychologists would examine personality factors for goodness of fit and the likely manner of role implementation. It is likely that this assessment process, although obviously more time consuming and expensive, will result in a more accurate prediction.

Issues in Clinical Interpretation

To summarize, the integrative model of career assessment suggests a complex view of personality assessment and asserts that personality measures must have demonstrated job and career relevance before they are used in clinical practice. The results of personality evaluations should be considered in relation to other aspects of the overall career profile, including vocational interests and ability.

Unfortunately, much of the personality research in the context of career issues has not examined individual characteristics of personality (e.g., need for achievement, extraversion–introversion) as they relate to other personality variables, much less to abilities, interests, or job performance. It is not certain that isolated personality variables adequately predict simple criteria of job success (e.g, one-time supervisory ratings or productivity measures) for the purposes of personnel selection or individual counseling. This sort of gross "cut-score" mentality, especially related to crude, dichotomous, hire–do not hire decisions, ignores the potential richness and complexities of individual assessment. Still, the psychologist learning career assessment methodologies must begin step by step. In this chapter, therefore, I have identified several promising personality variables that have demonstrated relevance for career assessment and counseling.

To summarize, personality characteristics may be appropriate or inappropriate to the career context and may complement or deviate from the results of measurement in other domains. The assessor must proceed cautiously when comparing a person's score on personality variables with the average scores of incumbents in various occupational groups. The personality scores of various occupational groups may be similar to one another. For example, a group of physicians and a group of executives may both score high on a measure of dominance, yet a person who individually scores high on dominance will not necessarily make either a good executive or a good physician. On the other hand, scoring low on a measure of dominance may constitute grounds for exclusion from certain occupations (e.g., management), provided that the variable is clearly associated with failure or poor performance in an occupation. Put another way, one can be extraverted and a good salesperson or a good executive (the specific fit being guided by other variables), but one is unlikely, as an introvert, to be effective in sales (except, perhaps, in sales of a highly technical product). In such cases, personality variables may constitute exclusionary rather than inclusionary criteria.

Which Personality Variables Should Be Measured?

Given the complexity of the personality domain, which variables should the practicing career assessor measure? No easy or well-validated answers emerge. Ideally, career assessors would work with clearly defined variables appropriate for each occupational assessment. Practically, however, they are likely to continue measuring personality with broadbrush instrumentation originally designed for noncareer purposes. There is a need to reduce data from such measures to a relatively small set of promising occupationally relevant personality measures and to be especially careful while interpreting test results that have demonstrated limited occupational relevance.

Recent advances in theory and measurement point to a reduction in the number of cross-situationally significant personality variables to five or so. Each of these is thought to encompass relatively stable characteristics of personality (e.g., McCrae & Costa, 1986, 1987; McCrae, Costa, & Busch, 1986). These reduced variable sets have yet to be adequately examined for their career implications, although emerging personality instruments, notably by Costa and McCrae (1985b, 1988; Costa, McCrae, & Holland, 1984) and Hogan (1986), have begun to examine the relevant research questions. A variety of other personality measures have also shown varying degrees of research support for occupational purposes including the Myers-Briggs Type Indicator (MBTI; I. B. Myers, 1980, 1987; P. B. Myers & Myers, 1985), the CPI (Gough, 1987), the Edwards Personal Preference Schedule (EPPS; A. L. Edwards, 1959), and the Guilford-Zimmerman Temperament Survey (GZTS; J. S. Guilford et al., 1976).

If the trend in recent years, especially since Norman's (1963) and R. B. Cattell's (1946; Cattell & Kline, 1977) important contributions, has been to reduce personality characteristics to a small number of cross-situational variables, personality theorists are not yet in agreement on the specific variables that are most important and overarching (Borkenau, 1988; Livenh & Livenh, 1989). Neither, however, do various models of the primary personality variables so far put forth by key theorists differ radically from one another. Table 4.1 shows a comparison of the primary personality variables advanced by current researchers. From these variables, those with the most implications for career assessment are expected to be found.

Desirable Characteristics of Career-Relevant Personality Dimensions

In evaluating the relevance of personality variables for career assessment, criteria similar to those recommended for evaluating ability measures can be used. A career-relevant

Table 4.1

Four Alternative Models of the "Big Five" Personality Variables

Norman[a]	Kamp and Gough[b]	Hogan[c]	Costa and McCrae[d]
Surgency	Ascendancy	Ascendance	Assertiveness[e]
Emotional Stability	Adjustment	Adjustment	Neuroticism
Agreeableness		Likeability and Agreeableness	Agreeableness
Conscientiousness	Self-Control	Conscientiousness	Conscientiousness
Culture	Intellectance Masculinity	Intellection	
			Openness
			Extraversion

[a]Norman (1963).
[b]Kamp and Gough (1986).
[c]Hogan (1986).
[d]Costa and McCrae (1985a).
[e]Facet scale of Extraversion scale.

personality variable will ideally be one with demonstrated theoretical and empirical relevance and with norms for various occupational groups of sufficient size and diversity. The variable will also demonstrate a pattern of differential performance: Those people scoring in the desired direction will be more likely to perform successfully in a given career path; those scoring in the opposite direction will be shown to perform more poorly in the same occupation. In addition, the variable will be relatively stable over time (I. Jackson, 1982).

The specific assessment task must also be considered. To determine the fit of an individual to various occupational groups, it is appropriate to examine interoccupational differences. However, to determine how high one will rise in a particular occupation (for which a good fit has been suggested by other measures), intraoccupational patterns may be the most relevant. Finally, age at the time of assessment must also be considered because certain personality variables vary as a function of age (see Gruff, Ramseyer, & Richardson, 1968; Howard & Bray, 1988; Martin, Blair, Dannennaier, Jones, & Asako, 1981).

I review variables with theoretical or empirical relevance to occupational assessment next. I review the variables one at a time, even though, as the case example at end of the chapter demonstrates, it is the *integration* of personality data that is important for the clinical practice of career assessment. Nevertheless, the assessor must first understand the nature of the independent variables and the research literature on their career relevance before attempting the more complex task of integration.

Achievement Orientation

Conceptual issues. Originally conceptualized as a stable and generalized characteristic of personality, need for achievement in relation to occupational accomplishments has been extensively studied, at least compared with some of the other personality variables. Much of the early research literature was conducted or inspired by the theories and research of McClelland (e.g., 1961) and his associates. McClelland discussed need for achievement in terms of the interaction between personological and sociological factors and helped to develop a measurement methodology based on projective testing. Societies that value achievement have transmitted the importance of getting ahead and the need for a strong work ethic in many ways through the culture. The theory is not without its critics and revisionists (Frey, 1984).

Achievement orientation generally refers to a persistent striving to get ahead and a liking for activities in which one's abilities are goal directed. For some people, this includes a preference for competitive activities in which efforts are directed against those of others, whereas for others, the preference is for competing against a standard of excellence (Spence & Helmreich, 1983). Spence and Helmreich defined achievement orientation as "task-oriented behavior that allows the individual's performance to be evaluated according to some internally or externally imposed criterion, that involves the individual in competing with others, or that otherwise involves some standard of excellence" (p. 12). R. B. Cattell and Horn's (1964) now somewhat dated Motivation Analysis Test (MAT) identified assertiveness (achievement) as an "erg" or motive that relates to the drive for self-assertion, mastery, and achievement. In this model, ergs can be directed toward a variety of different "sentiments," including career.

McClelland and Pilon (1983) suggested that need for achievement and need for power may be strongly influenced by early child-rearing practices, including the scheduling of feeding and severity of toilet training. O'Malley and Schubarth (1984) noted that people high in need for achievement tend to distribute rewards in accord with performance differences, whereas those high in need for affiliation base their reward patterns on the response tendencies of the partner.

There is evidence that achievement orientation is not unidimensional. Researchers examining the dimensionality of the need for achievement variable have tended to identify multiple factors, including competitiveness, status aspirations, dominance, and striving (Bendig, 1963, 1964; Bendig & Martin, 1962; D. N. Jackson, Ahmed, & Heapy, 1976). Gough's (1987) CPI differentiates achievement through conformity and achievement through independence. Derman, French, and Harman (1978) identified factors reflecting both a desire to get ahead and a liking of competition; however, not all agree on the latter as a necessary component of need for achievement (see Lipman-Blumen, Handley-Isaksen, & Leavitt, 1983). Supporting the multidimensional conception of need for achievement is the finding of an association between the need for achievement and authoritarianism (Teevan, Heinzen, & Hartsough, 1988).

Spence (1983) and Spence and Helmreich (1983) identified at least three dimensions of achievement orientation: work orientation (high in those with elevated need for achievement scores), need for mastery (also high), and interpersonal competitiveness (generally low in the most successful). Elaborating on the interpersonal aspects of achievement orientation, Lipman-Blumen et al. (1983) identified three *types* of styles used to achieve goals: direct, in which one uses one's own efforts to accomplish goals; instrumental, in which others may also be used to accomplish goals; and relational, in which one contributes actively or passively to the accomplishment of others' goals. These conceptualizations help to move the construct away from a simple high–low dichotomization to the recognition that preferred style may help to determine how achievement is manifested in real-world behavior. The assessing clinician may therefore need to be sensitive to the varieties of achievement that can be manifested by the same individual.

Complex interactive relations are suggested between need for achievement and other personality variables. R. B. Cattell and Kline (1977), for example, objected not so much to the construct of need for achievement as to its isolation as a distinct measure of personality. Those researchers conceptualized need for achievement as an amalgam of self-assertion, career orientation, and self-sentiment. Higher need for achievement scores were reported for teenagers scoring high on a factor indicating perceived control over their environment (Metcalfe & Dobson, 1983). Such teens were more competitive and enjoyed novel and creative activities. Chusmir and Hood (1988) reported a sex difference for men and women on need for achievement as it related to Type A and Type B behavior patterns. Specifically, the need for achievement predicted the Type A behavior pattern for women but not for men.

Reeve, Olson, and Cole (1987) found complex relations among the need for achievement, the experience of success and failure, and locus of control. They noted that need for achievement is affected both by individual difference variables and by the results one achieves (or thinks one has achieved) on a task. Using a female sample, Schroth (1987) reported relations between need for achievement scores on the Thematic Apperception Test (TAT) and EPPS and scores on other variables such as need for affiliation and need for power on the TAT. Parvathi and Rama-Rao (1982) found no relation between social desirability and need for achievement.

The presence of a sex difference on need for achievement has been considered by several researchers (Lipman-Blumen, Leavitt, Patterson, Bies, & Handley-Isaksen, 1980; see also Deaux, 1985). Schroth (1987) found that college men scored higher than women on need for achievement (and dominance), whereas women scored higher on need for affiliation. These results held for both the TAT and EPPS. Rao and Murthy (1984) also reported a sex difference in favor of men on internal locus of control and higher levels of need for achievement. Elder and MacInnis (1983) noted that women assessed in their youth could be classified into two motivational groupings in a sample whose members were first assessed in 1932. Those who were grouped in the social–marital path had lower initially rated levels of need for achievement, whereas those in the worklife–career path were more likely to finish school, marry, and have children later and were more oriented toward a career over the life span.

However, other studies measuring need for achievement in different ways and with different samples have disputed a sex difference. Chusmir (1985a), for example, examined a group of male and female managers and found the women to have higher scores on need for achievement and need for power and that there were no sex differences on need for affiliation. Chusmir (1984b) also noted that these findings run counter to the beliefs of personnel administrators, who believed that male and female personnel administrators were about equal in need for achievement but viewed women as being higher in need for affiliation and men as being higher in need for power. However, people who become managers are presumably selected, both by employers and by themselves, on the basis of their personality characteristics. Thus, it is possible that female managers differ from women (or college women) in general.

Crew (1982) also found no sex difference between Black male and Black female business majors when measuring need for achievement with the TAT. Similarly, Stahl (1983), in a variety of samples, found no sex or racial differences on a managerial motivation measure (managerial talent was measured by high need for achievement and high need for power). No sex differences were reported by Waller and Rothschild (1983), but their sample was limited to music students. Schroth and

Andrew (1987) reported that in a Hawaiian college student sample, men and women differed on subscales of a need for achievement measure. Men scored higher on the Competitiveness scale, women on the Work Dimension scale. A third subscale, Mastery, showed no sex difference. Faver (1984) also noted that age may interact with sex such that younger women high in need for achievement are more likely to pursue a career than older women.

Need for achievement levels can change. Levels can also moderate as the result of psychological intervention (Craig & Olson, 1988; McClelland & Winter, 1969) or the passage of time. Several researchers (e.g., Howard & Bray, 1988; McClelland, 1961) have reported that the need for achievement tends to decline with age. This may occur as people come to terms with their actual levels of accomplishment and accept the lowered possibilities of mobility as they rise within an occupational or organizational hierarchy. Because the number of vacancies at the higher levels is small, with age comes a greater recognition that continued advancement may not be likely.

Need for achievement may change differentially over time for the sexes. Jenkins (1987), for example, measured need for achievement in 117 female college seniors and again 14 years later. She found that for the women in her sample, businesswomen and college professors showed larger increases in achievement motivation over time than did the other occupational groups. Faver (1984) reported that there were cross-sectional differences in the likelihood of pursuing a career; younger women were more likely than older women to express need for achievement by pursuing a career.

Although many theorists conceptualize need for achievement as being stable across situations, there is evidence that it may be influenced by them. For example, Hollenbek, Williams, and Klein (1989) found the commitment to difficult goals to be predicted by need for achievement scores, but only as they interacted with locus of control (internal vs. external), the public expression of goals and self-set (vs. assigned) goals. Similarly, D. Eden (1988) noted that the motivation to expend effort must be differentiated from the motivation to choose a task. Characteristic levels of achievement motivation may therefore interact with the specific task undertaken and the extent to which the individual has an interest in it. Aspects of the task and situation also appear to affect the role of need for achievement influencing outcomes. Niebuhr and Norris (1982), for example, found in an undergraduate sample that subjects high in need for achievement did better than those low in the dimension in complex or stressful situations, a difference that was attenuated when the situational elements were favorable.

Career relevance. Relatively few studies have been published examining the effects of the variable in specific occupational groups, especially among nonbusiness occupations. However, some literature does exist, probably more than for most of the personality variables discussed in this chapter, which is to say, not much.

Within entrepreneurial and managerial occupations, need for achievement has received research support for its ability to predict level of management reached (e.g., Orpen, 1983), and there is evidence that individuals who rate themselves as having a high need for achievement value advancement and promotion more than pay (e.g., Terpstra, 1983). Ghiselli (1971) published data showing that a need for occupational achievement variable differentiated between managers, supervisors, and workers, with the managerial sample scoring significantly higher, on average, than the other two groups. McClelland (1961) focused primarily on the societal rather than the individual implications of the need for achievement variable. He argued that individuals high in need for achievement find especially good outlets for it in Enterprising occupations, which might partially explain why much of the need for achievement literature has been conducted with people in or aspiring to managerial careers. Other researchers have also noted the importance of need for achievement in managerial occupations (e.g., Grant, Katkovsky, & Bray, 1967). Stahl (1983) found that in a variety of occupational and student samples, high need for achievement paired with high need for power predicted higher levels of managerial performance. McClelland and Boyatzis (1982) reported that the so-called leadership motive pattern (elevated needs for power, low needs for affiliation, high inhibition of activity) predicted long-term managerial success and that need for achievement predicted only lower levels of success within the organization. The results held only for nontechnical managers. Miller and Droge (1986) reported data that suggested that chief executive officers who are high in need for achievement may structure their organizations differently from those low in the dimension. Schilit (1986) noted that middle-level managers with a high need for achievement (and those with a high need for power or those scoring in the internal direction on a locus of control measure) had more influence on their superiors in the organizations than did those scoring in the opposite direction on these variables. Kernan and Lord (1988) reported in an undergraduate sample that need for achievement moderated the relation between work motivation and type of goal setting (participatory vs. assigned). High need for achievement students performed better when they participated in setting the goals; low need for achievement subjects did best when the goals were assigned.

Bretz, Ash, and Dreher (1989) examined the relation between need structures (including achievement, power, and affiliation) and preference for a particular type of organization in which to work. Although some differences were noted in occupational choice, the intervention was so weak (deciding which of two companies college students would want to work for after viewing a videotape staged to represent different organizational reward structures) that it severely limited generalizability. W. H. Cooper (1983) reported data suggesting that achievement motivation (defined as the desire to approach success and to avoid failure) was associated with several other variables, including initial task choice, persistence, performance, value attached to success and failure, and task difficulty estimates.

Other research has examined the relation between need for achievement and productivity among nonbusiness professions. M. F. Peterson (1983) reported that health care staff were more likely to have high intrinsic reward satisfaction and lower turnover than others in the same organizational setting. Schroth (1987) reported that whether a task condition was intrinsic or extrinsic affected the interaction with need for achievement. The interaction was strongest between need for achievement and intrinsic task performance. Misra and Jain (1986) found that need for achievement (along with self-esteem and need for autonomy) moderated the job performance–job satisfaction relation.

Spence and Helmreich's (1983) need for achievement instrument demonstrated some interoccupational differences consistent with presumed occupational differences. They also reported correlations between salary earned among business professionals and need for achievement and, for scientists, between a scientific citation index and need for achievement. However, for both groups, need for achievement interacted with competitiveness. Those who had high needs for mastery and high work motivation did better than those who also had high interpersonal competitiveness.

Other studies have been less positive, reporting little relation between need for achievement and workplace effectiveness (Mohan & Brar, 1986). Mehta and Agrawal (1986) found no relation between need for achievement and job satisfaction among a sample of male Indian bank clerks. Moreover, need for achievement has been reported to be trainable (McClelland & Winter, 1969) and thus subject to change, suggesting that some of the relations outlined here may be different if active efforts are made to change individual achievement needs.

Measurement issues. Many omnibus measures of personality (e.g., the EPPS, CPI, 16PF) include some sort of need for achievement variable. However, the variable's conceptualization may vary from one measure to another. Need for achievement scores are included in many paper-and-pencil measures of personality, including the CPI, the EPPS, and the MAT. Measures of need for need for achievement have been used for preschool children (Carr & Mednick, 1988) and with physically and behaviorally challenged children (Pagdiwalla & Pestonjee, 1988).

The most widely used projective measure of need for achievement appears to be the TAT. An objective procedure exists for scoring TAT stories on need for achievement (see Winter, 1973); a short-cut method for scoring has also been reported (Chusmir, 1985b). Lundy (1988) reported that instructional set can influence the validity of need for achievement themes on the TAT. Orpen (1983) noted an adjective checklist for measuring need for achievement, a variation of Ghiselli's (1971) Self-Description Inventory. Reuman (1982) also noted that TAT measures of need for achievement may demonstrate construct validity, even in the absence of high internal consistency. Sid and Lindgren (1982) reported a 30-item questionnaire for differentiating between need for achievement and need for affiliation. Stahl and Harrell (1982) reported a behavioral measure of needs for achievement, affiliation, and power.

Important new measures of achievement have been put forth by Spence, Helmreich, and their associates, including the Work and Family Orientation Questionnaire (see Spence & Helmreich, 1983). The L-BLA Achieving Styles Inventory (Lipman-Blumen et al., 1980) is based on a complex model of *type* of achievement behavior (relational, direct, and instrumental) and on subtypes within each major grouping. Little research exists comparing the various achievement measures for their relative predictive validity or examining which instrument works best under which situations with which type of client.

Introversion–Extraversion

Conceptual issues. Introversion–extraversion is well established in the literature (although Derman et al., 1978, did not include the variable in their factor-referenced temperament scales), and it has at least some evidence of occupational relevance. Many studies (see Morris, 1979) have suggested that introversion–extraversion is a temperament variable that is established early in life and appears to be relatively immutable.

Yet, specific definitions (and even the labels attached to the concepts) of introversion and extraversion are not yet universally established. From Jung (1923) to H. J. Eysenck (e.g., 1953) to Cattell (e.g., R. B. Cattell & Kline, 1977), researchers and theorists have posited extraversion–intraversion (or "exvia–invia" in the case of R. B. Cattell, whose creativity, especially in labeling, knows few bounds) as an individual-difference variable. Introverts and extraverts have been reported to differ in their degree of social inhibition; in their level of arousal (with introverts higher in cortical arousal); and, by implication, in their preference for arousal reduction (introverts) or stimulation (extraverts) from the external world (Morris, 1979). Costa and McCrae (1985b) included extraversion as one of three primary personality variables and noted that extraverts are generally more sociable, active, cheerful, energetic, and optimistic than introverts. Introverts are characterized by these researchers as being reserved, submissive, and even-paced.

The dimensionality of extraversion–introversion has been examined by some researchers. Costa and McCrae (1985b), for example, identified the following dimensions in their Extraversion scale: warmth, gregariousness, assertiveness, activity, excitement seeking, and the tendency to experience positive emotions. Morris (1979) identified the following dimensions: social activity (time spent in social and interpersonal activities, talkativeness); social facility (dominance, leadership, and social skills); risk taking and adventuresomeness (vs. restraint and inhibition); and action orientation (vs. preference for introspective, abstract intellectual pursuits).

Interactions between extraversion–introversion and other personality variables have been reported. Heaven, Connors, and Trevethan (1987) reported that antisubmissiveness was associated with extraversion for women. A study by Nauss (1973) indicated that among a sample of clergy, extraversion (e.g., friendliness and sociability) combined with more introverted-like, scholarly personality traits (seriousness, introspection), suggesting that extraversion may indeed be multidimensional, at least in its career manifestations. Morris (1979) reviewed relations between introversion–extraversion and other personality variables, including field dependence–independence, impulsiveness, and sociability. R. B. Cattell (1987) reported that extraversion and creativity are negatively related and hypothesized, at a societal level, that an increase in introversion may be a likely concomitant of the increasing complexity of modern life. This thesis suggests an interesting analogue to McClelland's (1961) characterizations of need for achievement as being a culturally influenced variable.

Career relevance. There appears to be a difference in the relative incidence of people scoring in the introverted and extraverted direction in various occupational groupings. Using the census approach (tabulating the number of respondents in each of the personality measure groupings), Myers and McCaulley (1985, pp. 244–246) reported on the results of MBTI scores. This popularly used measure includes an Introversion–Extraversion scale.

Applying a dichotomous split on the Introversion–Extraversion scale of the MBTI (i.e., each respondent is categorized as being introverted or extraverted depending on his or her score on the scale), more extraverts were found in business and industry occupational groups, whereas engineers, physicians, librarians, and various technical groups more commonly scored in the introverted direction. However, not all groups scored in a direction that might have been predicted. For example, actors ($n = 62$) scored in the extraverted direction, as did musicians and composers ($n = 136$), whereas 59% of a group of 267 lawyers scored in the introverted direction. A sizable sample of writers and journalists ($n = 530$) included 52% who scored in the extraverted direction on the MBTI. Moreover, even for the occupational groups with the most extreme number of introverts or extraverts (extraverted, marketing personnel; introverted, electrical and electronic engineers), 25% and 37%, respectively, scored in the direction opposite that of the majority, suggesting that occupations may contain diverse personality styles, at least for the introversion–extraversion variable measured by the MBTI. (There is little assurance at this time that the various scales of introversion and extraversion are measuring the same thing.) It must also be noted that the census approach does not measure against a criterion, so one does not know, for example, if the quarter of the marketing personnel who were introverted were less effective than the majority who were extraverted.

Other census approaches have been reported in the literature, with results generally in the predicted direction. Banks, Mooney, Mucowski, and Williams (1984) found that successful candidates for the Catholic clergy scored in the extraverted direction, consistent with the findings of Nauss (1963). Costa, Fozard, and McCrae (1977) compared scores on the Strong Vocational Interest Blank and Introversion–Extraversion factors. They noted a distinction between people who preferred task-oriented occupations (e.g., engineer, chemist, artist, and dentist) to socially oriented occupations (e.g., YMCA secretary, social worker). Extraversion was positively associated with the second group, as would be predicted. Kemp (1982a) studied the personality characteristics of teachers of music compared with performers of music, concluding that teachers were more likely to be extraverted, tough-minded, and realistic compared with the performers, who were more likely to be sensitive and introverted. Kincel (1986) compared artists with dancers and found a predominance of introverted personality styles as measured by the Rorschach, although a higher percentage (25%) of the dance students scored in the extratensive direction.

Morris (1979) reviewed the literature on the occupational implications of introversion–extraversion and concluded that a variety of studies showed scores on this personality dimension to be associated with preferences for particular, predictable types of work (e.g., Johansson, 1970; R. W. Johnson, Flammer, & Nelson, 1975; Bendig & Martin, 1963), although a few exceptions were noted (e.g., Bartram & Dale, 1982; Ward, Cunningham, & Wakefield, 1976). In Holland's (1985a) interest scheme, there is reasonably convincing evidence that extraverts are more likely to be found in Social and Enterprising occupations and introverts in Investigative, Conventional, and Realistic occupations (see also R. W. Johnson, Flammer, & Nelson, 1975).

Other researchers have also examined these constructs in career assessment contexts. Costa et al. (1984), for example, fond a correlation between extraversion scores on the N–E–O (Neuroticism–Extraversion–Openness) model of personality and scores on Holland's (1985a) Self-Directed Search in the Social and Enterprising directions (as both theories would predict). Introverts generally do better with occupations demanding concentration and intellectual mastery. Indeed, a general tendency has been reported in the literature for introversion to be associated with higher grades in school after early adolescence and for higher performance in a variety of professions requiring mastery of complex, intellectually demanding material (see R. B. Cattell & Kline, 1977; Morris, 1979).

Some studies have not reported results in the expected direction. Turnbull (1976), for example, found that extraversion scores did not predict success in summer book sales by a group of male college students, although, conversely, extraversion scores did increase, apparently the result of work experience. However, because this was a temporary, part-time position and because books are a commodity often associated with introverts rather than extraverts, it is possible that this was not a good test of the relation between extraversion and sales, which generally has been reported to be positive. Dorr, Cowen, Sandler, and Pratt (1973) found little association between extraversion and job performance for adult mental health workers. Although the direction of the expected endorsement might be subject to disagreement, Bartram and Dale (1982) found higher extraversion scores than are found in the general population in a sample of military pilots, somewhat contrary to the expected Realistic personality characteristics. Again suggesting the importance of examining intraoccupational differences, K. H. Bradt (personal communication, September 16, 1989) reported that of 313 participants in the Leadership Development Program at Eckerd College, 49% scored in the introverted direction on the MBTI.

The potential complexity of extraversion in its career and work manifestations is further illustrated by R. B. Cattell's (1987) identification of a pattern of personality often associated with creativity. (On the ability side, high general intelligence and intensity of concentration, among other variables, are important in the creative profile.) This includes a pattern that may show up on test measures as introversion but that combines aspects typically associated with extraverts (e.g., boldness, Factor H on R. B. Cattell's personality measuring devices). R. B. Cattell (1987, p. 510) hypothesized, intriguingly, that high creativity may be manifested in personality as introversion in individuals who "constitutionally" would be extraverts but who have "somehow" been made extraverts, presumably by family or group influences against self-expression, as in dysfunctional families.

R. B. Cattell et al. (1970) also noted that the 16PF and the Clinical Analysis Questionnaire (CAQ) differentiate people on the basis of their occupational preference for working alone or with others. They reported that people scoring high on Factor A (i.e., those more oriented toward others) tend to prefer working with other people, whereas those scoring low (sizothymics) prefer working with things and ideas rather than with other people. For example, artists, electricians, and research scientists score in the A − direction, whereas social workers and business executives score in the A + direction.

Measurement issues. Many personality measures include measures of introversion and extraversion. Omnibus personality measures typically include Introversion–Extraversion scales either as first- or second-order scales or factors. These include the 16PF and the CAQ (both with the Sizothymia–Affectothymia scale and a second-order factor), the GZTS, the CPI (especially as a second-order factor), the MMPI-1 and MMPI-2 (Social Introversion scale, Scale 0), the MBTI (Introversion–Extraversion scale), the Comrey Personality Scales (see Morris, 1979), and the Eysenck Personality Inventory (H. J. Eysenck & Eysenck, 1964). The Strong Vocational Interest Blank (Campbell & Hansen, 1981) also includes an "occupational introversion" scale, which has at least some evidence of correlating highly with other measures of the construct (see Goodyear & Frank, 1977). More recent measures with Introversion–Extraversion scales include the NEO Personality Inventory (Costa & McCrae, 1985a), which has potentially valuable subscales, and the Hogan Personality Inventory (Hogan, 1986). R. B. Cattell's CAQ includes a second-order factor (invia vs. exvia) that is similar to other measures of introversion–extraversion; Factor A (Sizothymia vs. Affectothymia) also differentiates those oriented toward working and being with people and those preferring more reserved activities. Unfortunately, here, as elsewhere, there is little cross-instrument research available to determine which instrument is superior for particular types of measurement tasks, particularly in the occupational arena. High correlations would be expected among the various alternative measures.

Ascendance–Dominance and Need for Power

Conceptual issues. Ascendance or dominance generally refers to a tendency to assume directive roles in one's interactions with others and to be assertive and "bossy" rather than accommodating or easily led (Institute for Personality and Ability

Testing, 1986). The Educational Testing Service (ETS) personality factors include dominance in the factor-referenced temperament scales. Most omnibus personality measures include a measure of dominance or ascendance, including the CPI, the 16PF, and the GZTS.

Although there is scant literature examining the overlap between the two constructs, a fair amount of literature has been published on the need for power variable, and it is reasonable to believe that the variables are highly similar. Winter (1973) and McClelland (1975) have provided the most definitive statements on the power motive. Winter defined social power as "the ability or capacity of [one person] to produce (consciously or unconsciously) intended effects on the behavior or emotions of another person" (Winter, 1973, p. 5). McClelland, who was somewhat better at describing the experience than defining the concept, depicted power as an individual difference variable associated with having impact on others (McClelland, 1975, p. 7). People scoring high on need for power seek outlets in activities such as accumulating possessions, joining clubs and organizations (especially seeking or holding officer positions in them), and participating in competitive interactions with others (McClelland & Burnham, 1976).

The Derman et al. (1978) dominance construct suggests strong similarity to the need for power construct. They hypothesized three Dominance subscales: *Do1*, wants power over others versus being submissive; *Do2*, pushes own ideas versus respecting others' ideas; and *Do3*, being conscious of one's own rights versus being tolerant. However, these subscales did not factor in the predicted direction, so no marker scales were included in these researchers' personality measures (Derman et al., 1976). Bouchard, Lalonde, and Gagnon (1988), on the other hand, found a correlation between assertiveness and extraversion and between peer-rated assertiveness and agreeableness and conscientiousness, suggesting that dominance is not an isolated personality characteristic.

Concerning sex differences in the power and assertiveness motives, a variety of studies (e.g., E. E. Maccoby & Jacklin, 1974) have shown sex differences on aggression (a form of dominance) in favor of men. Schroth (1985) found that college men scored higher than women on need for dominance. Other researchers have indicated that this difference extends to the occupational setting (e.g., Radecki & Jennings, 1980). More recent analyses have shown the sex difference to be less influential than sometimes assumed (see Deaux, 1985).

The power motive can be experimentally manipulated, which implies that it is able to be changed. Increases in the expression of power have been associated with perceiving threats from others, with viewing others exercising power, and with feeling inhibited by symbols that connote power (e.g., uniforms and titles; House & Singh, 1987).

Career relevance. Winter (1973) provided data from an elite college sample (Wesleyan undergraduates) showing different need for power scores among people indicating a preference for different occupations. Specifically, people indicating a preference for people-oriented occupations (teaching, psychology, clergy, and business) tended to have the highest need for power scores. Aspirants to jobs in medicine, the creative arts, architecture, and (surprisingly) government and politics scored relatively low on the expressed need for power. In a group of Harvard students whose actual (rather than preferential) career choices were charted, similar patterns were noted, and the findings have been replicated with other occupational groups. However, findings on the Ascendance scale of the GZTS (J. P. Guilford et al., 1976) measuring occupational groups have not always supported these findings, especially for the clergy and, to a lesser extent, for teachers. Managers, however, scored very high on the variable and people in the creative arts, especially men, typically scored low.

Other occupational groups have also been studied. Jacobs & Dunlap (1976; see also Kumar & Matha, 1985) suggested that teachers of young elementary school students generally represent a nondominant group, whereas teachers of the older grades need a certain amount of dominance to be able to sell the subject (and, it is today presumed, to maintain order and discipline). Helson (1978) found important personality differences among writers and critics of children's books. The critics were found to be more socially ascendant and conventional, whereas the writers were less conventional, less dominant, and more in touch with alternative states of consciousness. Chusmir (1984a) reported that need for power was found for almost every position in a police force. Chusmir claimed that the desired profile for most police positions would include a high need for power, a moderately high need for achievement, and a low need for affiliation. Cattell and Kline (1977, p. 306) reported average scores on the dominance (E) scale on the 16PF for a variety of occupational groups. Although many of the findings are understandable (e.g., nurses and physicians scored low on the E scale, police, high), others are not. For example, a sample of writers had the highest score on the E scale of all of the occupational groups and business executives were actually lower than a group of male elementary school teachers. These results are of course limited by reliance on only one measure of dominance and, in some cases, by small and possibly nonrepresentative samples.

More literature has been published on the occupational implications of the need for power related to managerial occupations. McClelland (1975) suggested that the essence of the managerial job is influence over others and that the modal manager scores high on need for power (as well as on need for achievement). D. N. Jackson, Paunonen, and Rothstein (1987) reported that personnel executives (especially women) scored much higher than the normative population on a dominance measure. Sedge (1985) found dominance to be one of the factors that differentiated a group of engineer managers from practicing engineers. Cornelius and Lane (1984), however, assessed the need for power, along with needs for achievement and affiliation. They found that for first-line supervisors in a for-profit foreign-language instruction organization, need for affiliation more than need for power or achievement predicted job performance and (not surprisingly) favorable attitudes of subordinates. However, the so-called "leadership motive profile" (above-average need for power, higher need for power than need for affiliation, and at least moderate levels of action inhibition [constraints on the expression of power needs]) predicted only whether subjects were in a high-status office, not job performance or subordinate morale. Cornelius and Lane noted that foreign-language instructors and administrators may be more similar to technical than to generic managers and that to date, the motive pattern assessed in this study does not appear to predict success in technical management. House and Singh's recent review presented a more favorable review of the leadership motive pattern (McClelland, 1985) and concluded that need for power is a promising construct in organizational assessment and research. It is especially relevant for positions in which social and interpersonal managerial skills (rather than technical expertise) are demanded.

A variety of studies have demonstrated that various measures of ascendance or dominance relate differentially to job outcomes. Generally, there is a positive association between scores on personality measures of dominance and ascendance and success on the job, at least for occupational groups in which dominance is a modal characteristic. Bentz (1985), for example, found that a dominance–masculine scale was the best predictor of several personality variables of success in the managerial ranks.

The need for power relates positively to certain managerial outcomes, but the projective measures (especially the TAT and the Miner Sentence Completion Scale) have not been found to predict technical (vs. bureaucratic) managerial positions (House & Singh, 1987).

The GZTS (J. P. Guilford et al., 1976), for example, has yielded some of the most extensive data on the role of the Ascendance scale (its dominance factor) in career and occupational issues. In several occupational samples, vocations in the Enterprising area (especially managers and sales personnel) scored, on average, considerably above the mean on the Ascendance scale. Moreover, the Ascendance scale was often an effective predictor for differentiating high-achieving managers from low-achieving ones. Other occupational groups (e.g., artists, dentists, scientists, counselors, and engineers) tended to score at or below average on this scale, as would be expected.

When nonmanagerial occupations are considered, dominance sometimes predicts career success in occupational groups in which dominance is not expected to be a characteristic personality trait. For example, although the *average* scores for a particular occupational group may be average on the

Ascendance scale, scores on this measure may differentiate more and less successful career paths, especially for women (J. P. Guilford et al., 1976). However, within some occupational groups, the opposite relation holds. For example, among people in training for the clergy, several studies have shown that people scoring higher on the Ascendance scale have tended to be more likely to leave the training program.

Dominant individuals have been reported to be more decisive and decided about career choice (S. E. Cooper, Fuqua, & Hartman, 1984). Phillips and Bruch (1988) found that shyness (presumably the antithesis of at least interpersonal dominance) was associated with less career information seeking, an avoidance of less interpersonally oriented career fields, and a lack of understanding about how appearing assertive in employment interviews might enhance the likelihood of a favorable outcome. Wiener and Vaitenas (1977) provided evidence that a group of 45 midcareer job changers scored lower on ascendancy and dominance (along with endurance and order) than a group of vocationally stable individuals.

Measurement issues. Most broadbrush personality measures include some measure of dominance or ascendance. Gough's (1987) CPI includes a well-validated measure of dominance, the EPPS has a Need for Dominance scale, the NEO Personality Inventory includes Assertiveness as a facet scale under the Extraversion category, and the GZTS includes an Ascendance scale. R. B. Cattell's 16PF and CAQ (R. B. Cattell et al., 1970; Krug, 1980) include a factor (E) that measures the tendency to be dominant versus submissive. Cattell and Horn's (1964) Motivation Analysis Test (MAT) also includes an assertion scale. McClelland and Winter's (see Winter, 1973) adaptation of the TAT is probably the most widely used projective measure of the need for power construct. The relation between the various measures of ascendance and dominance is not well established empirically and is badly in need of examination.

Bouchard, Lalonde, and Gagnon (1988) found poor convergence among self-reported, laboratory role-played, self-observed, and peer-rated measures of assertiveness, implying that behavioral and paper-and-pencil measures of the construct may yield different results. It should also be noted that ascendance scales may be influenced by one's test-taking orientation so that the desire to "fake good" (especially in the prosocial, controlling manner that generally characterizes managers) must be evaluated when considering individual scores.

Concerning the fake good issue, J. P. Guilford et al. (1976) reported that the Ascendance (A) scale on the GZTS was easily faked. Under normal conditions, fewer than 50% of test takers would be expected to have elevated A scale scores. However, when given instructions to "fake good," more than 50% had elevations on this scale. This implies that measuring assertiveness, ascendance, or need for power under conditions in which a positive test-taking orientation would be expected (e.g., in personnel selection contexts), assertiveness and need for power or ascendance will need to be confirmed by means other than paper-and-pencil tests.

Emotional Stability–Neuroticism

Conceptual issues. Derman et al. (1978) identified Emotional Stability (Factor ES) as one of their primary personality variables. Three subfactors were noted: Emotionally Stable versus Irritable and Sensitive, Optimistic versus Overly Worrisome, and Healthy versus Hypochondriacal. The first factor comes closest to the sense in which the construct has been used by other investigators in the career context.

R. B. Cattell et al., (1970) identified Ego Strength (Factor C) and Ergic Tension (Factor Q_4) as two factors related to adjustment. People scoring high in ego strength differ from those scoring low in being more emotionally mature, showing restraint in behavior, and separating the demands of a situation from their own emotional needs. Low scorers tend to show a pattern of emotional instability and ego weakness. They are also prone to worry and are easily disturbed. A variation of this variable is the Q_4 factor, which is thought to represent a generalized energy that, in high scorers, exceeds the capacity of the ego strength to integrate it and may be converted to neurotic problems. These and other 16PF factors are combined to make a generic factor, Anxiety (*Ax*; frustration vs. apprehension), and two adjustment scales, Psychoticism (*P*; well-integrated vs.

disorganized) and Neuroticism (*N*; well-adjusted vs. unstable). Trait ratings that had loadings across occupational samples on the Adjustment factor in Kamp and Gough's (1986) study included personal soundness, likeability, social acuity, good judgment and an absence of rigidity, self-defensiveness, and deceitfulness. This conception of adjustment suggests more of a self-assertive, absence-of-guile definition of the construct.

In assessing personality in career contexts, it is probably best to conceptualize neuroticism and adjustment, as did Costa and McCrae (1985b), as being variations of normal personality. Thus, in a study by McCrae and Costa (1985b), the Neuroticism variable of the NEO Personality Inventory corresponded well with the Neuroticism scale of the Eysenck Personality Inventory; the Psychoticism scale did not. However, it may be best to use traditional assessment devices to evaluate individuals who seek career assessment and are suspected of having more serious forms of psychopathology.

Career relevance. It is generally presumed that emotional stability and the absence of neuroticism are associated with positive performance on the job or, put another way, that neuroticism is associated with poor performance on the job. However, this assumption is not always valid. As previously noted, certain occupations, especially the creative arts, seem to be associated with higher than average levels of psychiatric disturbance. J. S. Guilford et al., (1976), for example, summarized the results of numerous occupational groups taking the GZTS, which includes an Emotional Stability scale. Except for a group of female telephone operators and a group of religious trainees, all of the groups with average scores in the less well-adjusted direction were in the artistic areas.

Popular stereotypes do suggest that people in Artistic professions are more prone to mental disturbance than are people in general (e.g., Edel, 1975; Frosch, 1987; Gotz & Gotz, 1979; Wittkower & Wittkower, 1963). However, Bryan (1942) found no tendency for students in art education, architecture, and design to be more neurotic than typical college students, as measured by the Bernreuter Personality Inventory. Frosch (1987), although noting the stereotype about the "misunderstood musical genius," found no reason to think that psychopathology was an essential part of musical creativity among composers. On the other hand, Fisher and Fisher (1981) reported differences in comedians and actors, finding that the latter group was more psychologically disturbed than the former. Wills (1984) examined personality differences among professional musicians working in the field of popular music. He found some differences according to a subject's instrument of choice: Trumpeters had the lowest Neuroticism scores on the Eysenck Personality Questionnaire, and guitarists had the highest scores on both the Psychoticism and Neuroticism scales. Goodwin and Jamison (1990) have summarized important findings on the unusually high rate of affective disorders among those in creative occupations. Emotional instability in the form of substance abuse is reported to be high among many artistic occupations (Goodwin, 1988).

Getzels and Csikszenthmihalyi's (1976) important study of artists found different profiles of successful male and successful female art students. For men, those whose work was rated highest presented a characteristic personality profile that included aloofness, low ego strength, introspection, sensitivity, imaginativeness, self-sufficiency, and lack of conformity to social norms, which is the stereotype of the artistic temperament. For women artists, success was predicted more by ability measures (spatial ability and perceptual memory ability) than by personality factors. Piechowski and Cunningham (1985) reported five patterns of overexcitability found in a small sample of artists: psychomotor, emotional, sensual, intellectual, and imaginational. Restlessness, emotional vulnerability, and conflict between balance and integration were found to characterize the artists, suggesting that what may be perceived as psychopathology may actually be an essential component of the creative process.

Within other occupational groups, especially managers (Bentz, 1985), teachers, and other people-oriented professions (J. S. Guilford et al., 1976), emotional stability is generally the expected and reported condition found, on average. Bartram and Dale (1982) reported that lower neuroticism scores were associated with success in training for a group of 607 male pilots and trainee pilots. Stewart and Latham (1986) found that emotional stability was a factor in leadership performance evaluation. Bentz (1985) reported that Sears executives scored very high on measures of adjustment and emotional control.

Measurement issues. A number of paper-and-pencil personality measures assess emotional stability. Neuroticism constitutes one of the three original and primary variables on Costa and McCrae's (1985a) NEO Personality Inventory. The Eysenck Personality Inventory also has an adjustment measure. The 16PF (R. B. Cattell et al., 1970) and the CAQ (Krug, 1980) both contain adjustment variables. The GZTS (J. S. Guilford et al., 1976) also includes an Emotional Stability factor.

It is important to determine whether measures of adjustment or neuroticism were validated on "normal" or psychopathological populations. Measures normed and validated on the general population are generally more appropriate for career assessment. When preliminary results suggest the presence of psychopathology that may be job dysfunctional, the psychologist may wish to conduct or suggest a formal assessment of psychopathology. (For a more detailed discussion of the issues involved in the career-related assessment of psychopathology, see Lowman, 1989.)

Perhaps the most important measurement issue is the finding that neuroticism is not necessarily job dysfunctional, at least for certain career paths. Career assessors who encounter in their clients patterns of neuroticism may, in the face of congruent abilities and interests, need to consider fit to occupational groups in which the so-called instability is functional. Treatment or counseling to resolve the neurotic conflicts may be neither desirable nor a precursor of successful career placement.

Masculinity–Femininity

Conceptual issues. Although controversy has been associated with this variable for the last few decades, masculinity–femininity remains an important variable for career assessment because sex differences in preferences for various occupational groupings clearly exist (e.g., Holland, 1985a) and appear to persist despite major changes in the sex composition of many professions (e.g., Hansen, 1986).

J. S. Guilford et al. (1976)'s conceptualization of masculinity describes a preference for "masculine activities and vocations" and a fear-resistant, emotionally inhibited style versus (in the feminine direction) emotional expressiveness, interest in clothes and fashion, and a sympathetic and easily disgusted manner. Ghiselli (1971) differentiated robustness, forcibleness, and high activity levels (masculine) from gentleness, understanding, and passivity (feminine). Gough (1987) added sensitivity to criticism and vulnerability to the feminine side versus action-oriented, initiative-taking, and unsentimental to the low-femininity polarity. However, scores in the feminine direction in Gough's normative samples described people who were esthetically oriented, thinkers, had wide-ranging interests, held unusual versus popular perceptions, and were conservative and conventional in orientation. These findings suggest that, at least as measured by the CPI, femininity may be an amalgam of several behavioral constructs.

Although in principle Holland's (1985a) theory would predict that Realistic, Investigative, and Enterprising types would be more masculine and male dominated and that Artistic, Social, and Conventional types would be more feminine, it is important to differentiate between masculinity in the sense of male gender and psychological masculinity (see Adams, Priest, & Prince, 1985). Goal-directed behavior, competitiveness, and strong work orientation are often associated in cultural stereotype with men, whereas femininity is protypically characterized by nurturing and support. Although occupations clearly differ in their sex distributions and in the extent to which their members fit the "masculine" or "feminine" stereotypes, it is important to separate male gender and psychological "masculinity" because women can embody the masculine stereotype as well as men, even though there is an apparent tenacity to sex stereotypes that persists beyond societal and occupational changes (see Heilman, Block, Martell, & Simon, 1989).

Early measures of masculinity and femininity such as those of the Strong Vocational Interest Blank were based on items on which men and women had clearly differentiated interest patterns (Constantinople, 1973). Thus, items highly endorsed by women and seldom endorsed by men constituted the feminine direction of the scale (and vice versa for men), independently of theory or rationale. The Femininity scale of the MMPI, in contrast, was initially developed for its ability to differentiate a small sample of gay men. Since then, it has been used less as a scale of sexual preference than as a measure of feminine or even creative interests. The scale has apparently worked better with men than with women and was changed in the MMPI-2 only by the deletion of four "objectionable" items from the original scales (Hathaway & McKinley, 1989).

There is still controversy about the dimensionality of the masculinity–femininity construct (Feather, 1984; Lubinski, Tellegen, & Butcher, 1983). Constantinople (1973) noted that femininity and masculinity may not, contrary to common measurement approaches, constitute a single dimension, with masculinity at one end and femininity at the other. Bem (1974) proposed the psychological construct of androgyny, the notion that a third type of person, the androgynous, incorporates aspects of both masculinity (as traditionally defined) and femininity (as traditionally defined), with the androgynous scoring approximately equally on separate scales of masculinity and femininity (M. C. Taylor & Hall, 1982). Spence and Helmreich (1978) posited the existence of a masculinity dimension, a femininity dimension, and a separate masculinity–femininity dimension. Deaux's (1985) more recent review (raising important questions about popular research constructs such as androgyny) concluded that masculinity and femininity are broad constructs representing, as typically measured, dominance and self-assertion versus interpersonal warmth and nurturance. When these underlying behaviors are relevant, masculinity and femininity scales predict well; when they are not relevant, the constructs have less viability.

Career relevance. Occupation-specific norms are generally insufficient in size to establish the extent of occupational differences on this variable reliably. Moreover, most occupational studies have been based on unidimensional measures of the construct. Nevertheless, preliminary studies do suggest that members of certain occupations score, on average, higher or lower on traditional masculinity–femininity measures than do others. For example, in a study of teachers, K. E. Smith (1986) reported that male preschool teachers were more feminine than male high school teachers and that female high school teachers were more masculine than female preschool teachers. Creative occupations often show an androgynous pattern of sex interests. Kapalka and Lachenmeyer (1988) reported that female managers were the most likely to be androgynous on the Bem Sex-Role Inventory and male managers to be either masculine or androgynous. Roe's (1946) study of the personality of 20 leading American painters (all men living in New York) found a feminization (what today would probably be called adrogyny) among male painters. She found that these painters were markedly nonaggressive in their general personality structure, exhibiting more feminine than masculine qualities without being overtly gay. Kemp (1982b) examined sex differences in the personality structure of music students and professional musicians and concluded, in a cross-sectional study, that psychologically androgynous people are best suited by temperament for success in the field of music. Hassler and Birbaumer (1984) also noted that androgyny was related to musical talent, but only for men.

J. S. Guilford et al. (1976) reported occupational averages on a Masculinity–Femininity scale. Most groups scored at about the average compared with general population norms. However, male artist and musician samples tended to score in the feminine direction, and many of their female counterparts scored slightly in the masculine direction. Slight differences were found by occupational level (e.g., mid- vs. top-management levels). Ghiselli (1971) found that the M–F scale on his Self-Description Inventory (an adjective checklist) did not differentiate between successful and less successful managers, although there were small differences among managers, line supervisors, and rank-and-file workers, in the order listed (managers scored the highest on masculinity). Gough (1987) reported results from the CPI with a variety of occupational samples. Groups scoring in the feminine direction (i.e., above the 50th percentile on the scale) included architects, mathematicians, and Catholic priests. Among the lower (i.e., more "masculine" groups) were bankers, correctional officers, and military officers.

Masculinity–femininity, as it is typically measured by personality inventories, appears to show a sex difference for career assessment issues. Achievement and career-oriented women, somewhat independently of occupation and the measuring device used, appear more likely to score in the "masculine" direction on traditional masculinity–femininity measures, whereas femininity is not necessarily associated with lower levels of achievement among men (especially, it would appear, among the creative occupations). On the other hand, men may be more likely to express a preference for gender-congruent occupations (see Feather & Said, 1983). Wong, Kettlewell, and Sproule (1985) reported that women classified as feminine on the Bem Sex-Role Inventory were less achieving in their careers. Westbrook and Nordholm (1984) found that women in the health care professions had higher masculinity scores on the Bem Sex-Role Inventory when they had vertical or lateral advancement ambitions than when they were content to remain in their current position. Williams and McCullers (1983) reported that women in traditional female-dominated occupations were lower in intelligence, achievement orientation, and masculinity than those who pursued atypical careers (e.g., law), a finding mirrored by Waddell (1983) in comparing female secretaries and female managers and business owners. That the high-achieving woman's masculine interests were present from youth and presumably were not just an artifact of adult career choice is suggested by several researchers (e.g., Metzler, Lewis, & Gerrard, 1985; Williams & McCullers, 1983). Antill and Cunningham (1982) reported sex differences in ability test performance as a function of masculinity–femininity. Bridges (1988) discussed sex differences as being associated with expectations in job peformance.

Measurement issues. Well-validated measures of masculinity–femininity are included on the CPI (Gough, 1987), the GZTS, Ghiselli's (1971) Self-Description Inventory, the MMPI-1, and the MMPI-2. The Bem Sex-Role Inventory (Bem, 1974) is based on the concept of psychological androgyny, which has been challenged in recent years (see Deaux, 1985). Still another model of masculinity–femininity is reflected in Spence, Helmreich, and Stapp's Personal Attributes Questionnaire (Spence & Helmreich, 1978).

Psychologists using masculinity–femininity variables in career assessment contexts should be careful to identify whatever they are measuring—masculinity, femininity, or androgyny—and the extent to which the test was validated against occupational norms. Because of the often misunderstood nature of the labels attached to this construct, assessors and counselors must be especially careful to differentiate masculinity–femininity and sexual orientation or preference.

Because masculinity–femininity is typically defined in terms of cultural stereotypes of male and female behavior, including the preference for certain types of occupations, care must be taken to change measures of masculinity and femininity to reflect changes in society (see Lunneborg & Lunneborg, 1985). Measures based on outmoded constructs of male- or female-appropriate behavior may result in inappropriate conclusions about the occupational profiles of career assessees.

Other Promising Personality Variables

Several other personality variables have shown promise for use in career assessment, but they have been less extensively researched. These include conscientiousness (Costa & McCrae, 1986); agreeableness and need for affiliation (Costa & McCrae, 1986; Schutz, 1978); energy and general activity level (J. S. Guilford et al., 1976; Derman et al., 1978); field dependence–independence (Fry & Thompson, 1977; Goodenough, 1985; Goodenough, Oltman, & Cox, 1987; McKenna, 1984; Witkin, Moore, Goodenough, & Cox, 1977); openness (Costa & McCrae, 1985b; McCrae, 1987); sensitivity versus tough-mindedness (Evans and Quarterman, 1983; Heaven, Connors, & Trevethan, 1987; Howard & Bray, 1988; Institute for Personality and Ability Testing, 1986; Kirkcaldy, 1982); persistence (Lamont & Lundstrom, 1977); and the MBTI (Briggs & Myers, 1977) variables of intuiting versus sensing, thinking versus feeling, and judging versus perceiving.

Summary

Research directions. This review illustrates the need for improving the clinical applicability of personality assessment measures and particularly for establishing a consensus on which variables should be measured in career assessment. The measurement of personality variables relevant for career assessment is still at the incipient stage, despite the large number of studies cited in this chapter. Missing from the literature is an examination of how scores in a particular direction on personality measures longitudinally predict job behavior. The relations among personality variables also need further exploration.

Unfortunately, much of the best current literature on the occupational implications of various personality constructs has been conducted with single test instruments, often by the authors of the tests themselves. Although the attempt to compare occupational profiles on a single personality measure can be lauded in principle, in practice no broadbrush instrument yet promulgated is the "best" measure of all constructs. To better understand how various personality measures relate to real-world occupational contexts, one must compare multiple measures of the same construct in the same study. Finally, one must identify subgroups of members of the same occupation who differ on personality characteristics. In this manner, people whose personality characteristics are being measured for career assessment may more appropriately be matched with relevant job groups.

Clinical issues in personality measurement. In assessing individual clients for occupational purposes, the clinician must keep in mind the differences between modal characteristics of occupational groups and the differences, within occupational groups, of more and less successful members of the occupation. Personality characteristics alone are unlikely to predict appropriate occupational placement, but these variables may provide important dimensions otherwise missing from the assessment of abilities and interests. To assume, for example, that an assessee scoring high on the Guilford–Zimmerman Ascendance scale would be appropriate only for a managerial occupation is erroneous because high scores on the Ascendance scale may be found in a variety of successful people in nonmanagerial occupations.

Within a given occupation, it is also important to recall the wide variability of personality scores even when the modal or mean profile is consistent with expected characteristics. Thus, on the basis of personality alone, the career assessor should not discourage individuals from following a particular career path (assuming that ability and interest patterns are appropriate for the intended occupation). On the other hand, the person being assessed does need to understand the modal characteristics of the occupation; how deviations from that profile may affect the individual; and, if there are better occupational matches with the profile, what they might be. The following case example is illustrative.

Personality Assessment: An Example

Freda F. was 30 years old at the time of her career assessment. As an adolescent, she had been fiercely independent and had experienced a great deal of conflict with her parents. After dropping out of high school, she eventually obtained a graduate equivalency degree and entered college. Although she had initially thought of law, she instead majored in business and entered a managerial training program with a large conservative corporation in New York. The firm specialized in financial matters. She found the work to be highly unsatisfying, feeling that the firm was especially unsupportive of women. She did not suffer in silence and, anticipating that job action would soon be taken against her, she quit. At the time of her career assessment, she had taken a job with a fashionable restaurant in New York working as a waitress and special assistant to the manager. She was making a good deal of money through her tips and salary and enjoyed interacting with the "high society" crowd. However, she secretly felt that her youth was rapidly vanishing and that it was time for her to get on with what really interested her. She contemplated joining a social service organization or, alternatively, going back to school for a degree in social work or clinical psychology to enable her to assist needy children, with whom she felt great affinity.

For Freda, the validity indicator on the CAQ fell within normal limits. As shown in Table 4.2, she had high scores on the clinical scales of the CAQ intended to measure lack of inhibition

Table 4.2
Results of the Clinical Analysis Questionnaire

16PF factor	Sten score[a]	Direction
A. Warmth	7	Personable
B. Intelligence	8+	Abstract
C. Emotional Stability	6	Average
E. Dominance	9	Competitive
F. Impulsivity	9	Impulsive
G. Conformity	3	Nonconforming
H. Boldness	7	Bold
I. Sensitivity	10	Tender-minded
L. Suspiciousness	5	Average
M. Imagination	7	Highly imaginative
N. Shrewdness	5	Average
O. Insecurity	6	Average
Q1. Radicalism	8	Innovative
Q2. Self-Sufficiency	8	Self-resourceful
Q3. Self-Discipline	3	Undisciplined
Q4. Tension	7	Frustrated

Note. 16PF = Sixteen Personality Factor Questionnaire. Sten score source: Krug (1980).
[a]Compared with adult female normal personality norms.

and excitement seeking as well as (somewhat inconsistently) obsessiveness. Her second-order factors profiled her as extraverted, easily swayed by feelings, independent, unrestrained, immature, and nonneurotic.

On other measures of personality, similar characteristics were found. For example, on the EPPS (on which her consistency score was at the 66th percentile), she earned high scores on needs for exhibition (97th percentile), intraception (93rd percentile), dominance (94th percentile), and change (98th percentile) and earned low scores on needs for order (1st percentile), deference (9th percentile), and endurance (2nd percentile). Curiously, for one who found teaching roles appealing, her scores on the measures of nurturance (13th percentile) and affiliation (20th percentile) were low.

Of note was her average score on the need for achievement scale on the EPPS (50th percentile), suggesting the absence of a driving desire to get ahead, which might have accounted for some of her vacillation from one occupational and educational pursuit to the next.

Her results on the CPI presented a somewhat consistent picture (see Table 4.3). On this test, two themes were noted: a strongly prosocial, self-assertive tendency coupled with the tendency to rebel against authority. Her nontraditional views suggested a pattern of rebelliousness, perhaps from adolescence, not yet resolved. The scores on the Tolerance and Flexibility scales were low for someone aspiring to the helping professions, and her difficulty presenting herself in a positive light might have made her unsuited to business. Again, the achievement scores have shown that she feels no need to get ahead, and she may therefore be almost too comfortable with the absence of direction and achievement in her occupational life. Although Gough's (1987) second-order variables are not yet sufficiently cross-validated for routine clinical use, it is noteworthy that Freda scored in both the prosocial (extraverted) and the norm-questioning directions. She appears to be in conflict over her present life circumstances (V3), but her basic "type" (gamma) makes her tend to be rebellious and self-indulgent unless she can find a way to channel her energies and innovation more effectively. Interestingly, in Gough's (1987, pp. 22–23) occupational samples, modal gammas included both juvenile delinquents and psychology, social work, and nursing graduate students.

On the projective measures, several additional findings help to clarify the specific issues important in working with this client. To Card 1 of the TAT, for example, Freda gave the following story:

> John is an 8-year-old and his mother is making him take violin lessons against his will. He's supposed to practice every day while the rest of the kids are out playing. He's sitting in his room depressed. You want an outcome, eh?

Table 4.3

Results of the California Psychological Inventory

Scale	Score	Direction
Dominance	33	Dominant
Capacity for Status	24	Ambitious, independent
Sociability	26	Sociable
Social Presence	28	Self-assured
Self-Acceptance	23	High self-opinion
Independence	23	Self-sufficient
Empathy	25	Empathetic
Responsibility	22	Duty unbound
Socialization	26	Rule resistant
Self-Control	13	Inappropriately direct
Good Impression	13	Low interest in pleasing others
Communality	38	Sees self as fitting in
Well-Being	28	Worried about personal problems
Tolerance	20	Skeptical of others
Achievement (Conformity)	30	Driven to do well
Achievement (Independence)	22	Average
Intellectual Efficiency	29	Not intellectual
Psychological Mindedness	13	Not intellectual
Flexibility	8	Dislikes change
Masculinity–Femininity	13	Action-oriented, "masculine"
V1 Norm Favoring vs. Questioning[a]	7	Norm questioning
V2 Externality–Internality[a]	22	Externality
V3 Realization[a]	36	Level 4 (midlevel)

Note. The sources of the scale descriptions are Gough (1987) and Megargee (1972).

[a]Second-order variable, gamma type.

The outcome is he walks over to his bed and picks up a book instead.

Her other stories confirmed her tendency to have conflict with authority, often in a dramatic way. She appeared to view herself as unjustly treated by others but willing to fight the battle valiantly, even while expecting an inglorious end. For example, to Card 17BM on the TAT, she gave the following story:

> This takes place back in ancient Rome. This man committed a crime. Either they would cut off his hand—eye for eye and tooth for tooth—or he would be sent to the pit and have to fight off something—a wild boar—and at this moment he's still 3–4 feet away from the pit. He hears cheering and knows they want him to die. . . .He falls into a trance, falls into a daydream about his wife and children. What he stole were just staples. It seems so unfair that just a few had any wealth and the majority were led around by the nose. He got so angry he forgot where he was, lost his grip, let go and was trampled to death—ate him—which is exactly what the crowd wanted.

This story also illustrates a possible theme of narcissism (the "hero" in the story is certainly the center of great attention, albeit negative) and of conflict over succeeding (needs must be met surreptiously and, when one tries and is successful, there may be punishment). She identifies with the man who has (presumably for his and his family's survival) stolen food items yet is being killed, to the delight of the crowd. In the end, however, it is the victim's anger rather than the crowd itself that kills him because it is only when he "lets go" (quite literally in this case) of his anger, when he lets it loose, that he falls to his death.

On sentence-completion measures, Freda continued the aforementioned themes: "Bosses . . . must earn my respect if they want me to do as I'm told"; "I regret . . . nothing I have ever done in my entire life"; "Too many people . . . pass judgment and are narrow minded." However, another, more vulnerable side was shown to underly the client's outward strength.

For example: "I often think of myself as . . . outwardly strong and independent, but inwardly emotionally needy"; "If I don't succeed, I . . . am my worst critic"; "My greatest fear . . . is that I'll just coast through life"; "I . . . hate being lost, confused and unsure."

In summary, Freda F. presents with a variety of personality issues that will be important in understanding her career choice and adjustment on the job. The characteristic theme of rebelliousness must be examined further. If she is to make a satisfactory adjustment in many occupational settings, this feature must be more effectively channelled or directed. Depending on the rest of the occupational profile, Freda may wish to consider occupations such as those involving work with adolescents. Alternatively, again depending on the ability and personality pattern, counseling to better understand and control the apparent authority conflicts may be needed.

5

Integrating Interest, Ability, and Personality Data

I n this chapter I discuss methods for combining complex psychological assessment data to obtain a comprehensive understanding of the assessee. This difficult clinical task requires
careful analysis of diverse data in order to develop a comprehensive career portrait of the assessee and capture the assessee's complexity and diversity. In this chapter, the emphasis is
on understanding methodologies for combining across data sets;
in chapter 6, I address issues of providing feedback to the assessee or the corporate client.

Cross-Domain Relationships

A major premise of this book is the necessity of combining
ability, interest, and personality data to arrive at a comprehensive understanding of career dynamics. Although there is a rich
and diverse literature on the occupational applications of the
various intradomain variables just discussed, there is a paucity
of literature on the relationship across domains. This appears
to be changing, albeit slowly.

Cross-domain relationships include ability–personality interactions, ability–interest interactions, interest–personality interactions, and, most complexly, ability–interest–personality
combinations. Except for clinical writings on the subject (e.g.,

Blatt & Allison, 1981; Murray, 1938), little systematic research attention has yet been given to the cross-domain relationships.

An exception is R. B. Cattell and his associates' (especially Horn, 1976) important work in the ability–personality area. R. B. Cattell (1987), as much as anyone else, has appreciated that personality and ability characteristics are related and that both must be examined to understand differential patterns of performance. Cattell's attention to this area is not recent (see R. B. Cattell, 1945a, 1945b). Although Cattell's models have not formally integrated contemporary occupational interest theories, they have addressed the ability–personality interaction, particularly the relation between ability and motivation and interests in the sense of "sentiments" that direct the types of activities that one will find appealing (see R. B. Cattell & Horn, 1964). Although Cattell's work in this area must be criticized for too-frequent reliance on his own measures of ability and personality, which are not without problems, he has helped to demonstrate that ability and personality are conceptually not separable constructs (see especially R. B. Cattell, 1987; Hakstian & Cattell, 1978a). Horn (1977) concluded, probably overstating the case, "abilities are traits of personality. They constitute an important part of the total personality and a part that has been studied more thoroughly than most other parts" (p. 164).

Ability–Personality Relationships

Although it is true that there is extensive literature on ability measurement, the literature examining the personality–ability interaction is more limited than Horn's (1977) generalization might suggest. In fact, Horn's review of "suggestive relationships" between abilities and "other aspects of personality" gives a much less overarching, but more realistic and intriguing, state of the personality–ability interaction literature. The personality variables mentioned include relations between speed of closure, flexibility of closure (akin to field independence–dependence), verbal and numerical skills, and spatial abilities. People scoring high on speed of closure, Horn noted, tend to score high on personality factors indicating an absence of learned inhibition, whereas those scoring high on flexibility of closure tend to be free-thinking, cold and distant in interpersonal relationships, and uninfluenced by others (the essence of the Investigative interest type in Holland's, 1985a, model). High verbal and numerical abilities tend to be associated with high ego strength and superego development, whereas high spatial ability, at least for men, leans the individual toward "masculine reticence" (Horn, 1976).

R. B. Cattell's (1987) most recent definitive statement on ability–personality interactions identified similar and additional ability–personality relations. He also noted that there are personality traits that simulate ability in their behavioral manifestations. These included the aforementioned field dependence–independence, general inhibition factors, and ego strength, among others. Similarly, intelligence appears to predispose the individual toward certain personality characteristics (e.g., conscientiousness, behavioral control, superego strength, persistence, and certain aspects of assertiveness).

R. B. Cattell (1987) suggested other promising modal personality–ability interactions, including the relation between Realistic-related abilities (e.g., mechanical and spatial abilities) and an introverted, tough-minded, "realistic," nonemotional personality orientation. In contrast, drawing ability (measured primitively, I believe, in Cattell's instrumentation) tends to correlate with an intuitive, warm, and extraverted interpersonal nature. Social intelligence was reported by Cattell to be associated with the following personality portrait: high warmth, extraversion, interpersonal ability, high ego strength, low guilt, and high self-sentiment. The "creative" ability–personality profile is characterized by high intelligence, introversion, high dominance (suggesting that the Sixteen Personality Factor Questionnaire [16PF] measure is something other than interpersonal dominance in the California Psychological Inventory [CPI] sense), sensitive (rather than tough-minded), high in imagination, self-sufficient, and radical rather than conservative (R. B. Cattell, 1987; see also Drevedahl & Cattell, 1958). However, in that similar patterns of personality emerge for both creative artists and creative scientists, it must be presumed that interests and ability patterns (when ability is defined more complexly than simply intelligence) would in such circumstances predict whether science or arts constitute a better outlet for the creativity. These and other findings with potential career assessment implications are reported as suggestive, not definitive, and Cattell noted, appropriately, that

> achievement is a many-faceted thing, and, except for a few, relatively carefully studied occupations and examination performances . . . the greater number of achievements—from driving fifty years without an accident to raising a family of effective citizens—as yet remain undocumented and experimentally unanalyzed. (R. B. Cattell, 1987, p. 464)

Although he did present some quantitative equations to suggest the combination of personality–ability variables that predict criteria such as freedom from accidents and success in sales or as a psychiatric technician, the underlying data base and ability measures may be unacceptably small and the suggested precision of prediction too extreme to apply the results in routine clinical practice. Hakstian and Cattell (1978a) also provided a methodology for examining interbattery factor structures.

More recently, Hough (1990) examined the relation between selected characteristics of ability and personality in a large U.S. Army sample. Although the results are just now beginning to appear in the professional literature, job performance was influenced (using a predictive validity paradigm) by the following groupings of personality variables: potency (dominance and energy level), achievement (self-esteem and work orientation), dependability (traditional values, nondelinquency, and conscientiousness) and agreeableness (cooperativeness). Hough noted that personality factors were the only variables that added significant predictive validity to the ability measures. Similar findings suggesting that personality provides additive explanatory power to ability variables in personnel research contexts have been reported by Bentz (1985) and by Howard and Bray (1988).

Although intriguing, ability–personality research does not yet yield a clear and coherent theory of the nature of ability–personality variable interactions. The findings of Horn, R. B. Cattell, and the handful of other researchers working at the ability–personality interface are intriguing and suggestive of the ultimate validity of the interdomain model. However, the current state of the research literature is handicapping for the clinician who must deal with individual scores on tests and real-life career concerns. At an operational level, the clinician currently receives little help from the literature in determining how to best combine across ability interest and personality measures, how to differentially weight personality and ability data (not to mention interest variables), especially when there are inconsistencies across the domains. Even if it were to be demonstrated that fit in one domain (say, abilities) is more important for career success than fit in another domain (e.g., interests or personality), there would still be the problem of determining which variables in the ability domain were most predictive of positive outcomes for each career path. Also needed would be a methodology to assess degree of fit or misfit. As the literature is now, there is no theoretical or well-validated empirical basis for predicting quantitatively the appropriate variables to measure and the calculus for determining greater and lesser fit except for the congruency measures in the vocational interests (see chap. 2). Accordingly, for the present, judging degree of fit between person and occupation remains a matter of clinical judgment and calls for much work on the client's part in sorting out, from the various findings, which have the most personal salience and need for expression.

Interest–Personality Relationships

Concerning interest–personality interactions, Holland (1985a) viewed vocational interests as measures of personality; therefore, cross-domain relations between personality and interest variables would be expected. An important study by Costa et al. (1984) showed predictable relations between interests and personality consistent with what both theories would predict. Specifically, both the Extraversion and Openness scales of the NEO Personality Inventory (Costa & McCrae, 1985b) were differentially associated with the Holland interest types. For both sexes, Openness scores were strongly associated with Artistic and Investigative scale scores (and less strongly with Social and Enterprising scores), whereas Extraversion scores were highly associated with Social and Enterprising scores for both sexes. For women, there was also a positive and statistically significant correlation between Artistic and Extraversion scores.

Much of the earlier research literature on the relation between vocational interests and personality factors relied on comparison of scores on an interest measure with scores on a broad-brush personality measure. Generally, a mixed pattern has been reported with this methodology, an understandable finding because such studies have often been atheoretical. Studies by Wakefield and Cunningham (1975) and Utz and Korben (1976) compared scores on the Edwards Personal Preference Schedule (EPPS) with, respectively, the Vocational Preference Inventory and the Strong Vocational Interest Blank (SVIB). Both studies showed a mixed pattern of results on the relation between the interest variables and the personality variables. Modest commonalities were found between the two domains. Turner and Horn (1975) found that sex moderated the personality–interest relation, with a stronger association between the two domains being found for men than for women.

Other researchers have examined different aspects of the personality–interest relationship. R. W. Johnson et al. (1975) examined the relation between CPI factors and SVIB occupational scales. The most overlap occurred between CPI Extraversion, Emotional Sensitivity, and Independent Thought factors. S. G. Murray (1981) examined the relation of one aspect of vocational interests: Low Profile (LP) and High Profile (HP) scores on the SVIB and scores on the CPI. LPs, in contrast to HPs, scored lower on the CPI Dominance, Capacity for Status, and Sociability scores, whereas HPs scored higher than LPs on Authority, Creativity, and Responsibility scales on the Minnesota Importance Questionnaire.

Still other, more behaviorally anchored research has relied on an independent classification of occupations, examining personality characteristics of individuals in certain defined occupations. Peraino and Willerman (1983), for example, administered the 16PF to adult men in four occupational groups (Realistic, Investigative, Social, and Enterprising). Enterprising types had the highest scores on a second-order Extraversion factor and Investigative workers scored the highest on a scale measuring cognitive (vs. emotive) orientation and on a scale measuring independence. Witkin, Moore, Goodenough, and Cox (1977) found an association between field independence and expressed interests in the Realistic and Investigative areas and, among field-dependent people, increased interests in the Social and Enterprising interests. More recent research (York & Tinsley, 1986) raises questions about the relation between the defined interest types and field independence and dependence.

Interest–Ability Relationships

Modern literature on the relation between abilities and interests is beginning to emerge. Early studies (e.g., Berdie, 1943; Darley, 1941; R. W. Johnson, 1965; Strong, 1943; see Randahl, 1990, and Lowman et al., 1985, for literature reviews) predated recent developments in vocational interest theory, especially the emergence of Holland's (1985b) six-factor model. Such studies (and even more contemporary ones, such as Kelso, Holland, & Gottfredson, 1977; R. G. Turner & Hibbs, 1977) have tended to find little common variance between interests and abilities. However, those studies have typically been limited in the use of relatively narrow tests of abilities (primarily variations of measures of intelligence, especially verbal intelligence), male rather than mixed-sex samples, and highly select samples (mostly intellectually able college students).

More recent studies, however, have corrected some of the early deficits and have extended the literature. Lowman et al. (1985), using a sample of college women, examined associations between abilities corresponding to each of the six Holland interest types and vocational interests as measured by the Self-Directed Search (Holland, 1979, 1987). These researchers found a similar factor structure between these ability measures and the six-factor interest model, except that (a) no ability factor analogous to the Realistic area emerged in this all-women sample and (b) there were two abilities rather than one ability corresponding to the Artistic area. Common variance between the abilities and the interest variables, however, was low.

Using a different methodology, different tests of ability and interest and a heterogeneous sample, Randahl's (1990) recent research provides new perspectives on the relation between interests and abilities. In that study, profile analyses rather than correlational and canonical analyses were used. The SVIB (Campbell, 1981) was used as the measure of interest and the subtests of the General Ability Test Battery (GATB); U.S. Department of Labor, 1970, 1979) as the measure of abilities. The results, using a complex methodology, demonstrated a pattern of relationships between abilities and interests that was much more supportive of the predicted ability–interest relationship than has been found by other studies. Note, however, that unlike the Lowman et al. (1985) study, this one did not include measures of music, art, social–interpersonal, or managerial abilities. Moreover, the samples were, on average, higher than average on intellectual levels, had a higher than expected level of endorsed Artistic interest codes, and were all vocational clinic clients and therefore presumably not representative of the general population.

Overall, there is a need for considerably more research on ability–interest relationships. Especially needed are studies conducted (as in the Lowman et al., 1985, study) with nonclinical populations, but covering both sexes and a representative sample of the population, not just the highly intelligent.

Interest–Ability–Personality Relationships

No recent studies were found in the literature addressing the ability–interest–personality interactions simultaneously except, within the Social occupational area, for the research of Lowman and Leeman (1988), which was limited by the abbreviated nature of the personality measure used. The ancient call (e.g., Altender, 1940) for measuring across ability, interest, and personality domains in career assessment has yet to be routinely translated into either research or practice.

In the absence of research literature, a conceptual rationale must be used for combining clinically across interest, ability, and personality data. Table 5.1 shows a summary of the six Holland types (Holland, 1985a), the ability relationships that theoretically would be expected to be associated with the type, and the expected personality characteristics from among the variables discussed in chapter 4 that would have a reasonable rationale for scoring in a particular direction on the basis of the research literature already reviewed. This table is not a practical guideline to be routinely incorporated into clinical practice but rather as a guide to expected relationships and a source of research hypotheses for further exploration and study.

Clinical Principles for Integrating Complex Career Assessment Data

Clearly, the research literature on cross-domain relationships is just beginning to emerge. However, because the predictive power of each of the domains in career issues has been separately demonstrated, the practicing clinician must decide to either focus only on one or two domains (e.g., abilities and interests) or to attempt to integrate cross-domain data more clinically. The latter task is similar to the methodology used by clinicians in integrating ability (intellectual) data and personality data in doing clinical assessments with psychologically disturbed clients.

To improve the likelihood of drawing valid interdomain conclusions about career assessees, I provide a preliminary statement on principles for clinically interpreting and integrating complex psychological assessment results in this section. These principles are intentionally generic until the research literature

Table 5.1
Integration of Interest, Ability, and Personality Variables

Interest	Abilities	Personality

Realistic	+ Mechanical
	+ Spatial
	− Verbal reasoning
	− "g"
	− Social and
	   interpersonal
		+ Reserved and introverted
		− Intellectance
		− Ascendance
		+ Masculinity
		− /○Adjustment and Self-
		   control
		+ Tough-mindedness

Investigative	+ Reasoning + "g" + Convergent thinking	+ Adjustment − Agreeableness − Ascendance + Intellectance + Introversive + Masculinity + Self-control + Tough-mindedness

Artistic	+ Aesthetic ability
	+ Judgment and
	+ Spatial *or*
	+ Musical ability
	   and/or
	+ Divergent
	   thinking
		− Adjustment
		− Agreeablenes
		− Ascendance
		+ / − Intellectance
		+ Introversion (with
		   exceptions)
		Masculinity + female;
		   − male self-control
		+ / − Self-control[a]
		− Tough-mindedness

Social	+ Social and
	   interpersonal
	   abilities
		+ Adjustment
		+ Ascendance[b]
		+ Intellectance
		− Introversion
		+ Likeability
		− Masculinity
		+ Self-control
		− Tough-mindedness

(table continues)

Table 5.1   (*Continued*)

Interest	Abilities	Personality
Enterprising	+ Organizing and "managing" skills + "g" + Social and interpersonal skills	+ Adjustment + Ascendance + Intellectance − Introversion + Masculinity + Self-control + Tough-mindedness
Conventional	+ Perceptual speed and accuracy + Computational	○ Adjustment − Ascendance − Intellectance + Introversion − Masculinity + Self-control + Tough-mindedness

Note. "+" = high scores, "−" = low scores, and "○" = medium scores.
[a] "+" = Self-control in work and "−" = in personal life.
[b] High interpersonal ascendance; low need for power over others.

provides clearer guidance on the relative weight of the various variables used in career assessments.

1. *Separately evaluate the data in each domain (interests, ability, and personality) as if the other data did not exist.* The assessor should independently review the data from each of the three domains to determine the data's implications for the assessee's career concerns. This process requires that the career assessor or counselor have expertise in all three of the major career assessment domains discussed in this book: vocational interests, personality, and abilities. Hypotheses about the career implications of the data should be generated at each stage of the process. For

example, in considering interest data, one would want to know which occupational choices are the most and least compatible with the high-point scores. Are there areas of potential conflict within interests or, for abilities, does the client show "too many" abilities such that integrated expression may be difficult? No effort should be initially made to integrate the domain-specific data at this stage.

The career assessor proceeds in the evaluation of each set of data independently, generating hypotheses and issues requiring further clarification and elaboration that can be checked against the findings from other domains. For example, in reviewing a client's vocational interest data, the assessor might note an apparent conflict between managerial and helping (Enterprising and Social) interests and the scientific (Investigative) interests. In such instances, the counselor would want to know the origin of the Investigative interests: Are there strong intellectual abilities that might be receiving limited expression in the client's current position? Has the client worked in any managerial or sales position in which intellectual or scientific interests might have been needed (e.g., selling technical products for a computer firm)? Is there some way to clarify whether the interests are more Enterprising than Social or more Social than Enterprising? For example, is there a history of doing volunteer and other helping work? What about the relative conflict between financial and helping interests? These sorts of questions cannot be resolved on the basis of the test scores alone; additional work in career counseling sessions may be needed to help define and clarify these issues.

2. *After hypotheses have been separately generated in each domain, cross-domain comparisons can be made.* One way to begin the process of intregrating complex career assessment findings is to generate a table with three separate columns, one each for abilities, interests, and personality. The major findings for each domain can then be listed side by side, along with questions that cannot be resolved on the basis of these findings alone. For example, in the Fred D. case (presented later in this chapter), a portion of these columns might appear as follows:

Interests	Abilities	Personality
Highest interests in Enterprising, Social, and Investigative. What accounts for the Investigative interests in a managerial or sales profile? How does this interest get expressed? Is the apparent conflict in interests accounting for his job unhappiness?	Greatest strengths in Investigative, Social, and Enterprising areas. Is he an underachiever? How does his high intelligence get manifested?	Generally positive, prosocial, but has tendencies toward nonconformity. Does he conflict with authority? Is he passive-aggressive?

3. *Each tentative conclusion ideally should be supported by at least two sources of data.* Because the practice of career assessment and counseling is not an exact science, and the measures used generally do not have good validity for career assessment, it is important to base conclusions and even hypotheses on more than one data source. This is not always possible, of course, because to include two measures of every variable in every case the long assessment process would become even more protracted. However, in some instances, comparable variables moving in a consistent direction provide sufficient basis for drawing conclusions. For example, the Dominance scale of the CPI, the Need for Dominance scale of the EPPS, the Dominance (E) scale of the 16PF, or the Clinical Analysis Questionnaire (CAQ) are all measuring conceptually similar variables, although each scale has been developed and validated differently. If, for a given client, these scales are all consistent with one another and moving in the opposite direction of scales that are conceptually opposite (such as in the case of dominance and the need for abasement on the

"I was born in a trunk at the Morosco Theatre, but, as it turned out, I went into wholesale office supplies."

Drawing by Weber; © 1979 The New Yorker Magazine, Inc.

EPPS), then there is more solid ground for reaching a conclusion about tendencies toward assertiveness as a general characteristic of personality than if these variables present an inconsistent pattern.

4. *Inconsistent hypotheses may not need to be fully resolved.* It is not necessary to resolve every source of disagreement or discrepancy in order to draw meaningful conclusions about an assessee. Some data simply raise difficult or inconclusive issues that will require either more data, time, or life experience to resolve. It is not the task of the testing and counseling process to resolve all of these conflicts. However, the career counselor does have an obligation to help the assessee to become aware of sources of potential inconsistency or conflict and to understand how the conflict might be worked on or through. Although method variance may account for some discrepancies in psychological test results, it is also possible that the obtained differences represent sources of conflict within the personality. In such cases, it is not the task of the career assessor to *resolve* the discrepancies but to make the issue and its dimensions clear to the assessee.

For example, Social and Realistic vocational interests are thought to represent theoretically opposing characteristics of personality (Holland, 1985a, 1987). If present in the same individual, they are a potential source of frustration and conflict because those aspects of the person will be trying to be expressed in ways that are fundamentally incompatible with one another. Similarly, if an individual has skills both in relating to others and in working with mechanical objects, these may be difficult to make use of in one job. Finally, a person may be, in personality, genuinely conflicted between aggressiveness and submission. On an objective measure of personality, such as the EPPS or the Guilford-Zimmerman Temperament Survey, the individual may demonstrate a high need for dominance, whereas on more complex projective measures such as the Thematic Apperception Test (TAT), the need or personality tendency may be more complexly understood as a source of possible conflict.

Too many psychologists examine single variables in isolation and determine the characteristics of people who score high and low on the variable. More complex research may venture out to more than one variable and investigate, for example, the relation between empathy and, say, internal–external locus of control. This individualistic variable approach to assessment may make for easier research, but it has limited application to the task of assessing individuals in real-life contexts. The real-life individual may be characterized on a number of dimensions and these dimensions are not always compatible with each other. People experience both internal and external sources of discrepancy and conflict, and the real-life reality is much more complex and hard to influence than unidimensional models suggest. The important point is that discrepancies on an array of test results may represent real sources of conflict for an individual, not just a measurement problem. When the conflict has been identified, it may be easier to work with. Moreover, conflicts in career issues are analogous to those of personality: They may need years of experience and work to become resolved or accepted.

5. *Major conclusions should be summarized in a point-by-point fashion.* These include the data that emerge with convincing consistency from the results. For example:

- This is a profile consistent with a career in the sciences.
- Although strong scientific interests were expressed by the client, there is limited support for abilities at the independent-scientist level. The individual might be directed to lower level positions within the Investigative or scientific arena, such as technician or laboratory assistant.
- This vocational profile is most consistent with Artistic interests and abilities. The presence of significant personality conflicts does not change this conclusion but may point to the need for assistance in working through some areas of emotional conflict. These conflicts may also be an important part of the creative process.

As Case 5.1 illustrates, matching individuals and their jobs is far more complex than present clinical practice or research findings acknowledge. There is indication that a mismatch between person and job characteristics will result in lower job outcomes such as productivity and satisfaction. This relationship thus far has been examined primarily as it relates to vocational interests rather than to abilities or personality. Case 5.1 gives an indication of the number of variables needing to be examined and the difficulties in combining across multiple domains. Clinical ability to integrate the various test findings with the problems experienced on the job is suggested until further research is developed. The task of career assessment and counseling is obviously made easier if the areas of emphasis and strength in one domain are matched by comparable areas of emphasis in the other two domains.

Integrative Career Assessment Hypotheses

Finally, in this section I offer several implicit hypotheses about the career assessment process in differentiating the relative importance of cross-domain findings.

1. The most appropriate career path for bringing lasting growth and satisfaction to an individual is the one most congruent with individual abilities, interests, and personality.

2. When there is a conflict between degree of fit to a job (or career) and the three domains, abilities and interests take precedence over personality characteristics (i.e., the major career choice should be dictated by the abilities and interests, and personality variables may help "fine tune" the particular avenues used for its expression).

3. Abilities, if possessed, must actively be used or will result in dissatisfaction and a push for expression.

4. Experientially and qualitatively, the degree of fit is not just a quantitative issue but a matter of careful and often tedious comparison of relative fits and misfits, likes and dislikes.

5. Within most career paths, there are generally multiple career paths that an individual can take that are reasonable congruent with self. This permits application of "additional variables" such as personality characteristics to help create a more maximal fit with the career. For example, two individuals with the same vocational interest pattern (say, Enterprising–Artistic–Social) may both attend and successfully graduate from law school. Both have high inductive reasoning ability and high verbal fluency, but one is extraverted and highly gregarious, whereas the other is shy and reserved. Although both may become excellent attorneys, the former may enter criminal trial law while the latter flourishes by specializing in antitrust law, especially doing research.

6. The choice of a general career path and fine tuning it to individual abilities and personality often may require considerable individualized work with a professionally trained vocational counselor or psychologist. Merely presenting the results of aptitude testing does not allow individuals adequate time to assimilate information and to translate understanding into behavioral terms. Most career counseling ends when it should be beginning.

7. Fantasized career changes do not necessarily represent the best course of action for treating dissatisfaction. In assessing the appropriateness of individuals wanting to change professions, a thorough analysis of what the client finds dissatisfying

in his or her present occupation is important. When someone is dissatisfied in a career, the individual typically fantasizes that something else, often anything else, would be superior. This may lead to the attribution of exaggerated and unrealistically positive characteristics to alternative career possibilities. Career counseling may help an individual be protected from a move away from rather than toward a career or job choice.

Thomas and Robbins (1979), for example, found in an empirical study of 61 middle-aged men who left managerial or professional careers that a majority ended up in jobs that were no more congruent with their vocational interests than their old jobs; even among those who did change to a more congruent career, there was no greater satisfaction experienced with the new than with the old occupation. The literature on middle-age career changers has been reviewed by D. Brown (1984a). Thus, there is suggestion that the decision to change careers midstream should not be undertaken without careful analysis of sources of dissatisfaction if another misfit is to be avoided. When changes are made precipitously, they are often driven by a desire to escape rather than by a genuine commitment to the new choice, potentially resulting in subsequent disappointment. Assessing sources of dissatisfaction that are associated with the desire for a change thus becomes an important part of the counseling process for those contemplating a career change.

Case 5.1: A Midlife Career Changer

The following case illustrates the complexities of combining across domains. It presents a typical array of personality, ability, and interest data recommended to be collected by those using the interdomain model of career assessment. As recommended, these data are interpreted both as data with normative importance and against the referral questions.

Background

Fred D., in his late 30s at the time of assessment, sought career counseling because he was contemplating leaving his position as a securities analyst. At the time of the assessment, he was seriously considering a change in careers, describing both generalized unhappiness in his work and a concern about his present employer's ethical practices. Although his performance in his profession had generally been acceptable, it was erratic, varying with the degree of his frustration. In thinking about his career options, Mr. D. had considered several alternatives to his present job, including professional writing, opening his own business, and becoming a real estate appraiser.

Mr. D. was the third of four children. His father, an attorney, worked successfully for a large law firm; his mother, who was a homemaker while her children were young, was employed in later years as a teacher. At the time of the assessment, all of the client's siblings were grown. A brother worked as an attorney and his other siblings were in administrative positions. He was moderately close to his family, especially his brother, but considerable family conflict in his youth had resulted in infrequent contact in adulthood.

The bulk of Mr. D.'s explicitly voiced dissatisfaction with his profession concerned values. He was upset about the apparent dishonesty of many securities advisors, including those with whom he worked, and felt that his basic honesty and desire to help others found limited outlets in this field. However, he had not seriously considered assisting those with limited resources or nonprofit organizations, which might result in work more compatible with his espoused values.

Mr. D. had generally received good evaluations of his work and felt that he did what was assigned to him fairly well. However, he seemed to have no identification with the profession and was not motivated to rise within the organization where he worked, the usual burning ambition of people in his occupation. He had worked for several large firms but typically had quit after a year or two when his dissatisfaction became intolerable. As a result, he was less far along in the hierarchy than were his same-aged peers.

At the time of the assessment, Mr. D. was trying to decide how best to reenter the workforce because he had been staying at home to help his wife, a writer, complete a book that had taken several years longer than expected. He did some work in editing but mostly helped by managing the household and taking care of the couple's two preschool children. A small inheritance and book royalty advance his wife had received allowed him to stay home during this period. A the time of his assessment, Mr. D.'s wife was in the final editing stages of the book, the oldest child was ready to enter kindergarten, and it was no longer necessary for Mr. D. to stay home. During his sabbatical from work, Mr. D. had not been able to do much with his avocation—fiction writing—but he did write a few short stories and a long poem, none of which he submitted for professional review or publication consideration.

As an undergraduate, Mr. D. had majored in sociology. With some difficulty, he was accepted into a graduate management program that he completed successfully but with little distinction and some difficulty. He first became interested in writing in his 20s. He took a few courses in the subject and unsuccessfully attempted to enroll in a highly select creative-writing course in his community. When he had felt encouraged but not accepted by the faculty in this program, he was frustrated and seemed to interpret this as a possible sign that he should not pursue a writing career. However, he had not been "tested" in the marketplace.

Mr. D. was ambivalent about seeking career assessment. At the time of the initial interview, he appeared to be recovering from clinical depression. An obviously bright and talkative, youthful-appearing man, Mr. D. expressed considerable confusion about the appropriate next direction of his career. He noted that his wife was urging him to go back to a traditional job and felt that he did not have the temperament to have a writing career. However, she was supportive of his thoughts of opening his own business and wondered if he might open a travel agency because he was well versed in this area and widely traveled.

Testing Results

Vocational interests. Different vocational interest systems code Mr. D.'s present occupation of securities analyst in different ways. Holland's systems (G. D. Gottfredson & Holland, 1989; Holland,

Table 5.2

Scores on Vocational Interest Measures

Self-Directed Search	Vocational Preference Inventory	Strong Vocational Interest Blank
Social, 43	Social, 9	Artistic, 59
Investigative, 37	Investigative, 8	Investigative, 55
Artistic, 27	Artistic, 7	Social, 55
Enterprising, 18	Enterprising, 5	Enterprising, 46
Conventional, 14	Realistic, 3	Conventional, 44
Realistic, 5	Conventional, 2	Realistic, 36
Code: S–I–A	Code: S–I–A	Code: A–I–S
	Average self-control	Academic comfort,
	Relatively low	68 (high)
	masculinity	Introversion–
	Moderate Status	Extraversion, 39
	scale score	(extraverted)

Note. S = Social, I = Investigative, and A = Artistic.

1985b) code it as Conventional–Investigative–Social, whereas the Strong Vocational Interest Blank (SVIB; Campbell & Hansen, 1981) classifies an investments manager as Enterprising–Conventional–Investigative (men) or Enterprising–Investigative–Conventional (women). Table 5.2 shows Mr. D.'s results on the vocational interest measures used in his assessment.

Interpretation. Mr. D.'s scores on the three measures of vocational interests were reasonably congruent with one another, although the order of endorsed codes varied slightly from one measure to the next. The Social–Investigative–Artistic or Investigative–Social–Artistic combination was more consistent with a social science interest profile than with his current occupation, whereas the Artistic–Investigative–Social combination might best be directed toward a more abstract profession such as philosophy or writing. The discrepancies of order require further interpretative work with the client in order to determine which is most applicable. However, the Enterprising, Conventional, and Realistic occupations would seem inappropriate for someone with this pattern of interests, raising serious questions about his current occupation as well as for his opening his own business. The pattern also clarifies why Mr. D. might dislike securities analysis with its enterprising and competitive components. Depending on the ability pattern, if Mr. D. continues to pursue his current career, he might do better in a teaching role than in professional practice.

Other important information was also provided by the supplementary scales on the interest measures. Specifically, Mr. D. had a high enough score on the Academic Comfort scale of the SVIB to suggest that he would be compatible with further education if necessary. He would also presumably be most comfortable in an intellectually demanding occupational setting rather than one that is routine and predictable. His low scores on the Vocational Preference Inventory (VPI) Masculinity scale were not surprising given his artistic vocational preferences. His score in the extraverted direction on the SVIB measure of this construct is curious because people in business (among other occupational pursuits) usually score in that direction, which may raise questions about his suitability for a writing career that typically involves limited contact with others. Finally, the Self-Control score was lower than would be expected for a professional and for someone who is considering an occupational choice involving much independent work. The lack of a high Status scale score, given his occupational achievements to date, should also be further explored with him.

The client's "Occupational Daydream" interest codes.

1. Writer: Artistic–Enterprising–Social (technical writer, Investigative–Realistic–Enterprising).

2. Manager of own business: Enterprising–Social–Artistic (varies with type of business).

3. Real estate appraiser: Social–Conventional–Enterprising.

The occupations listed by Mr. D. as ones he was actively considering included two that would be suggested to be inappropriate (running his own business and real estate appraiser) and one that had a better but still not perfect fit (writer).

Some occupations thought to be consistent with the client's codes. The following occupations are thought to be consistent with Mr. D.'s vocational interest coding possibilities. Holland (1985b) and G. D. Gottfredson and Holland (1989) suggested the following occupations for the client's codes just listed:

- *Social–Investigative–Artistic*
  Dictionary editor
  Clinical or counseling psychologist
- *Social–Artistic–Investigative*
  Clergy member
  Speech pathologist
  Librarian
- *Investigative–Social–Artistic*
  Psychiatrist
  Medical technologist
  Physician assistant
- *Investigative–Artistic–Social*
  Art appraiser
  Economist
- *Artistic–Investigative–Social*
  Paper and print restorer
- *Artistic–Social–Investigative*
  Copywriter
  Dance therapist
  Instrumental musician
  Laserist
  Painter
- *Other occupational codings*

The SVIB also compared the client's scores with those of individuals in various professions but did so quantitatively and empirically. The following are some occupations on the SVIB (Campbell & Hansen, 1981) on which the client had similar interests as samples of people in these occupations. Highly similar occupations included lawyer, reporter, librarian, English teacher, foreign language teacher, and social worker. Similar occupations included chiropractor, college professor, psychologist, musician, flight attendant, advertising executive, broadcaster, public relations director, public administrator, guidance counselor, social science teacher, special education teacher, and speech pathologist. Note that both coding methodologies result in occupations that seem farfetched for this client (e.g., dance therapist and chiropractor); however, particularly for the SVIB, there are several occupations listed that are similar to those being contemplated.

The SVIB also includes basic interest codes. The following were the highest interest codes endorsed by Mr. D.: writing (64), social service (62), teaching (61), medical science (57), art (57), mathematics (56), law or politics (56), science (55), music or drama (54), and public speaking (54).

Summary. From the interest perspective, Mr. D. would seem best suited to a teaching or helping role, preferably in an intellectually demanding occupation. Interactions with others would seem to be important enough that the consideration of a solitary activity (e.g., the pursuit of an independent writing career) must be questioned. However, depending on the ability test results, it is possible that the client might consider the teaching of writing (or, for that matter, some teaching role in his present occupation) as one way of combining his interests.

Abilities. The client completed a variety of measures of ability. For convenience in interpretation, these are summarized by grouping the ability measures according to their theoretical association with each of the six Holland interest areas. Although this makes discussion easier, as noted previously, the grouping presented here is based on a priori theorizing and is not yet well established empirically (see, e.g., Lowman, et al., 1985).

The client's scores on the mechanical ability measures were relatively low, as his low scores on Realistic interests would have predicted (see Table 5.3). He did especially poorly on a fine finger manipulation test. He does not appear to have special abilities either to manipulate objects physically or to manipulate objects mentally. Mr. D.'s understanding of mechanical principles is only about average compared with those in mechanical jobs. Recall that scores on spatial ability measures (e.g., the Minnesota Paper Form Board test) are not just associated with Realistic-related occupations such as pilot, navigator, and engineers, but such skills

Table 5.3

Summary of Realistic-Related Abilities for Mr. D. and Normative Samples

Test name and sample	Score[a]
Bennett Mechanical Comprehension Test	
Mr. D.	39
Academic high school, Grade 12	60th %ile
Mechanics at aviation company (applicants)	20th %ile
Minnesota Paper Form Board	
Mr. D.	38
Grade 12 males	30th %ile
Engineers and scientists	10th %ile
Draftsmen	10th %ile
Engineering students	5th %ile
Tweezer Dexterity Test	
Mr. D.	> 900 seconds
Standardization sample	< 1 %ile

[a]Sources for norms: Bennett (1969); Likert and Quasha (1970); and examiner's manual (undated).

are also needed in drafting and architecture (Likert & Quasha, 1970), some forms of science, and art (see chap. 3).

Investigative-related abilities. Table 5.4 shows the Investigative-related ability test scores. These results demonstrate that Mr. D. has excellent verbal intellectual abilities, functioning in the superior to very superior range on the Wechsler Adult Intelligence Scale–Revised (WAIS–R), but that he has much more limited nonverbal abilities, scoring only in the low average to average range on the WAIS–R. The 40-point difference in verbal and nonverbal intelligence on the WAIS–R is highly unusual (Whittington, 1988). A possible pattern of impairment in nonverbal intellectual skills is suggested, possibly a nonverbal learning deficit.

Table 5.4

*Summary of Investigative-Related Abilities for Mr. D. and
Normative Samples*

Test name and sample		Score
Watson-Glaser Critical Thinking Appraisal		
Mr. D.		73
College upper-division males		97
MBA students		85
3rd-year medical students		80
Raven Advanced Progressive Matrices		
Mr. D.		23
Adults in the general population		95
University of California, Berkeley,		
undergraduates (Paul, 1985–1986)		24
Weschler Adult Intelligence Scale–Revised subscales		
Information		16
Digit Span		12
Vocabulary		15
Arithmetic		17
Comprehension		14
Similarities		13
Picture Completion		7
Picture Arrangement		9
Block Design		8
Object Assembly		7
Digit Symbol		10
Verbal IQ	129 ± 5.3	age norms, superior
Nonverbal IQ	88 ± 7.8	low average
Full Scale IQ	109 ± 4.5	average

Note. Scores for norms: Watson and Glaser (1980); Raven, Court, and
Raven (1977a); Paul (1985–1986); and Wechsler (1981).

In exploring the educational history of the client, he described some early problems possibly suggestive of neurological impairment that reportedly cleared up with time. However, he always excelled in the verbally oriented subjects compared with a more average performance in the nonverbal subjects.

On the other Investigative ability measures, Mr. D. scored in the 95th percentile (using the British test-manual-supplied norms; see Raven et al., 1977a) on the very difficult Raven Advanced Progressive Matrices test. However, when the University of California, Berkeley, norms were used (Paul, 1985–1986), this score dropped to the 24th percentile. On a verbal measure requiring detailed verbal analytical reasoning—the Watson-Glaser Critical Thinking Appraisal—he scored high compared with all of the criterion groups, again suggesting that he has exceptional verbal abilities.

Artistic-related abilities. On the Artistic measures (see Table 5.5), the client scored low on measures of aesthetic judgment but did show some (presumably isolated) abilities in rhythm and tonal memory on the Seashore Measures of Musical Talents. Musical ability is not reflected in the client's vocational interest pattern and would therefore appear to be best used as an avocational interest or hobby rather than as a primary occupational pursuit.

Social-related abilities. The ability scores in the Social area (see Table 5.6) suggest that social intelligence is an area of strength. Unfortunately, the measurement of social abilities is still primitive. Normative and validity data for these types of measures are currently insufficient. The client appears to have good social abilities as reflected both by a paper-and-pencil measure (the Interpersonal Problem-Solving Ability Test) of knowing the "correct" social response, but his slightly higher than the norm score on avoidant responses suggests a behavioral style that creates difficulties for him when more direct confrontation is needed. This would be particularly relevant in a managerial or social service type of occupation. The client's interpersonal style is also affected by personality factors, which I discuss in more detail later, and by his characteristic style of interacting in the assessment process. His behavior suggested social engagement, a highly interpersonally oriented style, but one that may

Table 5.5

Summary of Artistic-Related Abilities for Mr. D. and Normative Samples

Test name and sample	Raw score[a]	Norm[b]
Meier Art Judgment Test		
Mr. D.	95	
High School students		33rd %ile
College art students		19th %ile
Seashore Measures of Musical Talents		
Pitch	32	13th %ile[c]
Rhythm	28	73rd %ile[c]
Tonal Memory	27	61st %ile[c]
CAB Reproductive Drawing Ability test		
Mr. D.	22	
High school students		27th %ile

Note. CAB = Comprehensive Ability Battery.
[a]Mr. D.'s score.
[b]Sources for norms: Meier (1940); Seashore, Lewis, and Saetveit (1960); Hakstian, Cattell, and IPAT Staff (1982).
[c]Although this norm is not age specific, musical talent tends to appear and mature early, making this an appropriate normative group.

be somewhat narcissistic or self-centered, making it difficult for him to focus on others' needs. Nevertheless, his genuine warmth and involvement with those with whom he interacts, particularly those whom he perceives to be in need of his help, suggests generally strong social and interpersonal abilities.

Enterprising-related abilities. Typically, the promising managerial candidate fits the following profile: high-average or above-average intelligence; managerial vocational interests; good organizing and prioritizing skills; "tough-mindedness"; a moderately high need for power over others; high need for

Table 5.6

Summary of Social-Related Abilities on the Interpersonal Problem-Solving Ability Test for Mr. D. and Normative Samples

	Averages		
Response	Mr. D.[a]	College students[b]	Career counselees[b]
Effective	15	13	15
Avoidant	6	4	5
Inappropriate	1	4	1
Dependent	0	1	1
Unscorable	0	1	< 1

[a]Responses Mr. D. indicated he would actually make (see Getter & Nowinski, 1981).
[b]Sources for norms: Career Development Laboratory, Inc. (1990).

achievement; a moderate need for affiliation; and a generally positive, optimistic outlook.

Overall, Mr. D.'s fit with the Enterprising profile is poor. The one exception is his high overall verbal intelligence, but this is an attribute that can be applied in many different ways, with management being only one domain. When combined with other aspects of the overall pattern, management would seem an unlikely outlet for positive expression of his intellectual ability. On the other hand, his strong verbal and verbal reasoning abilities may allow him to perform reasonably well in areas in which his interests and personality would not normally direct him. Of special concern is the absence of Enterprising interests in his occupational interest profile and a personality profile that is generally the antithesis of that found among managers and people in business. His strong creative and artistic interests, estrangement from values involving conformity to existing norms, tender-mindedness, and fertile imagination all suggest limited

Table 5.7

Summary of Conventional-Related Abilities for Mr. D. and Normative Data[a]

Test	Client	Grade 12 males	Male clerks	Female clerks	Female tellers	General population[b]
Minnesota Clerical Test						
Names	151	90	97	95		
Numbers	186	95	99	99		
Wide Range Achievement Test (Arithmetic subtest)	42					79

[a]Sources for norms: Andrew, Paterson, and Longstaff (1979) and Jastak and Wilkinson (1984). All norms are in percentiles.
[b]Age specific.

correspondence to the characteristic Enterprising profile. As elaborated in more detail later, there is little reason to believe that Mr. D. would be happy in a conforming or routine occupation.

Conventional-related abilities. On the Conventional ability measures (see Table 5.7), Mr. D. performed well. Note that his scores on the Minnesota Clerical Test were strong compared with a variety of relevant occupational groups. His scores on the computational arithmetic measure, although not outstanding, were certainly respectable. Because Conventional interests are virtually absent in his occupational interest profile, one must conclude that the abilities measured by these tests are unlikely to find primary expression in a Conventional occupation.

Other ability measures. A variety of other tests were administered (see Table 5.8), which can be briefly summarized here. His scores on a measure of field dependence–independence (the Comprehensive Ability Battery [CAB] Flexibility of Closure test) suggested a more field-dependent than field-independent

Table 5.8

Summary of Other Abilities Measured for Mr. D. and Normative Samples

Ability and test	Client	Normative[a]
Field dependence– independence[b]	4	11th percentile high school males, 1st percentile freshman males
Memory		
WAIS–R Digit Span	19	12[c]
WAIS–Digit Symbol	58	10[c]
Creative imagination		
CAB-Original Uses	5	12th percentile high school males, 1st percentile college males
CAB-Fi	49	99th percentile high school males, 99th percentile college males
Writing	214	224[c] adult career assessment sample

Note. WAIS–R = Wechsler Adult Intelligence Scale–Revised.
[a]Sources for norms: Hakstian, Cattell, and IPAT Staff (1982); Wechsler (1981); and Career Development Laboratory, Inc. (1990).
[b]Measured with the Comprehensive Ability Battery (CAB) Flexibility of Closure test.
[c]Standard scores compared with general population ($M = 10$). Raw score average.

approach. The field-dependent pattern is commonly found among writers, artists, and helping professions, whereas a field-independent cognitive style is more likely to be found in the sciences.

Mr. D. scored very highly on a measure of creative abilities involving words (CAB-Fi) but did not score high on a measure requiring the creative integration of objects (CAB-O). Somewhat surprisingly, he scored only about average on verbal fluency in a writing sample. It is possible that he has a general disposition toward creativity, especially with words, but that it is not yet channeled in a constructive direction and is primarily raw talent.

Summary of ability data. Mr. D.'s chief strengths on the ability measures were in areas analogous to Investigative, Social, and Conventional areas. A very bright man in terms of verbal intelligence, his profile is lackluster in the nonverbal area, perhaps even suggesting a nonverbal learning disability. He had little manifest ability in the Artistic area and only isolated strengths in the Realistic and Conventional areas. Of continuing concern is the reason for the discrepancy between his performance on intellectual measures and his academic and occupational accomplishments to date. Although his apparent social needs may be being met in his sales job, it is less clear that his intellectual and managerial abilities receive adequate utilization.

Personality. A variety of personality measures were used: the CPI, the NEO Personality Inventory, the Fundamental Interpersonal Relations Orientation-Behavior (FIRO-B), selected cards of the TAT, and the EPPS. These measures help to clarify aspects of personality relevant to implementation of the work role and how these personality factors may moderate or ameliorate particular areas of vocational interest and ability.

Myers-Briggs Type Indicator. Mr. D. scored identically on the Extraversion and Introversion scales of the Myers-Briggs (see Table 5.9), contrary to the other measures on which he generally scored in the extraverted direction. However, on the other three dimensions of the test, he scored strongly in one direction. His orientation toward intuition rather than sensing is consistent and is to be expected given his essentially creative rather than conforming orientation. He is strongly oriented in the feeling rather than thinking direction, contrary to what one might expect of someone in business. This direction is found mostly in people in the creative or helping professions or in sales. A possible problem for Mr. D. is suggested by his score in the perceiving direction on the Judging–Perceiving scale. This implies the comfort with ambiguity and multiple projects that one might expect of a creative individual, but is also suggests that he would have difficulty bringing things to closure, especially when an external structure is absent.

FIRO-B. The FIRO-B (Schutz, 1978) is, on the surface, a transparent measure of need strength in three areas: inclusion (wanting

Table 5.9
Client's Myers-Briggs Type Indicator Scores

Scale	Raw score	Standard score of difference[a]
Extraversion	13	
Introversion	13	1
Sensing	3	
Intuiting	19	33
Thinking	4	
Feeling	12	17
Judging	9	
Perceiving	16	15

Note. Type: Extraverted–Introverted, Intuitive, Feeling, Perceiving.
[a]Source for norms: Myers and McCaulley (1985).

to be with others), control (wanting to have power over others or to be controlled by others), and affection (desire for close, intimate relationships). His scores on this measure are shown in Table 5.10.

Overall, his need for affection is higher than the needs for control and inclusion. He has good balance in the expression and wanting of affection, but the control pattern suggests that he prefers structure and influence to come from others than for him to have control or power over others. Although he publicly expresses desire for involvement with others, he actually may want somewhat less involvement than his behavior may suggest, perhaps sending mixed messages to those with whom he comes into contact. This issue is further reflected on the confusing results on the Extraversion and Introversion scales of the various personality measure (see the next section).

California Psychological Inventory. Table 5.11 shows Mr. D.'s scale scores on the CPI compared with the results of normative and reference groups. These findings should be interpreted as follows: On the validity scales, Mr. D. scored in an acceptable range. His above-average score on the Communality scale

Table 5.10

Client's Fundamental Interpersonal Relations Orientation-Behavior Scores

Need	Expressed	Wanted	Total
Inclusion	4	0	4
Affection	2	6	8
Control	5	6	11
Total	11	12	23

Source for scores: Schutz (1978).

suggests that despite his creative orientation, he still can function within the generally accepted societal norms. This measure suggests he is generally prosocial (as measured by the Social Presence [Sp], Sociability [Sy], Dominance [Do], and Empathy [Em] subscales) and oriented toward others, rather forcefully so (high Do). The Do scale is one of the best validated of the CPI scales (see Megargee & Carbonell, 1988), and he scored about the average of people in the managerial professions, who generally have standard scores averaging in the high 50s. At the same time, he is independent of others and may be overly sensitive in his support of others, at least compared with the typical manager (high scores on the Independence [In], Em, and Tolerance [To] scales; very high Self-Acceptance [Sa] scores). The results suggest that he is able to function responsibly (Responsibility [Re] scale) but may occasionally be rebellious (Socialization [So] scale, one of the better validated scales on the CPI; see Megargee, 1972). The client's scores on the CPI were similar to those of juvenile delinquents and were not much higher than a group of prison inmates.

The CPI scores also suggest that Mr. D. is bright (Intellectual Efficiency [Ie] scale), achievement oriented (high scores on the Achievement-Conformity [Ac] and Achievement-Independence [Ai] scales), flexible, and tolerant, as a creative pattern

Table 5.11

Results of the California Psychological Inventory

Subscale	Raw score	Standard score[a]
Dominance	25	59
Capacity for Status	18	54
Sociability	24	56
Social Presence	31	64
Self Acceptance	24	68
Independence	21	58
Empathy	30	68
Responsibility	33	66
Socialization	27	44
Self Control	24	54
Good Impression	18	50
Communality	37	58
Well-Being	35	58
Tolerance	29	68
Achievement-Conformity	31	58
Achievement-Independence	31	66
Intellectual Efficiency	37	64
Psychological Mindedness	19	59
Flexibility	22	68
Femininity–Masculinity	11	42

Note. Type: gamma, Level 7.
[a]Adult male norms. Sources for norms: Gough (1987).

would suggest. This may imply that he has a tendency to be too dominant, too insistent on having his own way, and therefore not be as compromising as one would need to be in management or sales. Similarly, the *Sa* scale scores, although not as well validated as they could be, suggest that he accepts himself as he is and may experience little motivation to change. On the other hand, his scores on the Well-Being (*Wb*) scale indicate that this may be costly to his sense of well-being. His only slightly above average Capacity for Status (Cs) score may be lower than desirable for someone who aspires to a high-level occupation, but is generally consistent with his score on the VPI Status scale.

On the second-order factors, the gamma type is somewhat rebellious and poorly adjusted, although his score on the Self-Realization scale of the CPI was high, perhaps suggesting little motivation for change. However, his scores were not extreme in the gamma grouping, being close to the border between norm-favoring and norm-questioning, suggesting a possible area of conflict between doing what is expected and doing what he wants to do. Note again that he scored in the extraverted direction on the Externality–Internality second-order factor.

Edwards Personal Preference Schedule. On the EPPS (A. L. Edwards, 1959; see Table 5.12), the client had a consistency score in the 97th percentile, lending credence to the validity with which he completed the measures. Several of the themes on the CPI were duplicated on the EPPS, but there were some differences. He scored high on the measures of need for achievement, need for affiliation, and autonomy and low on the Deference and Abasement scales, all consistent with the CPI. However, his score on the Dominance scale of the EPPS was below average, contrary to the score on the CPI, although generally about where one might expect given the overall pattern of abilities, interests, and personality. His low scores on endurance and order suggest possible problem areas and are consistent with his tendency not to stick with anything for long. The high Intraception score might be an asset in writing or could just be reflective of his going through a self-searching process as part of the career evaluation. His slightly below-average score on the Exhibition scale is surprising given how he presented himself in the assessment process.

NEO Personality Inventory. Mr. D.'s scores on the NEO Personality Inventory (see Table 5.13) are also intriguing. Of the five major dimensions of this instrument, he scored the highest on the Openness scale. He also scored high on the Agreeableness and Extraversion scales. He bordered on scoring highly on the Neuroticism scale, suggesting some possible adjustment

Table 5.12

Results of the Edwards Personal Preference Schedule

Need	Raw score	Normative comparisons for adult men[a]
Achievement	20	91
Deference	7	4
Order	7	8
Exhibitionism	11	37
Autonomy	19	88
Affiliation	22	97
Intraception	22	97
Succorance	71	13
Dominance	44	13
Abasement	27	11
Nurturance	20	81
Change	17	76
Endurance	7	3
Heterosexuality	13	62
Aggression	7	11
Consistency	14	97

Note. Normative data are percentiles.
[a]Source for norms: Edwards (1959).

difficulties. Finally, his low score on the Conscientious scale is of concern as he considers occupations. Somehow his creative interests and abilities may need better channeling if he is to productively integrate them into his work life.

On the facet scales currently available for the Neuroticism, Extraversion, and Openness scales, Mr. D.'s tendency toward depression was confirmed, and his high score on vulnerability may reflect an overall personality tendency or a transitory difficulty. Interestingly, on the Extraversion facet scales, he scored high on only three of the six scales. His tendencies toward extraversion would be expected to be manifest in his warmth

Table 5.13

Results of NEO Personality Inventory

Variable	Raw score	Percentile[a]
Neuroticism	80	Average +
Anxiety	12	Average
Hostility	8	Low
Depression	21	Very high
Self-consciousness	13	Average
Impulsiveness	13	Average
Vulnerability	13	High
Extraversion	115	High
Warmth	27	High
Gregariousness	18	High
Assertiveness	16	Average
Activity	16	Average
Excitement-seeking	17	Average
Positive emotions	21	High
Openness	147	Very high
Fantasy	24	Average +
Aesthetics	22	High
Feelings	26	Very high
Actions	21	Average +
Ideas	27	Average +
Values	27	Average +
Agreeableness	52	High −
Conscientiousness	42	Low

[a]Norms compared with normal adult populations; "+" and "−" indicate a score at the border between two classification categories. Source for norms: Costa and McCrae (1985a).

and sociability rather than in assertiveness or activity. On the other hand, he scored high on all of the Openness facet scales, particularly on openness to new feelings. Again, a "creative" profile is suggested, one that would presumably find little outlet in an occupation in which he must do the same things repetitiously.

Clinical Analysis Questionnaire. The CAQ includes both the 16 factors of normal personality of the 16PF and several clinical scales. Second-order factors are based on the integration of the various scales. Mr. D.'s results are summarized in Table 5.14.

On the first set of measures, he had extreme scores on several of the scales (including scoring in the submissive direction on the Dominance scale) that indicate tender-mindedness, imaginativeness, willingness to experiment, self-sufficiency, and lack of discipline. He scored in the midrange on the other variables. The clinical scales confirmed depression and suggested a possible need for professional assistance. His low self-esteem at the time of the evaluation was suggested by the Psychological Inadequacy (*Ps*) scale.

Interestingly, on the second-order factors, he scored in the midrange on the Extraversion factor, again communicating that he was not responding consistently to the various measures of this variable. It is possible that each scale was measuring something slightly different from the other or that he has characteristics of both polarities. His orientation toward feelings and away from objectivity was again suggested, contrary to the business career path. He is highly independent and self-reliant but probably not as disciplined as necessary to get his occupational goals accomplished.

Projective test results. Three projective measures were used: the TAT and two sentence-completion measures. Several themes emerged from these measures. Unresolved parent–child issues were suggested by the measures. The story generated in response to the first TAT card, which often succinctly captures the major work conflicts of the client, is illustrative:

> The boy is upper-class, lonely, and maladjusted. He rarely sees his parents, who are divorced. His father is a famous doctor. His mother is having a midlife crisis in her mid-30s and spends all of her time at the local theater. She imagines she is an actress. Her acting is lackluster at best. Other people take care of the boy. The boy regularly takes violin lessons, which he despises. His mother wants to show his "talents"

Table 5.14

Results of the Clinical Analysis Questionnaire

Measure	Raw	Sten[a]	Direction[a]
Normal personality traits			
Warmth	9	6	Average
Intelligence	6	7	Average
Emotional Stability	13	6	Average
Dominance	7	4	Submissive
Impulsivity	11	6	Average
Conformity	11	5	Average
Boldness	12	7	Bold
Sensitivity	11	8	Sensitive
Suspiciousness	8	5	Average
Imagination	15	10	Highly imaginative
Shrewdness	8	6	Average
Insecurity	7	6	Average
Radicalism	11	7	Innovative
Self-sufficiency	13	8	Self-sufficient
Self-discipline	8	4	Undisciplined
Tension	6	5	Average
Clinical factors			
Hypochondriasis	2	5	Average
Suicidal Depression	4	7	Depressed
Agitation	14	7	Hypomanic
Anxious Depression	8	7	Depressed
Low Energy Depression	7	6	Average
Guilt and Resentment	3	5	Average
Boredom and Withdrawal	4	6	Average
Paranoia	3	5	Average
Psychopathic Deviation	4	13	Inhibited
Schizophrenia	3	5	Average
Psychological Inadequacy	2	3	Noncompulsive

(*table continues*)

Table 5.14   (*Continued*)

Measure	Raw	Sten[a]	Direction[a]
Second-order factors			
Extraversion	53	5	Average
Anxiety	50	5	Average
Tough Poise	22	2	Feelings
Independence	85	9	Independent
Superego Strength	41	4	Unrestrained
Socialization	55	6	Average
Depression	66	7	Depressed
Psychoticism	56	6	Average
Neuroticism	70	7	Unstable

[a]Adult male norms. Sources for norms: Krug (1980).

off to her friends. The boy hates playing the violin. He wishes he was outside playing tackle football on the concrete. The boy refuses to learn how to play the violin. This stems partly from his lack of aptitude as well as a subconscious hostility toward his mother. He later ends up in reform school and is killed at age 17 in a high-speed race in his V-12 Jaguar.

The story is overdetermined and well-elaborated, the product of high imagination and high intelligence, but somewhat poorly channeled creativity. The story strongly suggests conflictual relationships with the parental figure and decided ambivalence about work and success. Identified with the boy, Mr. D.'s unresolved hostility toward the mother figure is blatant. The manner of channeling his hostility is aggressive and ultimately self-destructive. He is reacting to things rather than pursuing his own goals. The mother in the story is so self-absorbed (presumably narcissistic) that there is little time for the boy, whose "talents" are important only as an extension of her. Although the boy wants to direct his aggressive urges elsewhere (tackle football on the concrete), he instead rebels passively, feeling resentful and angry. The story is not atypical of neglected children "raised" by wealthy parents who have minimal interests in their children's activities or needs. Finally, a theme of conflict between upper-class values and pragmatic, real-world pleasures is suggested.

Themes of conflict between what is expected and what is wanted predominate many of the other stories as well. Coupled with resentment directed toward overly powerful parental figures, however, is guilt at breaking away and establishing his own identity, perhaps contrary to the perceived wishes of the parental figures, who are generally presented as being controlling and disapproving. Tragedies and death are experienced by most of the central characters in Mr. D.'s stories, even by those who apparently were on their way to successful outcomes. Defeat is snared from the jaws of victory. These stories imply intense, long-lasting, deeply felt conflict that is largely unresolved. His depressive features on the objective personality measures may require interpretation in this context.

On the sentence-completion measures, a few more themes emerged. The client acknowledged being stuck and noted that he "want[s] to grow again." A bit grandiose ("My mind. . .is a microscosm of the cosmos"; "My greatest worry is. . .to be a nobody"), he succinctly summarized a central issue in his life when he wrote, "I often think of myself as . . . unrealized aptitudes." His lack of interest in managing others was suggested by several responses (e.g., "Getting other people to do what I want . . . isn't that important, if they'll let me do what I want to do"). He also made frequent references to his disgust with close-minded individuals and offered glimpses of impaired relationships with both parents.

Summary of personality patterns. Offering a consistent but conflicted portrait, the personality measures point to an individual who is closer to the typical artist or writer than to someone in his current occupation. Complex and still struggling, at least unconsciously, with family issues, Mr. D. is imaginative, open, warm, and sensitive and generally oriented toward others. He does not want authority over others but is conflicted about achievement and accomplishment, which he both desires (in a grandiose sense) but fears. Perhaps he has seen what he perceives to be the consequences of success in his own family, with neglectful, somewhat narcissistic parents. Tender-minded and oriented toward feelings rather than thoughts, Mr. D. may struggle in an unproductive way with many of his conflicts, ending up with considerable energy being diverted from what might otherwise be creative accomplishment. His struggles between conventionality and conformity to his own strongly held values of freedom and independence from the dictates of others are largely unresolved, yet, if they can be channeled effectively, may provide a rich source of creative energy.

Summary and Integration

Mr. D. is a multitalented but conflicted man who appears to be stagnating in an occupation to which he is poorly suited. He must build on his strengths, especially the verbal and intellectual abilities, and work around his apparent nonverbal weaknesses. His occupational daydreams suggest paths both more and less consistent with his overall career profile. The thoughts of owning his own business or working as a real estate appraiser are career paths that presumably would leave him no better off than he is now. Becoming a writer suggests a potentially good fit except for the strongly socially oriented aspects of his personality, including those implying the need to work with and through others. Perhaps, ultimately, teaching might provide an appropriate outlet for this combination. Had he received career consultation earlier, a social sciences graduate education might have been recommended. This could still be possible but would be more difficult to execute at his current age. The hints of depression and possibly other psychopathology may need professional assistance if they do not spontaneously improve as he makes changes in his career and personal directions. There are likely many areas of unresolved conflict with his family, which could usefully be explored in ongoing psychotherapy, particularly if he pursues a career in an Artistic profession. Of great importance is the need for greater discipline in his professional life, so that his "raw aptitudes" are more properly working for him rather than against him.

6

Client Feedback and Report Preparation

W hat information should be given to the individual being assessed? In what manner should the results be reported? How should negative data be handled? In what form is the feedback most likely to be accepted and assimilated? What about the pragmatics of feedback? How many sessions are needed? Who should be in the session? Should follow-up be included as a standard practice?

The issues I discuss in this chapter refer both to the oral feedback reviewed with the client at the time of the assessment and the written report that, if properly prepared, will serve as a lifetime reference document on an individual's career concerns. As a general principle, feedback to individuals on the results of career assessments should match the comprehensiveness of the testing (or other assessment procedures administered) and should emphasize data germane to the reasons for which help was sought. This includes both negative and positive information. How the information is reported to the client will be largely influenced by the ability of the client to assimilate and make effective use of the findings. The client's psychological defenses must be respected and worked with in determining how best to report findings. It is possible to give too much and too little information in career feedback. To provide detailed explanations of every test and procedure to a client with limited intellect is not useful. On the other hand, focusing on conclusions without explanations of the procedures used or the limitations of results is also problematic. In my experience, career assessors are more likely to gloss over limitations of their methods and to present data in a much more conclusive sense than may be justified by the research literature.

Feedback must be contextually grounded. As in other types of clinical assessment, the context for feedback is established by the reasons for the referral. Even if a generic format is used for reporting assessment results, it is important to identify the idiographic reasons for which help was sought and to remind the client of these reasons, which may tend to become obscured with large data sets. Before the assessment begins, it is the assessor's responsibility to work with the client to determine goals for the assessment process. Such goals are obviously as varied as the type of client seeking referral but typically include issues such as (a) unhappiness in one's present occupation; (b) uncertainty about a contemplated career course; (c) confirmation that a previous decision is an appropriate one; (d) a need to satisfy someone else (typically a parent or supervisor) who has recommended or insisted that assessment take place; and (e) confirmation that one is ready for a change that might have been under consideration for several years.

The effective career assessor will anchor orally presented and written feedback to the referral questions, even though far more data may be gathered than are directly relevant to the referral questions. Especially in face-to-face feedback, information needs to be presented to the client in a way that creatively bypasses potential sources of resistance. This means that information must be presented both accurately *and* acceptably to the client, consistent with ethical guidelines and technical standards.

In the typical feedback process, information will be presented to a client that he or she will agree with and that will be inconsistent with his or her sense of self. Wise assessors know or soon learn that resistance will be encountered not just with negative information or areas of relative weakness. In fact, clients can be just as resistant, if not more so, to accepting positive information that is discrepant with their sense of self as they are to accepting negative information. For example, if an assessee has no musical background and does not have a self-perception that includes musical talent, the finding of low scores on a measure of psychoacoustical or musical ability may be readily accepted. On the other hand, if a client has a lifelong self-view as being below average in intellectual ability, it may be difficult to change this perception. Reframing information that may be difficult for the client to hear or accept may help. A client with average intellectual abilities, for example, who aspires to a profession in which superior intellectual functioning is necessary might be complimented on the high level of aspiration reflected by the interest and helped to explore whether that ambition might receive better expression in another direction. The client may be further assisted in thinking through problematic contemplated educational or career choices to their logical end. For an ambitious client with limited ability for desired career paths, heightened understanding that a misdirected career choice may result in a thwarting rather than obtaining of personal ambitions may assist the client in making more realistic choices.

Of course, it is also important in such cases for the clinician to work to understand the issues that might be motivating a seemingly inappropriate career choice. For example, it is possible that aspiration for a career in medicine or law may be associated with an unrealistic view of the rewards associated with one of these professions or may be heavily influenced by a significant other's (often a parent's) long-standing wishes. For these reasons, it is recommended that assessors routinely collect data on the occupational choices of the assessee's parents, spouse, or significant other, and the career ambitions, if any, that were expressed for the client by such parties. Further exploration may be needed in cases in which an assessee seems fixated on an inappropriate career choice yet who states that others important to the client have expressed no strong preference regarding the client's career. It is possible that more subtle influences and perceived pressures may be influencing the career decision process.

Concerning the pragmatics of the oral feedback process, these need to be tailored to the number of tests given and the specific referral questions. In my experience, using test batteries similar to those illustrated in this book, at least 3–4 hours should be allotted to the feedback process. This can be spread out over several sessions if necessary. Concerning the presence of people other than the client (e.g., parents or spouse), I do not routinely require or encourage such contact but am willing to do so when it is the client's wish or in cases in which the third party is clearly part of the career concern or problem. Finally, at least some follow-up should be expected if not encouraged. I believe that the full understanding of a comprehensive assessment can take a year or more. Follow-up should be available, and some career assessors make a follow-up session several weeks or months after the initial assessment a routine part of their practice.

General Principles of Report Preparation

With few exceptions, it is generally appropriate to provide the assessee with a written report summarizing the results of career assessment. If a third party has contracted for the assessment, then written reports may need to be provided for the third-party client and a separate report (or other type of feedback) provided to the assessee. For whomever it is prepared, the psychologist's report should be customized to the audience for whom it is intended. Thus, if career assessment is being done for someone other than the assessee (e.g., a potential employer), then different issues will be important than is the case when a report is being prepared for the individual. Few cases can be imagined in which the client should not receive a detailed written report as a permanent record of the assessment. Among other reasons, when a client is receiving verbal feedback on the results of an assessment, at least of the type advocated in this book, it is difficult to assimilate all of the data. Even taking notes or recording the feedback session, clients may not go away with a complete or accurate record of the important points being made or how they might guide future career decisions. Because the report, if it is done well, is likely to be used as a reference guide for many years, it should be written for posterity. The belief that a career report may be consulted by an assessee throughout his or her career should also temper rash or overly inclusive statements that might, years later, appear ridiculously ungrounded. A detailed written report, prepared in language the client can understand (see APA Ethical Principle 8-A, American Psychological Association, 1990), should be the goal. In my experience of reviewing hundreds of career assessment reports, too many appear to be written in a user-unfriendly way or in a misleading way. In such reports, technical terms may not be explained in language that the client can understand. Misleading, unexplained norms may be used. Overly zealous statements may be made about a personality characteristic or ability, or the assessor may make dogmatic statements about fitness for an occupation that are unjustified by supporting data.

There are many ways in which career feedback reports can be written, but each report should meet certain minimal standards. These include the following:

1. *The report should be accurate.*   It should not contain false statements or those that, in the context of the report, could potentially be misleading.

Example: "Because your score on the measure of spatial ability was low, you should avoid engineering or architectural careers."

Such a statement is entirely too off-putting and the recipient is likely to feel thwarted or inappropriately characterized, especially if it is directed toward an assessee who has been planning on a career in architecture. A better statement would be something such as the following:

Better: "Your score on the spatial ability test was at the 13th percentile compared with high school female students and at the 2nd percentile compared with a group of (primarily male) engineers and architects. Although this does not rule out fields such as engineering or architecture, they would likely be more difficult for you to master."

Example: "Your score on the Watson-Glaser Critical Thinking Appraisal (a measure of verbal reasoning) was at the 80th percentile."

This statement is not necessarily inaccurate but it certainly insufficient. The client needs both a context for interpreting the result (e.g., which level of percentiles are "high" and which are "low"?) and an explanation of the reference group used to make the normative comparison.

Better: "Your score of 66 on the measure of verbal reasoning ability (the Watson-Glaser Critical Thinking Appraisal measure) was at the 80th percentile compared with a group of upper division students in 4-year colleges and was at the 50th percentile compared with a group of MBA students. This score indicates well above-average verbal reasoning ability. Verbal reasoning ability is required in a variety of occupational pursuits, including. . . ."

Here, the specific name of the test is given so that a future assessor or career counselor can make use of the data, the reference groups are identified by name, and the general implications of the score are noted.

Caution should be used in drawing conclusions that exceed known facts. Psychologists trained in trait-and-factor models may be especially likely to overgeneralize from scores on specific variables on individual psychological tests to generic conclusions.

Example: "You scored highly on a measure of need for dominance. You are quick to express opinions and are seen by others as being self-assertive and aggressive. You like to influence others and to get ahead in the world."

Such statements are not necessarily wrong, but they may be unproved in occupational or work settings (in that studies to support such conclusions may not have been done); do not take into account potential method bias or threats to validity (e.g., "fake good"); and present a unidimensional view of the person.

Better: "Need for dominance refers to your tendency to want to have power and control over others. On three measures of personal characteristics related to the need for dominance (scales on the Edwards Personal Preference Schedule [EPPS], the California Psychological Inventory [CPI], and the Hogan Personality Inventory), you earned scores at or above the 90th percentile. This suggests consistency in presenting yourself as someone who enjoys having influence and control over others."

In career assessment, need for accuracy and validity generally necessarily means including appropriate qualifiers in a description. Even with well-validated and established measures, prudent circumspection in the generality of one's conclusions is recommended. The assessor should not let enthusiasm for a particular measure result in statements that exceed validity evidence. If a measure is experimental, or it is an internally developed test for which norms are being collected but not yet available, care should be taken not to present the measure as further along than it really is in the test-development process. Labels attached to scales do not always correspond to what is known about a measure and should not be used as the primary basis for identifying scale characteristics. For example, the Psychological Mindedness scale of the CPI appears to be related more to intelligence than to introspection (see Megargee, 1972).

2. *The report should be comprehensive and self sufficient.* Results of all tests administered should be included in the report. The measures that are administered experimentally or as part of a data collection effort can be labeled as such; it may be inappropriate to draw conclusions from such measures, but including information about such measures in the report provides a valuable reference in the future.

Self-sufficiency means that a career assessment report can be read and understood by the recipient audience. It means that the report can be readily understood by the person receiving the report. This requires a careful balance between technically accurate and pragmatically useful information. Thus, although it is important to include information that would be useful to another psychologist reviewing the results at a later date or faced with a later need for retesting, the primary consumer of the information should be kept in mind in preparing the report. If necessary, technical information can be put in parentheses or in an appendix.

When there is conflict between the need for technical accuracy and the need to be understood, it may be better to err in the former than in the latter direction. Unfortunately, there are many examples of career assessment reports that omit technical information and draw conclusions on the basis of unspecified tests. This is as inadequate as a medical report that contains conclusions about a person's condition without specifying the lab results on which the conclusions are based.

3. *The report should be written in language readily comprehended by the reader.* Psychologist's Ethical Principle 8-A states the following:

> In using assessment techniques, psychologists respect the right of clients to have full explanations of the nature and purpose of the techniques in language the clients can understand, unless an explicit exception to this right has been agreed upon in advance. (APA, 1990, p. 394)

It is possible to include too technical language and language that is not technical enough. The ideal feedback report strikes an effective balance between technical accuracy and ease of understanding.

Example: "You scored very high on our need for achievement measure. This means you will push ahead no matter what setting you are in and you will strive very hard to advance."

Even if generally true, a statement like this is problematic in that there is limited research literature to support the occupational and career assessment correlates of typical measures of need for achievement. Moreover, the reader does not know whether the measure used has an extensive validation base or even if minimal test standards have been met. Finally, the term is never really defined.

Better: "You scored at the 93rd and 99th percentiles on two measures of need for achievement (scales on the California Psychological Inventory and the Edwards Personal Preference Schedule, respectively). These scores are high compared with those of the general adult population with whom you were compared. People scoring in this manner typically have a strong drive to get ahead in the world and are usually highly motivated toward achievement in a variety of occupational and personal activities. Although researchers are not certain that these scales predict success in all occupations, people scoring as you did are thought to be strongly motivated toward high levels of achievement."

4. *The report should be tentative and hypothetical rather than definitive and dogmatic.* The competent career assessor attempts to guide and assist, to identify areas of conflict and opportunity but never to cut off avenues for pursuit. Accordingly, statements in the report or in oral feedback should be worded in such a way as to invite further exploration by the client, not as if they were divine and binding pronouncements.

Example: "Mr. Richardson does not belong in sales. He is ill-suited to management. He would probably make a good teacher."

Obviously, this statement is much too extreme. No psychologist can accurately say that a person does not "belong in" a particular occupation. Rather, degrees of fit can be approximated. Even when a candidate clearly seems to be a poor match with his or her occupation, the conclusion can be tempered and balanced.

Better: "Of the five candidates assessed, Mr. Richardson scored lowest in abilities and occupational interests commonly associated with success in sales. His scores on three measures of sales aptitude were all in the 25th percentile or below when compared with successful people in sales. Although he therefore would not be expected to be the best candidate for this position, he demonstrated strong scores on verbal reasoning and analytical abilities (95th percentile or higher on two measures of reasoning ability). Combined with his vocational interest scores, this may suggest a pattern better directed toward research and academic pursuits than toward sales."

5. *The report should be customized, not "canned."*   The mass production of computerized test results (Eyde & Kowal, 1987) has no doubt had many positive effects on the career assessment field, yet it has also resulted in the tendency to mass produce assessment "packages" that may have limited ability to address idiosyncratic concerns. Canned paragraphs from computerized testing reports are problematic if they are used exclusively with no thought or attempt at integration. Effective career assessment combines data from all three major domains (abilities, interests, and personality) and brings the data together into an integrated whole. It does not just present isolated variables as if they were independent of other variables. For example, to discuss intelligence independent of interests or motivation is inevitably limiting.

6. *Reports should express appropriate cautions.*   Whether intended or not, the results of an individual career assessment become lifetime companions of the assessee. To limit the potential misuse of the assessment report, it should contain appropriate cautions about potential sources of misuse. These include using a report after it may be reasonably presumed not

to be valid; inappropriately concluding that measured characteristics of people are unchanging or unchangeable; and using the report to draw conclusions about questions that were not studied in the initial evaluation. Reports prepared for third parties require even greater protection (see, e.g., Lounsbury, Bobrow, & Jensen, 1989) because it must be assumed that people other than the assessee will have access to the report. Despite multiple admonitions to the contrary, the psychologist may discover that a report prepared on an assessee became part of the individual's personnel file, was read by inappropriate parties, or was used for purposes other than those originally intended. The report should be written and labeled with these undesirable contingencies in mind. An expiration data is especially protective when preparing assessment reports for institutional settings or in situations in which people other than the assessee will have access to the report.

Case Examples

The following report provides an example of how a career assessment report might be prepared in a manner that is useful for a client. The report presented here is an abbreviated version of what would be given to the client. In the interests of continuity, the case is the same as the one discussed in chapter 5. Parts of the report have been deleted when the information is included in chapter 5 in a similar format or when space limitations dictated condensing detailed information that normally would be given to the client, such as the detailed explanation of the Holland vocational interest types.

Different approaches to the career assessment report would be needed if the assessment were done for a third party, such as a career assessment for an employer, as in the second example. The examples are not fool-proof models to be blindly emulated (nor are the tests included in each assessment to be blindly emulated), but they are illustrations of report formats that many clients have found to be helpful. Obviously, the specific format must be tailored to the purposes of the career assessment and to the needs of the individual. Although some have objected that the reports presented here are too long and overly detailed, I prefer the practice of including extensive data, which may have the potential to be useful throughout the client's career, to the alternative of having too little data or unexplained information.

Career Development Laboratory
3220 Louisiana Street, Suite 205
Houston, TX 77006
(713)-527-9235

Feedback on Your Career Assessment Process[1]

You have now completed a battery of tests intended to measure your vocational interests, skills, and abilities, and occupationally relevant personality characteristics. We believe that all three of these areas will help to identify career paths for which you are best suited and from which you are likely to derive the most enjoyment and success.

Your career counselor has reviewed the results of these tests in detail with you at the time of your feedback session. This summary will provide you with a written record of how you scored at the time of this testing and will give you a future reference should you receive additional testing in the future. We recommend that you keep this copy in a safe place and refer to it from time to time as you are faced with new career issues or decisions. Although some of the scores reported here are subject to change over time, and others may have been influenced by factors such as fatigue or level of development, many are relatively stable characteristics of personality or ability.

---

[1]Copyright © 1990, Career Development Laboratory, Inc. Reproduced by permission.

About Our Assessment Process

Our research suggests that there are three important aspects of people that determine their appropriateness for particular careers and types of work: abilities and aptitudes, vocational interests, and personality characteristics.

1. *Abilities and aptitudes.*   These are relatively stable characteristics that measure your capabilities and potential for doing certain types of things. You will most likely have areas of strength and weakness. We have arranged your abilities and aptitudes assessment results in a way that will make them somewhat easier to understand and remember.

2. *Vocational interests.*   These measure the types of work you like to do and find appealing. Vocational interests usually stabilize around the late teens and tend to be fairly constant after that. Vocational interests are an indication of preference for different types of work. We believe they also measure certain types of "occupational personalities" that will influence people's suitability for different types of work. Remember, though, that you can have interests in one area but not necessarily have the corresponding type of ability or aptitude for that type of work and vice versa.

3. *Personality characteristics.*   Increasingly, psychologists have come to recognize that one's success in an occupation depends on more than just having the ability or interests to pursue a line of work. There is more and more evidence suggesting that individuals in different occupations vary in the types of personality they have and that, within a given occupation, certain personality types will be appropriate for certain subspecialties and not for others. For example, lawyers usually share a common vocational interest pattern and pattern of abilities and aptitudes. However, there are many specialties within law. We believe that characteristics that make a good trial lawyer will differ from those associated with success as a research attorney. Two people may both be suited for law and one will make an excellent trial lawyer and the other will be unhappy and frustrated in that specialty area.

4. *Other factors.*   Career decisions are often made for reasons other than good fit. In the late 1960s and 1970s, the most

popular college major was psychology. In the 1980s, it was business. It is unlikely that the makeup of college students, on average, has changed substantially in that period of time. Rather, individuals have probably chosen business more often because of cultural factors, such as desire for economic rewards. Unfortunately, when career decisions are made on the basis of factors other than the person's aptitudes, interests, and personality type, the career choice may be regretted later.

We cannot choose your career for you, nor can we suggest that you ignore issues such as the likelihood of finding a good-paying job. However, we can provide you with feedback suggesting the likelihood of your contemplated career choices being well or poorly suited to your particular combination of abilities and aptitudes. We can also help you to become aware of cultural tendencies that may be pushing you in a direction that is poorly suited for you.[2]

Your Results

Vocational Interests

John Holland's widely respected theory of vocational interests suggests that there are six vocational interest types. The six Holland types will provide a useful organizing device to discuss your test results.

Each person will have a combination of types that best describe him or her. Some of these types are more compatible with each other than others.[3]

Your vocational interest scores. Three measures of vocational interest were administered: the Self-Directed Search, the Vocational Preference Inventory, and the Strong Vocational Interest Blank. On these measures, your highest scores were (from highest to lowest):

---

[2]At this point, the report includes current references for further reading, both general and tailored to the needs of the individual client when possible.

[3]The report here includes a detailed description, in lay language, of the six Holland interest types (see chap. 2).

Self-Directed Search		Vocational Preference Inventory		Strong Vocational Interest Blank	
Social	(43)	Social	(9)	Artistic	(59)
Investigative	(37)	Investigative	(8)	Investigative	(55)
Artistic	(27)	Artistic	(7)	Social	(55)
Enterprising	(18)	Enterprising	(5)	Enterprising	(46)
Conventional	(14)	Realistic	(3)	Conventional	(44)
Realistic	(5)	Conventional	(2)	Realistic	(36)
Code: S–I–A		Code: S–I–A		Code: A–I–S	

Other scores | Other scores

Average self-
  control
Relatively low
  Masculinity
Moderately high
  Status score

Academic
  Comfort = 68
  (high)
Introversion–
  Extraversion =
  39 (extraverted)

Your current occupation's code: Your present occupation of investments manager is coded in different ways by different coders. Holland's SDS codes it as Conventional–Investigative–Social, whereas the SVIB reports Enterprising–Conventional–Investigative.

Your "Occupational Daydream" interest codes: writer, A–E–S (technical writer, I–R–E); manager, own business, E–S–A (code varies with type of business); and real estate appraiser, S–C–E.

Some occupations thought to be consistent with your codes: The following occupations are thought to be consistent with your vocational interest coding possibilities. Considering the appeal of the following occupational groups' codings may help you to clarify your code. Note that not all of these codes are agreed on by all experts. Moreover, these represent *average* codes and will disguise important differences among members of the same occupation.[4]

Abilities

You were tested on a number of abilities and aptitudes. These have to do with your *ability*, or potential to have ability, as opposed to *interest* in doing particular types of activities. Although we have administered a comprehensive battery of tests, there are additional aptitudes and abilities that may also be vocationally relevant. We have grouped your ability measures into categories that are similar to the vocational interest measures. However, there is less certainty about the validity of the theoretical grouping listed here than there was in the case of Holland's theory of vocational interests. We therefore recommend that you first consider the results of each test one at a time and that you examine your areas of special strength and weakness.

Although there are no absolute rules, we believe that aptitudes and abilities at about the 75th percentile or higher compared with general population norms are very important to be used in your career choice. (*Percentile* refers to the percentage of people who took the test who did more poorly on the test than did you.) Aptitude scores below the 25th percentile are sufficiently low that you can generally avoid professions that make extensive use of this aptitude. Scores between the 25th and 75th percentiles are also probably not high enough to arrange your career around them. However, as you get closer to the 75th percentile, you may have enough of the aptitude to consider it in your career choice.

Note that in many cases we compare your scores not just with general population norm groups but also with speciality groups that make use of the ability in their daily work. In the latter cases, you would be expected to have lower percentile scores because the standard of comparison is much higher. If you score at about the 50th percentile (again, there are no

---

[4]In this section the occupational preference information discussed in chapter 5, using a similar format, is repeated.

absolutes) or above compared with a relevant, carefully screened normative group in which the ability is needed, this is probably confirmation that you do have enough of the aptitude or ability to use it occupationally.

When considering scores for which multiple norms are listed, look at the trends and compare yourself with the most appropriate comparison group. If, for example, on a measure involving strong intellectual skills you scored highly on the measure compared with high school and junior college students but only average compared with senior college students and low compared with graduate students, this may provide some feedback on how high you might expect to go in comparable occupations with defined educational requirements.

Realistic-Related Aptitudes and Abilities

Mechanical reasoning. This ability concerns one's understanding of mechanical concepts and principles similar to those used by mechanics and others who work with their hands and by certain scientists such as mechanical engineers, physicists, or certain medical specialists.

Your score on the measure used for this area (the Bennett Mechanical Comprehension Test) was 39. Here is how this score compares with other groups taking the test: 60th percentile, academic high school; 20th percentile, mechanical jobs, aviation company; and 1st percentile, machinists, steel company. This would not appear to be an area of special strength.

As a brief measure of fine finger ability, we administered the Tweezer Dexterity Test. You completed this test in over 15 minutes, which was below the 1st percentile compared with an adult male population. These norms are quite dated, however, and the results must therefore be interpreted conservatively.

Spatial ability. This concept refers to your ability to reason in space, that is, to manipulate three-dimensional objects in your mind. Spatial ability is often used by engineers, architects, and artists and also by pilots, navigators, and so forth. Your score of 38 on the test used in this area (the Minnesota Paper Form Board, AA series) can be compared with other groups as follows: 30th percentile, Grade 12 males; 5th percentile, engineering students; 10th percentile, engineers and scientists, research and development; 10th percentile, draftspeople; and 10th percentile, IBM customer service engineers. These results are low and suggest limited spatial abilities, at least as measured by this test.

Investigative-Related Aptitudes and Abilities

Nonverbal reasoning. This area refers to reasoning skills that can be done without words. The test we used to measure this (the Raven Advanced Progressive Matrices) requires you to complete a pattern in which one piece has been removed. You must use logical reasoning ability to do this, but the task is nonverbal. Your score on this measure was 23. Compared with the normative group on whom the test was standardized (primarily British people), you scored at the 95th percentile. Compared with a highly selected college-level normative population, your score was at the 24th percentile.

For comparison purposes, here are some average scores earned on this measure by various college student groups (note that these scores are averages obtained by each group, not percentiles)[5]: engineering, 25.7; law, 21.1; medicine, 24.0; mature-age students, 19.1; and career counseling students, 23.8. Your score suggests that nonverbal reasoning abilities are good but not your strongest ability.

Nonverbal reasoning ability can have different applications depending on whether spatial abilities are also present. For example, an architect may need both nonverbal reasoning ability and spatial ability. However, other, more verbally oriented professionals also tend to score highly on this measure, such as lawyers and other professionals.

Verbal reasoning ability. In this area of ability or aptitude, we examined your skill in the use of reasoning with words. In the test we used for this area (the Watson-Glaser Critical Thinking Appraisal), you had to carefully reason with fairly complex and demanding verbal material. You earned a score of 73 on this measure. Here are some normative comparisons to

[5]These norms were provided by the test authors (see Raven, Court, & Raven, 1977a).

interpret your score: 97th percentile, upper division 4-year college students; 85th percentile, MBA students; 80th percentile, 3rd-year medical students; and 63.3, average career assessment sample (this is a raw score average, not a percentile score)[6]. These results suggest verbal reasoning ability to be an area of special strength.

Overall Intellectual Ability

General Intelligence. General intellectual ability is probably the single most important career-related variable. Although general intelligence is grouped with the Investigative ability area, it relates to a number of other occupational pursuits. Some researchers believe that general intelligence is the best single predictor of how high an individual will rise within a particular career. Although we would not go that far, we do think general intelligence is very important in a variety of occupational pursuits.

We assessed your general intelligence with the Wechsler Adult Intelligence Scale–Revised. On this measure you earned scores on the Verbal intelligence in the superior to very superior range, but on the Performance intelligence in the low average range. The 41-point difference between verbal and nonverbal intelligence was very high and highly significant statistically and is suggestive of a true difference between these two areas of intelligence. A difference of this magnitude is unusual and possibly suggests a nonverbal learning disability, especially because the nonverbal intelligence score is below average. At the least, it suggests a major difference in your ability to process information verbally and nonverbally.

On the verbal tests, you did best on measures of vocabulary, arithmetic, general information, and the ability to abstract from verbal material. You did least well on a measure requiring you to repeat digits forward and backward. All subtest scores, however, were above average. On the Performance subtests,

---

[6]Note in this section that actual IQ scores are typically not presented because they are subject to such misuse and misinterpretation.

however, only your score on a digit symbol substitution task reached average. There was little variability among the other nonverbal tests, all of which were below average.

Overall, your results on the intelligence test suggest the ability to function at a very high level verbally and potentially at a below-average level nonverbally. Such a difference can possibly create strain in your ability to integrate information that requires both verbal and nonverbal processing. If present, a nonverbal learning disability could be associated with a possible pattern of underachievement compared with your very high verbal abilities. Difficulty concentrating on nonverbal tasks requiring sustained attention could be a problem.

Field dependence–independence. Research suggests that individuals often found to be either field dependent (i.e., rely primarily on their external environment for cues about how to act) or field independent (i.e., think independently of the environment in which they are functioning). Field dependence and independence is thought to measure your reliance on cues and stimuli from the environment to make judgments and form impressions. Scientists, mathematicians, and engineers tend, as groups, toward field independence, whereas people with skills in the helping professions and in highly verbal activities are more likely to be field dependent, and for that reason we group this concept here with the Investigative-related abilities.

The particular test we used to approximate this dimension (the Comprehensive Ability Battery Flexibility of Closure test) requires you to find drawings that have been "hidden" in a more complex drawing. Field-independent people usually can do this with a high degree of skill, whereas field-dependent people usually have trouble with the task. Your score of 4 on this measure compares with others as follows: 11th percentile, high school students (male), and 1st percentile, freshmen college students (male), suggesting more of a field-dependent than field-independent approach. (Our career assessment sample averaged 8.2.) The field-dependent pattern is commonly found among writers, artists, helping professionals, and othes, whereas a field-independent cognitive style is more likely to be found in the sciences.

Artistic-Related Aptitudes and Abilities

Aesthetic judgment. Aesthetic judgment is thought to relate to a number of different artistic-type professions, not just to those with drawing ability. Artists, interior decorators, and possibly musicians all would be expected to have a fine appreciation of things artistic.

To measure this construct, we used the Meier Art Judgement Test. This required you to compare two pictures and choose the one you found to be the most aesthetically pleasing. The criterion against which your scores were compared in this test was the ratings of the same pictures made by professional artists and other appropriate experts. Your score of 95 placed you at the 33rd percentile on this measure compared with high school students and at the 19th percentile compared with college art students. Our career counseling sample averaged 100 on this measure.

Artistic drawing ability was measured by a subtest of the Comprehensive Ability Battery. On this test you were required to reproduce two drawings. Your score of 22 (CAB-RD test) was at the 27th percentile compared with high school male norms. Of course, being able to reproduce a simple line drawing is not the same thing as being a great painter, but some similarities are shared.

Musical Aptitudes and Abilities

Musical abilities are thought to emerge at a relatively young age and to mature (reach a level at which they can effectively be integrated into important occupational, societal, or life tasks) fairly young (on average). There are a variety of ways to measure musical aptitude. We have included three subtests of one of the major musical talent measures (the Seashore Measures of Musical Talents). The specific aspects of musical talent measured by each of these three tests are explained.

Pitch: This is the ability to identify small differences in pitch. Musicians and singers need to be able to locate the appropriate pitch for reproducing musical sounds. Not all musical instruments require this to the same degree.

Rhythm: Much of music involves periodicity, that is, the perception or reproduction of notes in certain patterns. In this subtest, your ability to discriminate between different patterns of notes was examined.

Tonal Memory: This refers to the ability to remember series of musical notes or tones. It is important in many types of musical activities.

Here are your scores on these measures, using as norms comparison to a large number of people who have taken this test in the past. (The test was administered twice, on two different days, as a reliability check for the Pitch test score.)

Subtest	Raw score	Percentile
Pitch	32	13th
Rhythm	28	73rd
Tonal Memory	61	27th

These scores suggest low musical aptitudes except on Rhythm.

Social-Related Aptitudes and Abilities

Social abilities are important in jobs or careers that require that you get along well with others and in which you must work with and through other people. Most of the helping professionals would make strong use of these aptitudes, as would teachers, and, to some extent, managers. Unfortunately, our measures of social ability (sometimes called "social intelligence") are not as good as we would like.

You were assessed using a paper-and-pencil measure: the Interpersonal Problem-Solving Assessment Technique. This test was designed to measure your ability to judge the appropriate response in a social situation and to indicate which type of response you would be most likely to demonstrate in a variety of social situations. Because you had to indicate what you thought you would actually do in a given situation, obviously the results of the test will only be as good as the honesty with which you indicated what you think you would actually do in each instance. Here are your scores on this measure:

Response type	Your score[7]	Average college student sample	Average adult career counselees
Effective	15	13	15
Avoidant	6	4	5
Inappropriate	1	4	1
Dependent	0	1	1
Unscorable	0	1	< 1

These scores suggest good interpersonal behavioral abilities, assuming that your answers accurately reflected what you would really do in the described situations. Your avoidant responses were slightly higher than the college student sample, suggesting that you might sometimes work around conflict rather than address it directly. However, overall, this is an area of strength.

Enterprising-Related Aptitudes and Abilities

In this section, we present both "aptitudes and abilities" and interest and personality data because the modal managerial profile appears to be a composite of these types of measures. The typical managerial profile for middle-level managers and above includes the following[8]: high average or above intelligence, managerial vocational interests, tough-mindedness, a moderately high need for power over others, high prioritizing and organizing abilities, high interpersonal skills, leadership skills, high need for achievement, a moderate need for affiliation, and a generally positive, optimistic outlook.

Overall, your "fit" with business and management would appear to be low. Although your intellectual abilities are certainly adequate for this type of work, you had no manifest vocational interests in the Enterprising area. You showed little

---

[7]Responses the client said he would make.

[8]Currently we use a managerial in-basket to measure prioritizing and organizing abilities and, when possible, interpersonal simulations to measure leadership and interpersonal skills. This client was not administered these measures.

evidence of tough-mindedness and did not have a very positive outlook at the time of testing. Finally, you endorsed little interest in having power over others.

Although you were not tested on other managerial skills, we think it unlikely you would be content in a career primarily emphasizing managerial interests and skills. However, many people open their own businesses with other than a typical managerial profile. They rely on their knowledge of the business area (e.g., art appraising) for success rather than on generic managerial skills. In such instances, it is often desirable for the entrepreneur to hire a manager to assist with the management of the operation or the various details that must be accounted for with finances, taxes, and so on.

Conventional-Related Aptitudes and Abilities

Perceptual Speed and Accuracy. This variable measures your ability to rapidly compare numbers and names to determine whether they are the same or different. This is thought to be important in many clerical jobs, accounting, bookkeeping, and, on the verbal material side, in reading for speed and for accuracy. Many other career pursuits involve paperwork and reading verbal and numerical information.

On the measure we used (the Minnesota Clerical Test), you had to rapidly determine whether long lists of figures and letters were the same. Here is how your scores of 151 on the Number Comparison subtest and 186 on the Name Comparison subtest compared with selected normative groups:

| | Percentile | |
Group	Number comparison	Name comparison
Male clerks	97	99
Grade 12 college prep males	90	95
Female tellers	90	99
Female clerks	95	95

Our career assessment sample (all college educated) had

averages on this measure of 122 on Numbers and 124 on Names. Your scores indicate an area of strength. Note that the scores are somewhat higher than your nonverbal intelligence test results might suggest.

Computational and arithmetic skills. Computational and math skills are important in many clerical jobs, accounting, and, at the higher levels, in many aspects of science. On the measure we used to measure these skills—the Arithmetic subtest of the Wide Range Achievement Test–Revised—you earned a score of 43, which was at the 79th percentile compared with other people your age. The average of the career assessment sample was 39.7. Although this test is used in our battery primarily as a measure of computational skills, the more difficult items on this test require mathematical expertise. We note that you scored a bit better on the Arithmetic subtest of the intelligence test, which was orally presented. Perceptual speed and accuracy would appear to be an area of strength.

Other Tests of Ability

Writing sample. This was intended to provide a measure of your ability to organize thoughts quickly and to express yourself in a clear, coherent manner but mostly as a measure of verbal fluency. In addition, a number of other exercises and personality tests required the use of writing to complete unstructured assignments. The actual number of words you produced in the 15-minute time period (214) was about average (224) compared with our normative data for word flow and ideas, suggesting some ability in the free flow of ideas. Your topic chosen for this unstructured task was nonfiction. We did not score your writing sample for grammar or creativity.

Creative imagination. The Original Uses subtest of the Comprehensive Ability Battery required you to come up with new uses for two separate objects. Your score of 5 on this measure was at the 12th percentile compared with male high school students and at the 1st percentile compared with male college students. Our career assessment sample averaged 9.9.

On the Ideational Fluency subtest of the Comprehensive Ability Battery, you were required to generate as many adjectives to describe certain things as you could think of within a given time period. Your score of 49 was at the 99th percentile compared with high school males and at the 99th percentile compared with college males. Our career assessment sample's average score on this measure was 28. Overall, these measures suggest good to excellent ideational fluency, particularly in the verbal–descriptive area.

Memory. On a measure of memory for unrelated material (i.e., nonverbal "nonsense" material), you earned a score of 8, which scored at the 55th percentile for high school males and at the 36th percentile for male college freshmen, and was higher than the career assessment sample of 10.9.

Your scores on intelligence test subtests involving memory (e.g., Digit Span and the Digit Symbol substitution task) were average or above, although your scores on the Tonal Memory subtest of the Seashore Measures of Musical Talent was low. These results together suggest fair to good memory abilities, which may vary with the type of material to be memorized.

Personality

Your scores on the various personality tests were discussed with you in your feedback session. Highlights of some of these results are now summarized. The following are the tests you took: the California Psychological Inventory, the Clinical Analysis Questionnaire, the Fundamental Interpersonal Relations Orientation Scales-Behavior, the Edwards Personal Preference Schedule, the NEO Personality Inventory, the Myers-Briggs Type Indicator, selected cards from the Thematic Apperception Test, and two sentence-completion measures.

On the Fundamental Interpersonal Relations Orientation Scales-Behavior, a measure of need strength in three areas, you had the following scores:

| | Needs | | |
	Inclusion	Control	Affection
Expressed	4	2	5
Wanted	0	6	6
Total	4	8	11

These scores are thought to reflect your needs (wanted) for inclusion (involvement with others), control (of and by others), and affection (intimate relations). Your pattern of needs reflects little interest in having influence over others. The other areas suggest higher expressed needs for involvement with others than you may actually prefer.

On another measure of need strength (the Edwards Personal Preference Schedule), your score on a validity indicator (consistency, answering repeated items in the same direction) was high (97th percentile), suggesting that the results are internally consistent. On the Edwards, you expressed the following need pattern (compared with the adult male normative group): Your scores on this test indicated high needs for affiliation (97th percentile), intraception (introspection; 95th percentile), achievement (91st percentile), autonomy (88th percentile), succorance (a desire for nurturing and support from others; 87th percentile), nurturance (a desire to provide nurturing and support to others; 81st percentile), and change (76th percentile). You had low needs for endurance (3rd percentile), deference (4th percentile), and aggression (11th percentile).

On the Myers-Briggs Type Indicator, you scored in the following manner:

1. *Introversion–Extraversion:* Introverted people tend to require time alone, away from the distractions of other people, whereas extraverted people generally prefer continuous involvement with others. Introversion expresses a preference for working with things or ideas rather than with other people (the preference, typically, of extraverted people). Introverted people may also enjoy working with others but tend to prefer activities involving face-to-face contact with others in smaller doses. A "recovery period" may be required thereafter.

Extraverted people often feel invigorated by contact with others. Introversion can be helpful for working in areas involving high levels of concentration and attention to factual or other detail, whereas this may be more difficult for highly extraverted people to sustain.

Introversion–extraversion appears to express a characteristic of temperament (i.e., basic personality orientation) that may be present from a very early age and that may be relatively insensitive to change. Ideally, one's work is compatible with one's basic personality orientation.

Your scores for introversion and extraversion on this measure were the same, suggesting that characteristics of both types may be present. This is generally consistent with your scores on the Strong Vocational Interest Blank Introversion/Extroversion scale and the California Psychological Inventory, on both of which you showed a tendency toward the introverted direction, but only slightly. However, you scored in the extraverted direction on the NEO Personality Inventory and the Clinical Analysis Questionnaire, suggesting that there may be some inconsistency in your responses. Perhaps you have characteristics of both introversion and extraversion, not being strongly differentiated between these two dimensions. Managers, salespeople, therapists, and others who work with people (e.g., teachers and housewives) often score in the extraverted direction, whereas scientists and researchers often score in the introverted direction.

2. *Intuitive–Sensing:* Intuitive types of individuals may reach conclusions by "jumps" in logic rather than by careful, logical reasoning and tend to see possibilities rather than to master the detail of factual information. In contrast, Sensing types of individuals are thought to be more comfortable with doing things in a well-established routine and do not experience a continual need for change. Their thinking tends to be more orderly and predictable than the "conceptual leaps" of Intuitive types.

Intuitive types are often instigators of change and may feel very uncomfortable with consistency and sameness, whereas Sensing types can comfortably repeat things without getting bored. The two types can be complementary: Intuitive types tend to need Sensing types, who may have more of a factual orientation toward managing the daily grind and implementing their ideas. At the same time, however, Intuitive types tend to be impatient with such individuals, tending to conflict with them because of basic differences in style and personality. In contrast, Sensing types may find the constant innovation of the Intuitive type to be bizarre. At work, the Intuitive type often needs the Sensing type in order to get things done and to translate ideas from theory to practice.

You scored strongly (+16) in the intuitive direction, indicating a preference for doing things creatively rather than in a well-defined, repetitive way or for implementing an existing set of guidelines or structures rather than coming up with new ways to do things. According to this score, you would prefer to come up with new, innovative, creative methods rather than "more of the same."

3. *Thinking–Feeling:* People scoring in the Thinking direction seem more attuned to dispassionate, logical analysis of situations than to dealing with reactions to events. People scoring in the Feeling direction tend to be more reactive to their own emotions and to those of others and may be guided more by their affective reactions than by reason alone.

Many people in scientific and business occupations score in the Thinking direction. People in the artistic occupations and helping professions often score higher on the Feeling than the Thinking dimension.

It is important to note that this test measures a cognitive style preference; it does not measure actual feeling or thinking ability. Feeling-oriented styles are more often found in the arts, writing, and counseling and teaching professions.

You scored much more in the Feeling than in the Thinking direction (+8), suggesting greater orientation toward feelings than toward thoughts. The extent to which this has been affected by your therapeutic experiences is unknown. Typically, scientists, engineers, and men in general score in the Thinking rather than Feeling direction on this measure. Salespeople, more often than managers, would be expected to score in this direction.

4. *Perceiving–Judging:* Your score on the Perceiving–Judging dimension was moderately in the Judging direction (+7). The distinction here is the difference between desire for closure and willingness to tolerate open-endedness. As it relates to your work, this orientation is good for getting things done, sometimes in an unimaginative manner. This might present a potential problem area for you.

On the NEO Personality Inventory, you scored as follows:

1. *Adjustment:* This scale measures so-called "neurotic" traits within the normal range of personality. People scoring in the

nonadjusted direction tend to be seen as anxious, depressed, or poorly adjusted. You scored in the average range, but near the border of the nonadjusted direction. On the subtests in this area, you scored in the depressed and vulnerable direction. This may reflect situational depression at the time of testing or a common concern among creative people.

2. *Extraversion:* In contrast to your other test results, you scored strongly in the extraverted direction on this test.

3. *Openness:* You scored very high on this measure, something that is important in many of the artistic professions. Your scores also indicated a strong fantasy life and good access to your feelings.

4. *Agreeableness:* You scored slightly in the agreeable direction on this measure, suggesting a tendency to be seen by others as likeable and cooperative. Your score was near the average range.

5. *Conscientiousness:* You scored below average on this measure, suggesting a possible tendency toward poor organization or not finishing things. This is consistent with findings from some of the other measures.

Combining the results of other personality measures, we note that your scores showed a tendency toward "creative" personality characteristics, a preference for innovation rather than predictability and repetitiveness. Passivity and disorganization, however, can be a problem and you may pride yourself on your "differentness" and *potential* talents rather than on your accomplishments with these talents. As you stated on a sentence-completion measure, "I often think of myself as . . . unrealized aptitudes."

You generally scored fairly low on measures of assertiveness, suggesting that you would not naturally gravitate toward managerial or supervisory positions. You appear to be sensitive and oriented toward feeling somewhat submissive and avoidant of activities calling for dominance or control over others. On the other hand, you would appear to be sociable and accommodating, generally oriented toward the needs of others, warm, and somewhat gregarious.

Generally very open to new ideas, you would be expected to have an active fantasy life and to be receptive to new actions, values, and aesthetics. You may wait too often for "inspiration" and direction to come from others rather than attempting to plan for it for yourself. This is an area possibly needing attention and a plan for change. Greater focus is recommended in identifying your goals and committing them to paper. Continually reminding yourself of where you hope to get may help to keep you on track, especially because you may be easily distracted by external forces.

A number of themes run through your projective tests. These include a sense of abandonment and neglect by significant others, especially parental figures, and many unresolved issues of aggression and possibly passive-aggressiveness. There was also a theme of expecting the worst to happen or for good situations somehow to end negatively.

Your test results also suggest that you currently may be experiencing some degree of depression and vulnerability. This could influence how you view the world and, to some degree, your results on this assessment. A tendency toward interpersonal tension and instability may need attention if you find that it interferes with your desired future career directions.

Recommendations

1. *Career options:* Your major option now under consideration is choosing between returning to securities analysis or taking up writing, presumably on a full-time basis. The securities analysis area is generally a marginal fit to your areas of interests and abilities, but apparently it is an occupation in which you are able to function reasonably well. Your tendency to be disorganized and creative is a potential concern if this is a lasting career. Concerning the writing profession, you have many of the characteristics that are often found in writers, but there are areas of misfit, especially in the personality domain. Because you may be more extraverted than is common among writers, teaching writing might offer a slightly more consistent pattern. Running your own business and being a real estate appraiser do not appear to be good fits for you if pursued as full-time occupations. Social science occupations are also relevant but would require more training. Teaching would appear to

combine many of your characteristics, provided you were to instruct in a content area that you like.

2. *Personal concerns:* Currently, depression may be interfering with some of your occupational pursuits. We recommend that if depression or anxiety continues you may want to consider seeking professional assistance because such feelings can certainly interfere with your job pursuits.

3. *Watch these potential problem areas:* A tendency toward passivity and withdrawal may interfere with the career directions you find attractive. At this time, it is desirable to find a good-fitting job, not a perfect job.

A tendency was noted for your talent to be raw and undeveloped. Watch a possible trend toward disorganization and not taking your work or yourself very seriously.

4. *A simple solution to your career dilemmas is unlikely:* No one career choice emerges from your data. It therefore might be better to think as one possible approach in terms of having more than one job on a part-time basis as a way to bridge the various aspects of your training and interests. For example, you might work as a securities analyst (possibly in the public sector or in some manner you can direct toward helping others) on a part-time basis and do your writing or other desired activities in your spare time until you can support you and your family.

5. *Discipline:* Much more self-discipline will be needed to succeed in any of the options you are considering. The need for the raw talent to become directed is clear. Rather than waiting for external authority, you may need to go ahead and do *something*, but do it more consistently. For example, writing can be done now, not just after a training program is completed. You could immediately send samples of your work for publication consideration.

[Name of psychologist (and license number if required)]

[Title]

The next career assessment report illustrates some issues relevant when the assessment is done for a third party, in this case, the evaluation of a client for employment consideration. This is a composite report typical of what might be used with high-level, prescreened managerial candidates for employment or promotional consideration by an organization with which the psychologist has an ongoing consulting relationship. Different feedback reports might be used for other selection work, particularly when lower level jobs are considered and when personality and interest variables are less relevant.

Sample Career Assessment Report Prepared for a Potential Employer

CONFIDENTIAL

Executive Assessment Report[9]

Name of Candidate: Mark H.

Date of Examination:

Examiner:

> *Note:*   This report contains confidential and time-limited information about the person being assessed. It should not be considered to be an accurate statement of the assessee's career profile after 1 year because some of the variables measured may change.

---

[9]Copyright © 1988 by the Career Development Laboratory. Reproduced by permission.

The following tests were administered: a structured interview, the Wechsler Adult Intelligence Scale–Revised, the Self-Directed Search, the Thematic Apperception Test, the Rorschach[10], the California Psychological Inventory, and a sentence-completion measure.

Referral and Position Information

Mr. H. was referred for psychological assessment as part of the evaluation procedures being used in the final selection of candidates for the position of director of building management for the Arabesque Housing Authority. The purpose of this assessment was to identify a composite picture of some of each candidate's strengths and weaknesses for the organization and the particular position within the organization under consideration. Information generated by this approach was to be used as only one source of data in making final selection decisions and, for each candidate wanting feedback, would provide the basis for assisting the individual in identifying areas of strength and weakness and in creating a plan for personal development. Finally, a very limited amount of time was available for each candidate's assessment. Furthermore, because some candidates for this position were from out of town, group exercises in which all candidates participated were not possible with this particular assessment process.

Although no formal job analysis was performed for this position, the Arabesque Housing Authority had employed an executive recruiting firm to identify desirable characteristics of the successful candidate. The relevant identified psychological traits

---

[10]Because of its high potential for misuse, the Rorschach is not recommended for routine clinical use. Under the circumstances of this assessment, it was used primarily because most of the candidates were exceptionally verbally articulate and excellent at presenting themselves in a socially desirable manner on paper-and-pencil measures of personality. In addition, the candidates were senior managers with an anticipated restricted range (high) of intellectual ability. Psychologists are advised in general to use the Rorschach rarely in personnel selection contexts, to use standard administration and scoring procedures, and to interpret conservatively. To a lesser extent, these comments also apply to other projective personality measures.

to be evaluated included (a) a "team player" orientation as opposed to an orientation in which the individual seeks to overtly dominate or seeks rewards primarily for himself or herself; (b) good listening skills; (c) even-temperedness and a good sense of humor; (d) process oriented rather than directive oriented; (e) directness, strength, and independence in presenting and strongly defending professional convictions; and (f) optimism ("can-do attitude").

Although some of these desired characteristics are potentially at odds with one another (e.g., Examples a and e), the general themes emerging from the job description prepared by the recruiting firm suggested the importance of a high level of interpersonal skills, the ability to work more or less behind the scenes rather than as the focal point of attention, and the absence of personality characteristics that might be inhibiting in this position. These suggest that both ability and personality dimensions are relevant.

In addition, the psychological literature on leaders and managers suggests the importance for success in high-level positions in complex and structured organizational settings of several characteristics measurable by psychological instrumentation, including a high level of general intelligence, a high need for achievement, comfort with handling ambiguity, freedom from conflicts with authority, and managerial occupational interests.

Because the skills identified in the job analysis were largely interpersonal ones, the decision was made to focus primarily on the measurement of relevant personality variables. The aim was to identify limitations in candidates who might be expected, on the basis of the assessment results, to have difficulty in some aspect of interpersonal management skills that would be important in success with such a high-level position. In addition, we measured cognitive and intellectual and vocational interest variables judged to be important for this position.

It should be recognized that the psychological assessment task was directed both at determining whether candidates possessed any undesirable characteristics that might suggest ineffectiveness in the director of building management position and determining which candidates, among several who would likely be outstanding managers in general, would be best suited to the particular needs identified by the Arabesque Housing Authority. For this reason, the psychological assessment instruments selected included projective psychological tests as part of the evaluation. Because of the unusually short time period in which the assessments had to be completed, and the fact that half of the candidates would be visiting the client organization from out of town, an assessment center methodology was not possible to measure interpersonal skills through direct observation. A structured clinical interview was included, however.

Background Information

Mr. H. presently serves as director of building management for another employer, a position he has held for 3 years. An architect by training, Mr. H. initially worked as a building design supervisor and then as a senior planner before assuming his present duties. He currently supervises a staff of 15 employees, most of whom are professionally trained. He has assumed increasingly high managerial responsibilities within the last few years.

Mr. H. obtained his architectural degree from University A. He also received a Master's degree in urban planning from University B. He views his strengths as being his ability to "communicate in diverse settings," listening to others, and the ability to apply factual information to settle conflicts or disputes. He described his style of management as being participatory, although he noted that such a method works best with educated people. In describing a typical day, he noted that he often meets with his assistant directors in the morning and also spends considerable time working with members of the public such as developers. He tries to spend at least some time every day by himself working on planning and thinking through where his department is headed.

He takes particular pride in a special planning and development program that he helped instigate with his present employer and that he believes will prove to be the "single most important initiative" yet developed by the employer.

Behavioral Observations

Appropriately dressed in a conservative business suit, Mr. H. worked diligently and conscientiously on the testing materials. He was verbally articulate in his responses but often was overly attentive to detail. He did not shy away from ambiguous questions but frequently was abstract and perhaps overly intellectual in his responses. His wording was sometimes a bit stilted or pedantic (e.g., on one of the projective tests he said, "I see a butterflylike object, some kind of living organism").

Mr. H. readily commanded respect through his intellect. However, it was at times difficult to relate easily and directly to him other than through the discussion of intellectual ideas and abstractions. He appeared to be somewhat anxious about the assessment process, although he worked diligently and prodigiously regardless of how anxious he might have been.

He was viewed by our examiners as being serious, contemplative, and somewhat cerebral, someone who might readily be at home in a university or think tank. However, our examiners questioned how easily Mr. H. would be able to relate to nontechnical subordinates, especially in overseeing the daily detail of a job and when forced to interact with a diversity of types of people.

Cognitive and Intellectual Abilities

The Wechsler Adult Intelligence Scale–Revised is one of the most reliable and valid measures of general intellectual ability. On this test, Mr. H. earned scores at the low end of the superior range of intelligence (Verbal score = 120 ± 5.4; Full Scale score = 120 ± 4.4) to the high average (Performance score = 115 ± 7.4) range. However, he did relatively poorly on a Verbal scale, which might have been influenced by anxiety. If his Verbal intelligence scale score is recomputed removing the low score and substituting a prorated average, his overall Verbal and Full Scale scores would rise, respectively, by 6 and 4 points; they would still be in the superior range. He did especially well on subtests requiring the use of verbal and nonverbal reasoning abilities. His Performance intelligence score was lowered somewhat by a somewhat obsessive tendency to try to get every detail right and to check his work, such that he frequently missed bonus points given for rapid completion of a task.

Vocational Interests

On the Self-Directed Search, a vocational interest measure that Mr. H. was not familiar with, he completed the instrument to indicate that his highest three areas of vocational interest were (from highest to lowest) Social, Enterprising, and Artistic. However, his fourth and fifth highest areas of interest—Investigative and Realistic—were not significantly differentiated, and he might have been influenced somewhat by the desire to present himself in a manner consistent with what he thought to be the "desired" managerial code (Enterprising–Social–Conventional). (Interestingly, the client's area of original training—architecture—typically is coded as Realistic–Investigative–Artistic, which is highly discrepant from his endorsed preferences on the interest measure.

Overall, his vocational interest pattern, if accurate, would suggest an individual who would approach the manager's position creatively rather than conventionally and who might therefore conflict with individuals who are highly bureaucratic in orientation.

His occupational daydreams (the occupations he had thought of as possibilities for himself, either now or in the past) included many high-level managerial positions, such as president of an educational institution or a foundation. This suggests both high needs for advancement and achievement and, perhaps, comfort in high-level positions in which abstraction is important. It is possible that the more mundane day-to-day work in the position in question may be less challenging and interesting to him.

Personality Functioning

Several tests of personality were administered, for reasons discussed earlier. Mr. H. completed the California Psychological Inventory in a manner (as did most of the assessees) suggesting that he was presenting himself in a favorable light and potentially invalidating the remainder of the scales. His results, if valid, are consistent with those of a high-level manager, except that his score on a measure of traditionally masculine interests was in the nonmasculine direction. This pattern is typically found in people with diverse and intellectual interests and is job relevant only to the extent that the current position may require narrow and concrete rather than abstract interests.

On the projective personality tests, Mr. H. had a compulsive orientation. His style of dealing with others would be expected to be highly rational and logical. When dealing with emotionally charged issues, he would be expected to use the same methods and techniques, which may be limiting to a manager. However, in dealing with strictly abstract things, he was often highly creative, original, and integrative.

Mr. H.'s responses were often highly original and unusual, integrating the scientific and the artistic. He appears to view the world complexly rather than simplistically and is capable of deep insights and ideas that would not occur to others.

From a managerial perspective, Mr. H.'s personality characteristics are not those usually found in a manager. He may have more in common with leaders who are able to see the broad picture and look far ahead. Although valuable for high-level managers, such characteristics can sometimes prove dysfunctional in lower levels of management. Additional interviews with the candidate should therefore focus on the extent to which Mr. H. can work effectively with non-technically-oriented people who may not be responsive to a more intellectually oriented style.

Summary

Obviously very bright and verbally articulate, Mr. H. presents a number of attractive features for a high-level managerial position. He may be limited, however, by the lack of experience in non-technically-oriented management and limited experience in supervising very large organizations. Further exploration of the candidate's strengths and weaknesses in this particular context is suggested, with particular emphasis on investigating the potential areas of concern identified by this assessment.

Recommendations

Although a very impressive individual in many important respects, Mr. H.'s highly cognitive style may not work well in the position of director of building management without considerable assistance from others who could provide a more hands-on, pragmatic approach oriented toward overseeing the day-to-day details. Mr. H. would be expected to be outstanding in grasping the overall picture, providing direction and inspiration to his associates, but he does not appear to be particularly strong in fighting political battles or handling concrete details of projects as a primary focus. To the extent the current position demands such skills, further assessment of Mr. H.'s past and current experiences by those competent to discuss the technical details of his work is recommended. Although Mr. H. has apparently been highly successful in dealing in his current position (largely overseeing other technically trained professionals) using his rational style, it may have limits in a highly politicized position, such as the one described in the job description.

Because all of this candidate's experience has been basically within areas in which he is a specialist by training, it remains to be determined whether Mr. H. can function effectively as a manager in a position in which he must be a generalist, as appears to be needed in the current occupation. Although he appears to have a great deal of vision and to be able to provide a high level of complexity in approaching a managerial assignment, perhaps he should have a job in which he must manage others on a daily basis who have dissimilar backgrounds from his own before assuming a position such as the current one. This may help him to sort out a career path that is primarily administrative from one that he appears to presently be pursuing that is primarily technical and only secondarily administrative. Alternatively, Mr. H. might well aspire to a higher level of leadership within a technical institution, such as in a foundation or university.

Even if not chosen for this position, this is a very promising individual for whom other positions with the hiring institution should be considered, especially those for which long-range vision, conceptual adeptness, and an inspirational quality are considered important.

[Name of psychologist (license number if required)]

[Title]

Conclusion

As the two reports suggest, the assessment of career factors necessitates complexity. Detailed information should be provided to the client, at least in part to help assure that the results are not misused or misinterpreted. Particular care must be taken when the work is undertaken for a third party to ensure that the sometimes sensitive psychological information is not misused.

Above all, competent feedback must be cognitively and affectively on target. If the face-to-face feedback sessions are the place for addressing the affective reactions to career concerns, the written report will be available long after the specifics of the feedback work have been forgotten. As such, the written report can assist in the long-term integration of cognitive and emotional discoveries. Write your assessment reports from the perspective of how well they will read 25 years hence!

Afterword

The single most important message of this book is of the need for complexity in researching and clinically practicing career assessment: in theory, in measuring devices, and in integrating across diverse domains. The interdomain model of career assessment presented in this book demonstrates that career concerns are psychologically complicated, just as people are psychologically complex. Career assessors must consider each of the three domains (abilities, interests, and personality) and their interaction if they are to have success in capturing the complexity of real people and real career concerns.

It can be argued that important additional aspects of career assessment could appropriately have been targeted for discussion in this book. Thus, for example, career indecision (Barrett & Tinsley, 1977) and career immaturity (Crites, 1974)—two variables with emerging research literature and commercially available measuring devices (see Garbin & Stover, 1980; Super & Hall, 1978)—are two variables little noted here. Assuredly, there are others. It is not the case that such variables are irrelevant to career assessment. Neither, however, are they the place to begin and certainly they are not the place to end.

What is objectionable about so much of the recent literature on vocational assessment and selection is the tendency to isolate single individual difference variables and consider them as if they *were* the person. This may make for voluminous literature, but it does not necessarily make for good or clinically useful literature. Certainly, it is comparatively easier to measure one or a few variables at a time. Such a methodology is also conceptually simpler, and some might even say more elegant. As this book has repeatedly illustrated, however, interests, abilities, and personality characteristics encompass sets of individual difference variables that separately are part of a person's career profile. It is limiting to presume or pretend otherwise. To study isolated individual variables that may indeed have some relevance to career concerns without understanding the underlying context in which such variables are embedded is needlessly limiting.

For the practitioner, career assessment must never be regarded as a test-driven methodology. A measure is not worth using in career assessment or personnel selection work simply because its characteristics and methodology were learned in graduate school. To understand career concerns, the psychologist or other professional must measure broadly and integrate thoroughly. It is unlikely that the examiner will feel or in fact be competent in this area of practice much before completing at least 100 or so career assessments representing multiple patterns of interests, abilities, and personality. This is not an area of practice appropriate for dabbling.

For the researcher, it is time to refocus vocational assessment and guidance research from isolated variables that, although relatively easy to measure well, stand separately and in isolation from real-world concerns. The history of measurement of vocational interests illustrates the practical utility of good empiricism when combined with good theory. It also demonstrates that theory can emerge successfully after empirical findings rather than before.

There is still much work to be done just in the area of career assessment (not to mention career *counseling*, the focus of my next book). A valid theory of career assessment is of necessity a theory of interests, a theory of abilities, and a theory of personality. In each separate domain, psychologists are far from the finality of universally accepted understandings. Pressures to empiricize plentifully might have filled journals but have not yet resulted in integrated, and often not even in clinically applicable, findings.

Within the arena of career assessment, the researcher can do far worse than to start with the phenomenology as it is experienced by a variety of people functioning well and poorly in a multitude of careers. In addition, the clinician is well advised to examine the literature in each of the three domains and not to become distracted into creating pet theories supported only by the clinician's inevitably limited exposure to a necessarily biased and nonrepresentative client sample.

These are as demanding times as any. Work competence has never been in greater need. That psychologists and other relevant professionals can make a significant contribution to individuals' well-being while simultaneously enhancing society's productivity (by assisting individuals in becoming more productive in work to which they are well suited) can be doubly enriching.

In the end, it is difficult to imagine a more challenging area of psychology than career assessment for both practitioner and researcher alike. It is hoped that the lessons of this book will assist both groups in helping to modernize one of psychology's early and historic success stories.

References

Ackerman, T. A., & Smith, P. L. (1988). A comparison of the information provided by essay, multiple-choice, and free-response writing tests. *Applied Psychological Measurement, 12,* 117–128.

Adams, J., Priest, R. F., & Prince, H. T. (1985). Achievement motive: Analyzing the validity of the WOFO. *Psychology of Women Quarterly, 9,* 357–369.

Aderman, D., & Berkowitz, L. (1983). Self-concern and the unwillingness to be helpful. *Social Psychology Quarterly, 46,* 293–301.

Altender, L. E. (1940). The value of intelligence, personality, and vocational interest tests in a guidance program. *Journal of Educational Psychology, 31,* 449–459.

American Educational Research Association, American Psychological Association, & National council on Measurement in Education. (1985). *Standards for educational and psychological testing* (3rd ed.). Washington, DC: American Psychological Association.

American Psychological Association. (1987). *Casebook on ethical principles of psychologists.* Washington, DC: Author.

American Psychological Association. (1990). Ethical principles of psychologists (amended June 2, 1989). *American Psychologist, 45,* 390–395.

Anastasi, A. (1982). *Psychological testing* (5th ed). New York: Macmillan.

Anderson, L. R., & Thacker, J. (1985). Self-monitoring and sex as related to assessment center ratings and job performance. *Basic and Applied Social Psychology, 6,* 345–361.

Andreason, N., & Canter, A. (1974). The creative writer: Psychiatric symptoms and family history. *Comprehensive Psychiatry, 15,* 123–131.

Andreason, N., & Powers, P. S. (1975). Creativity and psychosis: An examination of conceptual style. *Archives of General Psychiatry, 32,* 70–73.

Andrew, D. M., Paterson, D. G., & Longstaff, H. P. (1979). *Minnesota Clerical Test manual: 1979 revision.* San Antonio, TX: Psychological Corporation.

Andrews, H. A. (1975). Beyond the high point code in testing Holland's theory. *Journal of Vocational Behavior, 6,* 101–108.

Ansari, M. A. (1982). The semantic-differential profiles of successful executives. *Indian Psychologist, 1,* 70–78.

Ansari, M. A. (1984). Psychodynamics of a successful executive. *Managerial Psychology, 5,* 25–43.

Ansari, M. A., Baumgarter, H., & Sullivan, G. (1982). The personal orientation-organizational climate fit and managerial success. *Human Relations, 35,* 1159–1177.

Ansley, T. N., Spratt, K. F., & Forsyth, R. A. (1989). The effects of using calculators to reduce the computational burden of a standardized test of mathematics problem solving. *Educational and Psychological Measurement, 49,* 277–286.

Antill, J. K., & Cunningham, J. D. (1982). Sex differences in performance on ability tests as a function of masculinity, femininity, and androgyny. *Journal of Personality and Social Psychology, 42,* 718–728.

Aranya, N., Barak, A., & Amernic, J. (1981). A test of Holland's theory in a population of accountants. *Journal of Vocational Behavior, 19,* 15–24.

Arenson, M. A. (1983). The validity of certain entrance tests as predictors of grades in music theory and ear training. *Bulletin of the Council for Research in Music Education, 75,* 33–39.

Arieti, S. (1976). *Creativity: The magic synthesis.* New York: Basic Books.

Arlien-Soborg, P. (1984). Chronic toxic encephalopathy in housepainters. *Acta Neurologica Scandinavica, 69*(Suppl. 99), 105–113.

Arvey, R. D. (1986). General ability in employment: A discussion. *Journal of Vocational Behavior, 29,* 415–420.

Bair, J. (1951). Factor analysis of clerical aptitude tests. *Journal of Applied Psychology, 35,* 245–249.

Baird, L. L. (1969). Testing Holland's theory. *Measurement and evaluation in guidance, 4,* 107–114.

Baird, L. L. (1985). Do grades and tests predict adult accomplishment? *Research in Higher Education, 23,* 3–85.

Bakker, F. C. (1988). Personality differences between young dancers and non-dancers. *Personality and Individual Differences, 9,* 121–131.

Bamberger, J. (1982). Growing up prodigies: The midlife crisis. *New Directions for Child Development, 17,* 61–77.

Banks, S., Mooney, W. T., Mucowski, R. J., & Williams, R. (1984). Progress in the evaluation and prediction of successful candidates for religious careers. *Counseling and Values, 28,* 82–91.

Barnes, M. L., & Sternberg, R. J. (1989). Social intelligence and decoding of nonverbal cues. *Intelligence, 13,* 263–287.

Barrett, D. W. (1945). Aptitude and interest patterns of art majors in a liberal arts college. *Journal of Applied Psychology, 29,* 483–492.

Barrett, H. O. (1949). An examination of certain standardized art tests to determine their relation to classroom achievement and to intelligence. *Journal of Educational Research, 42,* 398–400.

Barrett, T. C., & Tinsley, H. E. A. (1977). Vocational self-concept crystalli-
zation and vocational indecision. *Journal of Counseling Psychology, 24*, 301–
307.

Barron, F. (1972). *Artists in the making.* New York: Seminar Press.

Bartol, K. M., & Martin, D. C. (1987). Managerial motivation among MBA
students: A longitudinal assessment. *Journal of Occupational Psychology,
60*, 1–12.

Bartram, D., & Dale, H. C. (1982). The Eysenck Personality Inventory as a
selection test for military pilots. *Journal of Occupational Psychology, 55*,
287–296.

Beck, N. C., Tucker, D., Frank, R., Parker, J., Lichty, W., Horwitz, E., Horwitz, B., & Merritt, F. (1989). The latent factor structure of the WAIS-R:
A factor analysis of individual item responses. *Journal of Clinical Psychology, 45*, 281–293.

Begley, T. M., & Boyd, D. P. (1987). A comparison of entrepreneurs and
managers of small business firms. *Journal of Management, 13*, 99–108.

Bem, S. L. (1974). The measurement of psychological androgyny. *Journal of
Consulting and Clinical Psychology, 42*, 155–162.

Benbow, C. P. (1988). Neuropsychological perspectives on mathematical talent. In L. K. Obler & D. Fein (Eds.), *The exceptional brain: Neuropsychology
of talent and special abilities* (pp. 48–69). New York: Guilford Press.

Benbow, C. P., Stanley, J. C., Kirk, M. K., & Zonderman, A. B. (1983).
Structure of intelligence in intellectually precocious children and in their
parents. *Intelligence, 7*, 129–152.

Bendig, A. W. (1963). The relation of temperament traits of social extraversion
and emotionality to vocational interests. *Journal of General Psychology, 69*,
311–318.

Bendig, A. W. (1964). Factor analytic scales of need achievement. *Journal of
General Psychology, 70*, 59–67.

Bendig, A. W., & Martin, A. M. (1962). The factor structure and stability of
fifteen human needs. *Journal of General Psychology, 67*, 229–235.

Bennett, G. K. (1969). *Bennett Mechanical Comprehension Test manual: Forms S
and T.* San Antonio, TX: Psychological Corporation.

Bennett, G. K., & Cruikshank, R. M. (1942). *A summary of manual and mechanical ability tests.* New York: Psychological Corporation.

Bennett, G. K., Seashore, H. G., & Wesman, A. G. (1982). *Differential Aptitude
Tests: Administrator's handbook.* San Antonio, TX: Psychological Corporation.

Bennett, G. K., Seashore, H. G., & Wesman, A. G. (1989). *Differential Aptitude
Tests for Personnel and Career Assessment: Directions for administration and
scoring.* San Antonio, TX: Psychological Corporation.

Benninger, W. B., & Walsh, W. B. (1980). Holland's theory and non-college-
degreed working men and women. *Journal of Vocational Behavior, 17*, 81–88.

Benton, A. (1982). Spatial thinking in neurological aspects. In M. Portegal
(Ed.), *Spatial abilities: Development and physiological foundations* (pp. 301–
331). New York: Academic Press.

Bentz, V. J. (1985). Research findings from personality assessment of executives. In H. J. Bernardin & D. A. Bownas (Eds.), *Personality assessment in organizations* (pp. 82–144). New York: Praeger.

Berdie, R. F. (1943). Factors associated with vocational interests. *Journal of Educational Psychology, 34,* 257–277.

Berfield, K. A., Ray, W. J., & Newcombe, N. (1986). Sex role and spatial ability: An EEG study. *Neuropsychologia, 24,* 731–735.

Bernardin, H. J., & Bownas, D. A. (Eds.). (1985). *Personality assessment in organizations.* New York: Praeger.

Bingham, W. V. D. (1937). *Aptitudes and aptitude testing.* New York: Harper.

Bingham, R. P., & Walsh, W. B. (1978). Concurrent validity of Holland's theory for college-degreed black women. *Journal of Vocational Behavior, 13,* 242–250.

Blatt, S. J., & Allison, J. (1981). The intelligence test in personality assessment. In A. I. Rabin (Ed.), *Assessment with projective techniques: A concise introduction* (pp. 187–231). New York: Springer.

Borg, W. R. (1950). Some factors relating to art school success. *Journal of Educational Research, 43,* 35–40.

Borkenau, P. (1988). The multiple classification of acts and the big five factors of personality. *Journal of Research in Personality, 22,* 337–352.

Bouchard, M. A., Lalonde, F., & Gagnon, M. (1988). The construct validity of assertion: Contributions of four assessment procedures and Norman's personality factors. *Journal of Personality, 56,* 763–783.

Boyd, D. P., & Gumpert, D. E. (1983). Coping with entrepreneurial stress. *Harvard Business Review, 61,* 44–51.

Braisted, J. R., Mellin, L. G., Gong, E. J., & Irwin, C. E. (1985). The adolescent ballet dancer: Nutritional practices and characteristics associated with anorexia nervosa. *Journal of Adolescent Health Care, 6,* 365–371.

Bray, D. W., Campbell, R. J., & Grant, D. L. (1974). *Formative years in business: A long-term AT&T study of managerial lives.* Malabar, FL: Robert E. Krieger Publishing.

Brennan, F. M. (1926). The relation between musical capacity and performance. *Psychological Monographs, 36* (1, Whole No. 67).

Bretz, R. D., Jr., Ash, R. A., & Dreher, G. F. (1989). Do people make the place? An examination of the attraction-selection-attrition hypothesis. *Personnel Psychology, 42,* 561–581.

Bridges, J. S. (1988). Sex differences in occupational performance expectations. *Psychology of Women Quarterly, 12,* 75–90.

Briggs, K. C., & Myers, I. B. (1977). *Myers-Briggs Type Indicator.* Palo Alto, CA: Consulting Psychologists Press.

Bronfenbrenner, U., Harding, J., & Gallwey, M. (1958). The measurement of skill in social perception. In D. McClelland, A. Baldwin, U. Bronfenbrenner, & F. Strodtbeck (Eds.), *Talent and society: New perspectives in the identification of talent* (pp. 29–111). Princeton, NJ: Van Nostrand.

Brooks, G. J., Warren, M. P., & Hamilton, L. H. (1987). The relation of eating problems and amenorrhea in ballet dancers. *Medicine and Science in Sports and Exercise, 19,* 41–44.

Brown, D. (1984a). Mid-life career change. In D. Brown & L. Brooks (Eds.), *Career choice and development* (pp. 369–387). San Francisco: Jossey-Bass.

Brown, D. (1984b). Trait and factor theory. In D. Brown, L. Brooks, & Associates (Eds.), *Career choice and development* (pp. 8–30). San Francisco: Jossey-Bass.

Brown, D., Brooks, L., & Associates. (1984). *Career choice and development.* San Francisco: Jossey-Bass.

Brown, J. S., Grant, C. W., & Patton, M. J. (1981). A CPI comparison of engineers and managers. *Journal of Vocational Behavior, 18,* 255–264.

Bryan, A. I. (1942). Grades, intelligence, and personality of art school freshman. *Journal of Educational Psychology, 33,* 50–64.

Bulley, M. H. (1933). *Have you good taste?* London: Methuen.

Burbeck, E., & Furnham, A. (1985). Police officer selection: A criticial review of the literature. *Journal of Police Science and Administration, 13,* 58–69.

Burke, H. R. (1985). Raven's Progressive Matrices (1938): More on norms, reliability, and validity. *Journal of Clinical Psychology, 41,* 231–235.

Burnett, S. A., Lane, D. M., & Dratt, L. M. (1982). Spatial ability and handedness. *Intelligence, 6,* 57–68.

Campbell, J. P., Dunnette, M. D., Lawler, E. E., III, & Weick, K. E., Jr. (1970). *Managerial behavior, performance, and effectiveness.* New York: McGraw-Hill.

Campbell, J. P., & Hansen, J-I. C. (1981). *Manual for the SVIB-SCII.* Stanford, CA: Stanford University Press.

Canby, V. (1990, June 24). What's art all about? *New York Times,* pp. 1, 18–19.

Cantor, N., & Kihlstrom, J. F. (1987) *Personality and social intelligence.* Englewood Cliffs, NJ: Prentice-Hall.

Caro, R. A. (1989, November 6). Annals of politics. The Johnson years: A congressman goes to war. *The New Yorker,* pp. 62–125.

Carr, P. G., & Mednick, M. T. (1988). Sex role socialization and the development of achievement motivation in Black preschool children. *Sex Roles, 18,* 169–180.

Carroll, H. A. (1933). What do the Meier-Seashore and the McAdory Art Tests measure? *Journal of Education Research, 26,* 661–665.

Cartledge, G. (1987). Social skills, learning disabilities, and occupational success. *Journal of Reading, Writing, and Learning Disabilities International, 3,* 223–239.

Casey, M. B., Brabeck, M. M., & Ludlowk, L. H. (1986). Familial handedness and its relation to spatial ability following strategy instructions. *Intelligence, 10,* 389–406.

Cattell, H. E. (1982). Sex-roles and dyadic uniqueness in parent-child personality trait relationships. *Multivariate Experimental Clinical Research, 6,* 33–46.

Cattell, R. B. (1945a). Personality traits associated with abilities: I. With intelligence and drawing ability. *Educational and Psychological Measurement, 5*, 131–146.

Cattell, R. B. (1945b). Personality traits associated with abilities: II. With verbal and mathematical abilities. *Educational and Psychological Measurement, 5*, 475–486.

Cattell, R. B. (1946). *Description and measurement of personality.* Yonkers-on-Hudson, NY: World Book.

Cattell, R. B. (Ed.). (1987). *Intelligence: Its structure, growth and action.* (rev. ed.). Amsterdam: North-Holland.

Cattell, R. B., Eber, H. W., & Tatsuoka, M. M. (1970). *Handbook for the Sixteen Personality Factor Questionnaire.* Champaign, IL: Institute for Personality and Ability Testing.

Cattell, R. B., & Horn, J. L. (1964). *Handbook and individual assessment manual for the Motivation Analysis Test (MAT).* Champaign, IL: Institute for Personality and Ability Testing.

Cattell, R. B., & Kline, P. (1977). *The scientific analysis of personality and motivation.* New York: Academic Press.

Childs, A., & Klimoski, R. J. (1986). Successfully predicting career success: An application of the biographical inventory. *Journal of Applied Psychology, 71*, 3–8.

Chlopan, B. E., McCain M. L., Carbonell, J. L., & Hagen, R. L. (1985). Empathy: Review of available measures. *Journal of Personality and Social Psychology, 48*, 635–653.

Christiansen, K., & Knussmann, R. (1987). Sex hormones and cognitive functioning in men. *Neuropsychobiology, 18*, 27–36.

Churchill, G. A., Ford, N. M., Hartley, S. W., & Walker, O. C. (1985). The determination of salesperson performance: A meta-analysis. *Journal of Marketing Research, 22*, 103–118.

Chusmir, L. H. (1984a). Motivational need pattern for police officers. *Journal of Police Science and Administration, 12*, 141–145.

Chusmir, L. H. (1984b). Personnel administrators' perception of sex differences in motivation of managers: Research-based or stereotyped? *International Journal of Women's Studies, 7*, 17–23.

Chusmir, L. H. (1985a). Motivation of managers: Is gender a factor? *Psychology of Women Quarterly, 9*, 153–159.

Chusmir, L. H. (1985b). Short-form scoring for McClelland's version of the TAT. *Perceptual and Motor Skills, 61*, 1047–1052.

Chusmir, L. H., & Hood, J. N. (1988). Predictive characteristics of Type A behavior among working men and women. *Journal of Applied Social Psychology, 18*, 688–698.

Clark, G., & Zimmerman, E. (1983). At the age of six, I gave up a magnificent career as a painter: Seventy years of research about identifying students with superior abilities in the visual arts. *Gifted Child Quarterly, 27*, 180–184.

Clark, K. B. (1980). Empathy: A neglected topic in psychological research. *American Psychologist, 35,* 187–190.

Clifford, J. S. (1986). Neuropsychology: Implications for the treatment of alcoholism. *Journal of Counseling and Development, 65,* 31–34.

Colberg, M. (1985). Logic-based measurement of verbal reasoning: A key to increased validity and economy. *Personnel Psychology, 38,* 347–359.

Cole, N. S., & Hanson, G. (1971). *An analysis of the structure of vocational interests* (ACT Research Rep. No. 40). Iowa City, IA: American College Testing Program.

Cole, N. S., Whitney, D. R., & Holland, J. L. (1971). A spatial configuration of occupations. *Journal of Vocational Behavior, 1,* 1–9.

Coles, R. (1989, June 18). The gloom and the glory. *New York Times Book Review,* pp. 1, 30–31.

Colwell, R. (1985). Australian Test for Advanced Music Studies [Review]. In J. V. Mitchell (Ed.), *The ninth mental measurements yearbook* (pp. 117–119). Lincoln, NE: Buros Institute of Mental Measurement.

Conoley, J. C., & Kramer, J. J. (1989). *The tenth mental measurements yearbook.* Lincoln, NE: Buros Institute of Mental Measurements.

Constantinople, A. (1973). Masculinity-feminity: An exception to a famous dictum? *Psychological Bulletin, 80,* 389–407.

Cooper, S. E., Fuqua, D. R., & Hartman, B. W. (1984). The relationship of trait indecisiveness to vocational uncertainty, career indecision, and interpersonal characteristics. *Journal of College Student Personnel, 25,* 353–356.

Cooper, W. H. (1983). An achievement motivation nomological network. *Journal of Personality and Social Psychology, 44,* 841–861.

Cornelius, E. T., & Lane, F. B. (1984). The power motive and managerial success in a professionally oriented service industry organization. *Journal of Applied Psychology, 69,* 32–39.

Costa, P. T., Fozard, J. L., & McCrae, R. R. (1977). Personological interpretation of factors from the Strong Vocational Interest Blank scales. *Journal of Vocational Behavior, 10,* 231–243.

Costa, P. T., Jr., & McCrae, R. R. (1985a). *The NEO Personality Inventory manual.* Odessa, FL: Psychological Assessment Resources.

Costa, P. T., Jr., & McCrae, R. R. (1985b). *The NEO Personality Inventory manual:* Form S and Form R. Odessa, FL: Psychological Assessment Resources.

Costa, P. T., Jr., & McCrae, R. R. (1988). *The NEO PI/FFI manual supplement.* Odessa, FL: Psychological Assessment Resources.

Costa, P. T., Jr., McCrae, R. R., & Holland, J. L. (1984). Personality and vocational interests in an adult sample. *Journal of Applied Psychology, 69,* 390–400.

Court, J. H. (1983). Sex differences in performance on Raven's Progressive Matrices: A review. *Alberta Journal of Educational Research, 29,* 54–74.

Craig, R. J., & Olson, R. E. (1988). Changes in functional ego states following treatment for drug abuse. *Transactional Analysis Journal, 18,* 68–72.

Crew, J. C. (1982). An assessment of needs among Black business majors. *Psychology: A Quarterly Journal of Human Behavior, 19,* 18–22.

Crites, J. O. (1974). *Measuring vocational maturity for counseling and evaluation.* Washington, DC: National Vocational Guidance Association.

Crites, J. O. (1981). *Career counseling: Models, methods and materials.* New York: McGraw-Hill.

Csikszentmihalyi, M., & Csikszentmihalyi, I. S. (Eds.). (1988). *Optimal experience: Psychological studies of flow in consciousness.* New York: Cambridge University Press.

Dardis, T. (1989). *Thirsty muse: Alcohol and the American writer.* New York: Ticknor & Fields.

Darley, J. G. (1941). *Clinical aspects and interpretation of the Strong Vocational Interest Blank.* New York: Psychological Corporation.

Darley, J. G., & Hagenah, T. (1955). *Vocational interest measurement: Theory and practice.* Minneapolis: University of Minnesota Press.

Dash, A. S., & Rath, S. (1986). Testing the limits of Raven's Progressive Matrices: An experiment. *Psychological Studies, 31,* 82–89.

Deaux, K. (1985). Sex and gender. *Annual Review of Psychology, 36,* 49–81.

Deb, M. (1983). Sales effectiveness and personality characteristics. *Psychological Research Journal, 7,* 59–67.

Derman, D., French, J. W., & Harman, H. H. (1978). *Guide to Factor Referenced Temperament Scales 1978.* Princeton, NJ: Educational Testing Service.

Deutsch, D. (1978). Pitch memory: An advantage for the lefthand. *Science, 199,* 559–560.

Dewar, J. (1938). A comparison of tests of artistic appreciation. *British Journal of Educational Psychology, 8,* 29–49.

Diamond, R., Carey, S., & Black, K. J. (1983). Genetic influences on the development of spatial skills during early adolescence. *Cognition, 13,* 167–185.

Dillard, A. (1989). Write till you drop. *New York Times Book Review,* pp. 1, 23.

Dong, H. K., Sung, Y. H., & Goldman, S. H. (1985). The validity of the Ball Aptitude Battery (BAB): II. Relationship in training and occupational success. *Educational and Psychological Measurement, 45,* 951–957.

Dorr, D., Cowen, E. L., Sandler, I., & Pratt, D. M. (1973). Dimensionality of a test battery for nonprofessional mental health workers. *Journal of Consulting and Clinical Psychology, 41,* 181–185.

Dorval, M., & Pepin, M. (1986). Effect of playing a video game on a measure of spatial visualization. *Perceptual and Motor Skills, 62,* 159–162.

Doty, M. S., & Betz, N. E. (1979). Comparison of the concurrent validity of Holland's theory for men and women in an enterprising occupation. *Journal of Vocational Behavior, 15,* 207–216.

Drake, R. M. (1933). Validity and reliability of tests of musical talent. *Journal of Applied Psychology, 17,* 447–458.

Drake, R. M. (1939). Factor analysis of music tests. *Psychological Bulletin, 36,* 608–609.

Dreps, H. F. (1933). The psychological capacities and abilities of college art students. *Psychological Monographs, 45*(1, Whole No. 200).

Drevdahl, J. E., & Cattell, R. B. (1958). Personality and creativity in artists and writers. *Journal of Clinical Psychology, 14,* 107–111.

Dziurawiec, S., & Deregowski, J. B. (1986). Time as a factor in a spatial task. *International Journal of Psychology, 21,* 177–187.

Edel, L. (1975). The madness of art. *Psychiatry, 132,* 1005–1012.

Eden, D. (1988). Pygmalion, goal-setting, and expectancy: Compatible ways to boost productivity. *Academy of Management Review, 13,* 639–652.

Edwards, A. L. (1959). *Edwards Personal Preference Schedule manual.* San Antonio, TX: Psychological Corporation.

Edwards, K. J., & Whitney, D. R. (1972). Structural analysis of Holland's personality types using factor and configural analysis. *Journal of Counseling Psychology, 19,* 136–145.

Edwards, M. R. (1983). OJQ offers alternative to assessment center. *Public Personnel Management, 12,* 146–155.

Ekstrom, R. B., French, J. W., & Harman, H. H. (1976). *Manual for Kit of Factor-Referenced Cognitive Tests.* Princeton, NJ: Educational Testing Service.

Elder, G. H., & MacInnis, D. J. (1983). Achievement imagery in women's lives from adolescence to adulthood. *Journal of Personality and Social Psychology, 45,* 394–404.

Elias, P. K., Elias, M. F., Robbins, M. A., & Gage, P. (1987). Acquisition of word-processing skills by younger, middle-age, and older adults. *Psychology and Aging, 2,* 340–348.

Eliot, J. (1987). *Models of psychological space: Psychometric, developmental, and experimental approaches.* New York: Springer-Verlag.

Eliot, J., Medoff, D., & Kimmel, K. (1987). Development of a new spatial test. *Perceptual and Motor Skills, 64,* 479–483.

El Kousy, A. A. H. (1935). An investigation into the factors in tests involving the visual perception of space. *British Journal of Psychology Monograph Supplements* (No. 20). London: Cambridge University Press.

Elton, C. F. (1971). The interaction of environment and personality: A test of Holland's theory. *Journal of Applied Psychology, 56,* 114–118.

Embretson, S. E. (1987). Improving the measurement of spatial aptitude by dynamic testing. *Intelligence, 11,* 333–358.

Englert, C. S., Stewart, S. R., & Hiebert, E. H. (1988). Young writers' use of text structure in expository text generation. *Journal of Educational Psychology, 80,* 143–151.

Erez, M., & Shneorson, Z. (1980). Personality types and motivational characteristics of academics versus professionals in the same occupational discipline. *Journal of Vocational Behavior, 17,* 95–105.

Ericsson, K. A., & Faivre, I. A. (1988). What's exceptional about exceptional abilities? In L. K. Obler & D. Fein (Eds.), *The exceptional brain: Neuropsychology of talent and special abilities* (pp. 436–473). New York: Guilford Press.

Estes, S. G. (1942). A study of five tests of "spatial" ability. *Journal of Psychology, 13,* 265–267.

Ethics Committee of the American Psychological Association. (1988). Trends in ethics cases, common pitfalls, and published resources. *American Psychologist, 43,* 564–572.

Ethington, C. A., & Wolfle, L. M. (1984). Sex differences in a causal model of mathematics achievement. *Journal for Research in Mathematics Education, 15,* 361–377.

Evans, V., & Quarterman, J. (1983). Personality characteristics of successful and unsuccessful Black female basketball players. *International Journal of Sport Psychology, 14,* 105–115.

Examiner manual: 42070 M—O'Connor Tweezer Dexterity Test. (Undated). Chicago: Stoelting Co.

Eyde, L., & Kowal, D. M. (1987). Computerised test interpretation services. Ethical and professional concerns regarding U.S. producers and users: Computerised psychological testing. *Applied Psychology: An International Review, 3–4,* 401–417.

Eysenck, H. J. (1953). *The structure of human personality.* London: Methuen.

Eysenck, H. J., & Eysenck, S. B. G. (1964). *Manual of the Eysenck Personality Inventory.* London: London University Press.

Eysenck, J. J. (1986). Toward a new model of intelligence. *Personality and Individual Differences, 7,* 731–736.

Fabry, J. J. (1975). An extended concurrent validation of the vocational preferences of clergymen. *Psychological Reports, 36,* 947–950.

Farnsworth, P. R. (1931). An historical, critical, and experimental study of the Seashore-Kwalwasser test battery. *Genetic Psychology Monographs, 9,* 291–393.

Farnsworth, P. R. (1958). *The social psychology of music.* New York: Dryden Press.

Farnsworth, P. R., & Issei, M. (1931). Notes on the Meier-Seashore Art Judgment Test. *Journal of Applied Psychology, 15,* 418–420.

Faver, C. A. (1984). Women, achievement and careers: Age variations in attitudes. *Psychology: A Quarterly Journal of Human Behavior, 21,* 45–49.

Feather, N. T. (1984). Masculinity, femininity, psychological androgyny, and the structure of values. *Journal of Personality and Social Psychology, 47,* 604–620.

Feather, N. T., & Said, J. A. (1983). Preference for occupations in relation to masculinity, femininity, and gender. *British Journal of Social Psychology, 22,* 113–127.

Fennema, E., & Tartre, L. A. (1985). The use of spatial visualization in mathematics by girls and boys. *Journal for Research in Mathematics Education, 16,* 184–206.

Ferris, G. R., Bergin, T. G., & Gilmore, D. C. (1986). Personality and ability predictors of training performance for flight attendants. *Group and Organization Studies, 11,* 419–435.

Fishburne, F. J., Jr., & Walsh, W. B. (1976). Concurrent validity of Holland's theory for non-college degreed workers. *Journal of Vocational Behavior, 8,* 77–84.

Fisher, S., & Fisher, R. L. (1981). *Pretend the world is funny and forever: A psychological analysis of comedians, clowns, and actors.* Hillsdale, NJ: Erlbaum.

Fleishman, E. A. (1954). Dimensional analysis of psychomotor abilities. *Journal of Experimental Psychology, 48,* 437–454.

Fleishman, E. A. (1957). A comparative study of aptitude patterns in unskilled and skilled psychomotor performances. *Journal of Applied Psychology, 41,* 263–272.

Fleishman, E. A. (1964). *The structure and measurement of physical fitness.* Englewood Cliffs, NJ: Prentice-Hall.

Fleishman, E. A. (1982). *The structure and measurement of physical fitness.* Englewood Cliffs, NJ: Prentice-Hall.

Fleishman, E. A. (1984). *Taxonomies of human performance: The description of human tasks.* New York: Academic Press.

Fleishman, E. A., Gebhart, D. L., & Hogan, J. C. (1984). The measurement of effort. *Ergonomics, 27,* 947–954.

Fleishman, E. A., & Hempel, W. E., Jr. (1956). Factorial analysis of complex psychomotor performance and related skills. *Journal of Applied Psychology, 40,* 96–104.

Fleishman, E. A., & Quaintance, M. K. (1984). *Taxonomies of human performance.* New York: Academic Press.

Flicker, C., Bartus, R. T., Crook, T. H., & Ferris, S. H. (1984). Effects of aging and dementia upon recent visuospatial memory. *Neurobiology of Aging, 5,* 275–283.

Fontana, D., Lotwick, G., Simon, A., & Ward, L. O. (1983). A factor analysis of critical, convergent and divergent thinking tests in a group of male polytechnic students. *Personality and Individual Differences, 4,* 687–688.

Frederiksen, N. (1962). Factors in in-basket performance. *Psychological Monographs, 76*(22, Whole No. 541).

Frederiksen, N., Saunders, D. R., & Wand, B. (1957). The in-basket test. *Psychological Monographs, 71*(9, Whole No. 438).

Frederiksen, W., Carlson, C., & Ward, W. C. (1984). The place of social intelligence in a taxonomy of cognitive abilities. *Intelligence, 8,* 315–337.

Freeman, J. (1984). Talent in music and fine art. *Gifted Education International, 2,* 107–110.

Frey, R. S. (1984). Need for achievement, entrepreneurship, and economic growth: A critique of the McClelland thesis. *Social Science Journal, 21,* 125–134.

Fry, K. L., & Thompson, D. S. (1977). Comparison of selected measures of field dependence. *Perceptual and Motor Skills, 45,* 861–862.

Frosch, W. A. (1987). Moods, madness and music: I. Major affective disease and musical creativity. *Comprehensive Psychiatry, 28,* 315–322.

Gael, S., Grant, D. L., Ritchie, R. J. (1975). Employment test validation for minority and nonminority clerks with work sample criteria. *Journal of Applied Psychology, 60,* 420–426.

Gaffey, R. L., & Walsh, W. B. (1974). Concurrent validity of Holland's theory for non-college degreed workers. *Journal of Vocational Behavior, 5,* 41–51.

Gakhar, S. C. (1986). Correlational research-individual differences in intelligence, aptitude, personality and achievement among science, commerce and arts students. *Journal of Psychological Researches, 30,* 22–29.

Garbin, A. P., & Stover, R. G. (1980). Vocational behavior and career development, 1979: A review. *Journal of Vocational Behavior, 17,* 125–170.

Gardner, H. (1973). *The arts and human development.* New York: Wiley.

Gardner, H. (1982a). *Art, mind, and brain: A cognitive approach to creativity.* New York: Basic Books.

Gardner, H. (1982b). Giftedness: Speculations from a biological perspective. *New Directions for Child Development, 17,* 47–60.

Gardner, H. (1983). *Frames of mind.* New York: Basic Books.

Geschwind, N., & Galaburda, A. M. (1985a). Cerebral lateralization. Biological mechanisms, associations, and pathology: I. A hypothesis and a program for research. *Archives of Neurology, 42,* 428–459.

Geschwind, N., & Galaburda, A. M. (1985b). Cerebral lateralization. Biological mechanisms, associations, and pathology: II. A hypothesis and a program for research. *Archives of Neurology, 42,* 521–552.

Getter, H., & Nowinski, J. K. (1981). A free response test of interpersonal effectiveness. *Journal of Personality Assessment, 45,* 301–307.

Getzels, J. W., & Csikszentmihalyi, M. (1976). *The creative vision: A longitudinal study of problem finding in art.* New York: Wiley.

Ghiselli, E. E. (1963). Managerial talent. *American Psychologist, 18,* 631–642.

Ghiselli, E. E. (1966). *The validity of occupational aptitude tests.* New York: Wiley.

Ghiselli, E. E. (1968). Some motivational factors in the success of managers. *Personnel Psychology, 21,* 431–440.

Ghiselli, E. E. (1969). Managerial talent. In D. Wolfle (Ed.), *The discovery of talent* (pp. 212–239). Cambridge, MA: Harvard University Press.

Ghiselli, E. E. (1971). *Explorations in managerial talent.* Pacific Palisades, CA: Goodyear.

Ghiselli, E. E., & Barthol, R. P. (1953). The validity of personality inventories in selecting employees. *Journal of Applied Psychology, 37,* 18–20.

Gilbride, T. V. (1973). Holland's theory and resignations from the Catholic clergy. *Journal of Counseling Psychology, 20,* 190–191.

Glencross, D., & Bluhm, N. (1986). Intensive computer keyboard training programmes. *Applied Ergonomics, 17,* 191–194.

Goleman, D. (1986, February 2). The psyche of the entrepreneur. *New York Times Magazine,* pp. 30–36.

Goodenough, D. R. (1985). Styles of cognitive-personality functioning. In H. J. Bernardin & D. A. Bownas (Eds.), *Personality assessment in organizations* (pp. 217–235). New York: Praeger.

Goodenough, D. R., Oltman, P. K., & Cox, P. W. (1987). The nature of individual differences in field dependence. *Journal of Research in Personality, 21,* 81–89.

Goodenough, F. L., & Harris, D. B. (1963). *Goodenough-Harris Drawing Test: Test manual.* San Antonio, TX: Psychological Corporation.

Goodwin, D. W. (1988). *Alcohol and the writer.* Kansas City, MO: Andrews & McNeel.

Goodwin, F. K., & Jamison, K. (1990). *Manic-depression illness.* New York: Oxford University Press.

Goodyear, R. K., & Frank, A. C. (1977). Introversion-extraversion: Some comparisons of the SVIB and VPI scales. *Measurement and Evaluation in Guidance, 9,* 206–211.

Gordon, E. E. (1965). *Musical Aptitude Profile.* Chicago: Riverside Publishing.

Gordon, E. E. (1986). A factor analysis of the Musical Aptitude Profile, the Primary Measures of Music Audiation and the Intermediate Measures of Music Audiation. *Bulletin of the Council for Research in Music Education, 87,* 17–25.

Gordon, H. W. (1986). The Cognitive Laterality Battery: Tests of specialized cognitive function. *International Journal of Neuroscience, 29,* 223–244.

Gordon, H. W. (1988). Specialized cognitive function and school achievement. *Developmental Neuropsychology, 4,* 239–257.

Gordon, H. W., Charns, M. P., & Sherman, E. (1987). Management success as a function of performance on specialized cognitive tests. *Human Relations, 40,* 671–699.

Gordon, H. W., & Leighty, R. (1988). Importance of specialized cognitive function in the selection of military pilots. *Journal of Applied Psychology, 73,* 38–45.

Gordon, H. W., Silverberg-Shalev, R., & Czernilas, J. (1982). Hemispheric asymmetry in fighter and helicopter pilots. *Acta Psychologica, 52,* 33–40.

Gormly, J., & Gormly, A. (1986). Social introversion and spatial abilities. *Bulletin of the Psychonomic Society, 24,* 273–274.

Gottfredson, G. D., & Holland, J. L. (1989). *Dictionary of Holland occupational codes* (2nd ed.). Odessa, FL: Psychological Assessment Resources.

Gottfredson, G. D., Holland, J. L., & Gottfredson, L. (1975). The relation of vocational aspirations and assessments to employment reality. *Journal of Vocational Behavior, 7,* 135–148.

Gottfredson, G. D., Holland, J. L., & Ogawa, D. K. (1982). *Dictionary of Holland occupational codes.* Palo Alto, CA: Consulting Psychologists Press.

Gottfredson, L. (1980). Construct validity of Holland's occupational typology in terms of prestige, census, Department of Labor, and other classification systems. *Journal of Applied Psychology, 651,* 697–714.

Gottfredson, L. (Ed.). (1986a). The *g* factor in employment. *Journal of Vocational Behavior, 29,* 293–450.

Gottfredson, L. (1986b). Societal consequences of the *g* factor in employment. *Journal of Vocational Behavior, 29,* 279–410.

Gotz, K. O., & Gotz, K. (1978). Personality characteristics of successful artists. *Perceptual and Motor Skills, 49*, 919–924.

Gough, H. (1984). A managerial potential scale for the California Psychological Inventory. *Journal of Applied Psychology, 69*, 233–240.

Gough, H. (1987). *CPI: The California Psychological Inventory administrator's guide.* Palo Alto, CA: Consulting Psychologists Press.

Grant, D. L., Katkovsky, W., & Bray, D. W. (1967). Contributions of projective techniques to assessment of management potential. *Journal of Applied Psychology, 51*, 226–232.

Greeno, J. G. (1989). A perspective on thinking. *American Psychologist, 44*, 134–141.

Grudin, J. (1983). Non-hierarchic specification of components in transcription typewriting. *Acta Psychologica, 54*, 249–262.

Gruff, S., Ramseyer, G., & Richardson, J. (1968). The effect of age on four scales of the California Psychological Inventory. *Journal of General Psychology, 78*, 183–187.

Guilford, J. P. (1948). Some lessons from aviation psychology. *American Psychologist, 3*, 3–11.

Guilford, J. P. (1950). Creativity. *American Psychologist, 14*, 469–479.

Guilford, J. P. (1957). Creative abilities in the arts. *Psychological Review, 64*, 110–118.

Guilford, J. P. (1959). Traits of creativity. In H. H. Anderson (Ed.), *Creativity and its cultivation* (pp. 142–161). New York: Harper & Row.

Guilford, J. P. (1967). *The nature of human intelligence.* New York: McGraw-Hill.

Guilford, J. P., & Guilford, R. B. (1931). A prognostic test for students in design. *Journal of Applied Psychology, 15*, 335–345.

Guilford, J. S., Zimmerman, W. S., & Guilford, J. P. (1976). *Guilford-Zimmerman Temperament Survey Handbook: Twenty-five years of research and application.* San Diego, CA: EDITS.

Guion, R. M. (1987). Changing views for personnel selection research. *Personnel Psychology, 40*, 199–213.

Guion, R. M., & Gottier, R. F. (1965). Validity of personality measures in personnel selection. *Personnel Psychology, 18*, 135–164.

Hakstian, A. R., & Bennet, R. W. (1977). Validity studies using the Comprehensive Ability Battery (CAB): I. Academic achievement criteria. *Educational and Psychological Measurement, 37*, 425–437.

Hakstian, A. R., & Bennet, R. W. (1978). Validity studies using the Comprehensive Ability Battery (CAB): II. Relationships with the DAT and the GATB. *Educational and Psychological Measurement, 38*, 1003–1015.

Hakstian, A. R., & Cattell, R. B. (1974). The checking of primary ability structure on a broader basis of performances. *British Journal of Educational Psychology, 44*, 140–154.

Hakstian, A. R., & Cattell, R. B. (1978a). An examination of inter-domain relationships among some ability and personality traits. *Educational and Psychological Measurement, 38*, 275–290.

Hakstian, A. R., & Cattell, R. B. (1978b). Higher stratum ability structures on a basis of twenty primary abilities. *Journal of Educational Psychology, 70,* 657–669.

Hakstian, A. R., Cattell, R. B., & IPAT Staff. (1982). *Manual for the Comprehensive Ability Battery (CAB).* Champaign, IL: Institute for Personality and Ability Testing.

Hakstian, A. R., & Gale, C. A. (1979). Validity studies using the Comprehensive Ability Battery (CAB): III. Performance in conjunction with personality and motivational traits. *Educational and Psychological Measurement, 39,* 389–400.

Hakstian, A. R., Woolsey, L. K., & Schroeder, M. L. (1986). Development and application of a quickly-scored in-basket exercise in an organizational setting. *Educational and Psychological Measurement, 46,* 385–396.

Hall, D. T., & Associates. (1987). *Career development in organizations.* San Francisco: Jossey-Bass.

Halpern, A. R. (1984). Perception of structure in novel music. *Memory and Cognition, 12,* 163–170.

Hammond, S. M. (1984). An investigation into the factor structure of the General Aptitude Test Battery. *Journal of Occupational Psychology, 57,* 49–56.

Hansen, J. C. (1986). The Strong Vocational Interest Blank/The Strong Campbell Interest Inventory. In W. B. Walsh & S. H. Osipow (Eds.), *The assessment of interests* (pp. 1–29), Hillsdale, NJ: Erlbaum.

Hanson, G. R., & Raymon, J. R. (1976). Validity of sex-balanced interest inventory scales. *Journal of Vocational Behavior, 9,* 279–291.

Hargrave, G. E., & Berner, J. G. (1984). *POST psychological screening manual.* Sacramento, CA: Commission on Peace Officer Standards and Training.

Harrell, T. W. (1937). Validity of certain mechanical ability tests for selecting cotton mill machine fixers. *Journal of Social Psychology, 18,* 279–282.

Harrell, T. W. (1940). A factor analysis of mechanical ability tests. *Psychometrika, 5,* 17–33.

Harrell, T. W., & Harrell, M. S. (1973). The personality of MBA's who reach general management early. *Personnel Psychology, 26,* 127–134.

Harris, L. J. (1981). Sex-related variations in spatial skill. In L. S. Liben, A. H. Patterson, & N. Newcombe (Eds.), *Spatial representation across the life span: Theory and application* (pp. 83–125). New York: Academic Press.

Harrison, C. S. (1987a). The long-term predictive validity of the Musical Aptitude Profile relative to criteria of grades in music theory and applied music. *Educational and Psychological Measurement, 47,* 1107–1112.

Harrison, C. S. (1987b). The validity of the Musical Aptitude Profile for predicting grades in freshman music theory. *Educational and Psychological Measurement, 47,* 477–482.

Hartup, W. W. (1989). Social relationships and their developmental significance. *American Psychologist, 44,* 120–126.

Harvey, D. W., & Whinfield, R. W. (1973). Extending Holland's theory to adult women. *Journal of Vocational Behavior, 3,* 115–129.

Hassler, M., & Birbaumer, N. (1984). Musikalishches talent und raumliche begabung. *Archive-fur-Psychologie, 136*, 235–248. (From *Psychological Abstracts*, 1984, *73*, Abstract No. 3432).

Hassler, M., & Birbaumer, N. (1986). Witelson's Dichaptic Stimulation Test and children with different levels of musical talent. *Neuropsychologia, 24*, 435–440.

Hassler, M., Birbaumer, N., & Feil, A. (1985). Musical talent and visual spatial abilities: A longitudinal study. *Psychology of Music, 13*, 99–113.

Hathaway, S. R., & McKinley, S. R. (1989). *MMPI-2: Manual for administration and scoring.* Minneapolis: University of Minnesota Press.

Hayes, J. R., & Flower, L. S. (1986). Writing research and the writer. *American Psychologist, 41*, 1106–1113.

Hayter, A. (1988). *Opium and the romantic imagination: Addictions and creativity* (2nd ed.). Wellingbough, Northamptonshire, England: Crucible.

Heaven, P. C., Connors, J., & Trevethan, R. (1987). Authoritarianism and the EPQ. *Personality and Individual Differences, 8*, 677–680.

Heilman, M. E., Block, C. J., Martell, R. F., & Simon, M. C. (1989). Has anything changed? Current characterizations of men, women, and managers. *Journal of Applied Psychology, 74*, 935–942.

Heiner, T., & Meir, E. I. (1981). Congruency, consistency, and differentiation as predictors of job satisfaction within the nursing occupation. *Journal of Vocational Behavior, 18*, 304–309.

Helmes, E., & Fekken, G. C. (1986). Effects of psychotropic drugs and psychiatric illness on vocational aptitude and interest assessment. *Journal of Clinical Psychology, 42*, 569–576.

Helson, R. (1978). Writers and critics: Two types of vocational consciousness in the art system. *Journal of Vocational Behavior, 12*, 351–363.

Hendricks, M., Guilford, J. P., & Hoepfner, R. (1969). *Measuring creative social intelligence: Reports from the psychological laboratory* (Tech. Rep. No. 43). Los Angeles: University of Southern California.

Hennig, M., & Jardin, A. (1977). *The managerial woman.* Garden City, NY: Anchor Press.

Henson, R. A., & Wyke, M. A. (1982). The performance of professional musicians on the Seashore Measures of Musical Talent: An unexpected finding. *Cortex, 18*, 153–158.

Hermelin, B., & O'Connor, N. (1986). Spatial representations in mathematically and in artistically gifted children. *British Journal of Educational Psychology, 56*, 150–157.

Highsmith, J. A. (1929). Selecting musical talent. *Journal of Applied Psychology, 13*, 486–493.

Hisrich, R. D. (1990). Entrepreneurship/intrapreneurship. *American Psychologist, 45*, 209–222.

Hobbs, C. (1985). A comparison of the music aptitude, scholastic aptitude, and academic achievement of young children. *Psychology of Music, 13*, 93–98.

Hoepfner, R., & O'Sullivan, M. (1968). Social intelligence and IQ. *Educational and Psychological Measurement, 28*, 339–344.

Hoffman, M. L. (1981). Perspectives on the difference between understanding people and understanding things: The role of affect. In J. H. Flavell & L. Ross (Eds.), *Social cognitive development: Frontiers and possible futures* (pp. 67–81). Cambridge, England: Cambridge University Press.

Hogan, J. (1969). Development of an empathy scale. *Journal of Consulting and Clinical Psychology, 33*, 307–316.

Hogan, J. (1986). *Hogan Personality Inventory manual*. Minneapolis, MN: National Computer Systems.

Hogan, J., & Hogan, R. (1986). *Hogan Personnel Selection Series manual*. Minneapolis, MN: National Computer Systems.

Holland, B. (1989, November 6). Vladimir Horowitz, 86, virtuoso pianist, dies. *New York Times*, pp. 1, 13.

Holland, J. L. (1962). Some explorations of a theory of vocational choice: I. One- and two-year longitudinal studies. *Psychological Monographs, 76*(26, Whole No. 545).

Holland, J. L. (1963a). Explorations of a theory of vocational choice and achievement: II. A four year prediction study. *Psychological Reports, 12*, 545–594.

Holland, J. L. (1963b). Explorations of a theory of vocational choice: Part I. Vocational images and choice. *Vocational Guidance Quarterly, 11*, 232–239.

Holland, J. L. (1963c). Explorations of a theory of vocational choice: Part II. Self-descriptions and vocational preferences. *Vocational Guidance Quarterly, 12*, 17–21.

Holland, J. L. (1963d). Explorations of a theory of vocational choice: Part IV. Vocational daydreams. *Vocational Guidance Quarterly, 12*, 93–97.

Holland, J. L. (1966). *The psychology of vocational choice*. Waltham, MA: Blaisdell.

Holland, J. L. (1968). Explorations of a theory of vocational choice: VI. A longitudinal study using a sample of typical college students. *Journal of Applied Psychology, 52*, 1–37.

Holland, J. L. (1976a). The virtues of the SDS and its associated typology: A second response to Prediger and Hanson. *Journal of Vocational Behavior, 8*, 349–358.

Holland, J. L. (1976b). Vocational preferences. In M. D. Dunnette (Ed.), *Handbook of industrial/organizational psychology* (pp. 521–570). Chicago: Rand McNally.

Holland, J. L. (1979). *Professional manual for the Self-Directed Search 1979 edition*. Palo Alto, CA: Consulting Psychologists Press.

Holland, J. L. (1985a). *Making vocational choices: A theory of vocational choices and work environments* (2nd ed.). Englewood Cliffs, NJ: Prentice-Hall.

Holland, J. L. (1985b). *The Occupations Finder for use with the Self-Directed Search*. Odessa, FL: Psychological Assessment Resources.

Holland, J. L. (1985c). *Vocational Preference Inventory (VPI) manual—1985 edition*. Odessa, FL: Psychological Assessment Resources.

Holland, J. L. (1987). *1987 manual supplement for the Self-Directed Search*. Odessa, FL: Psychological Assessment Resources.

Holland, J. L., Gottfredson, G. D., & Gottfredson, L. S. (1975). Read our reports and examine the data: A response to Prediger and Cole. *Journal of Vocational Behavior, 7,* 253–259.

Holland, J. L., & Nichols, R. C. (1964a). Explorations of a theory of vocational choice: III. A longitudinal study of change in major field of study. *Personnel and Guidance Journal, 43,* 235–242.

Holland, J. L., & Nichols, R. C. (1964b). Prediction of academic and extra-curricular achievement in college. *Journal of Educational Psychology, 55,* 55–65.

Hollenbek, J. R., Williams, C. R., & Klein, H. J. (1989). An empirical examination of the antecedents of commitment to difficult goals. *Journal of Applied Psychology, 74,* 18–23.

Horn, J. L. (1976). Human abilities: A review of research and theory in the early 1970s. *Annual Review of Psychology, 27,* 437–485.

Horn, J. L. (1977). Personality and ability theory. In R. B. Cattell & R. M. Dregers (Eds.), *Handbook of modern personality theory* (pp. 139–165). Washington, DC: Hemisphere.

Horn, J. L., & Cattell, R. B. (1966). Refinement and test of the theory of fluid and crystallized intelligence. *Journal of Educational Psychology, 57,* 253–270.

Horton, J., & Walsh, W. B. (1976). Concurrent validity of Holland's theory for college degreed working women. *Journal of Vocational Behavior, 9,* 201–208.

Hough, L. (1990, October 12). *Personality variables and criterion-related validity: Construct confusion.* Paper presented at the Personnel Testing Council of Southern California Conference, Newport Beach, CA.

House, R. J., & Singh, J. V. (1987). Organizational behavior: Some new directions for I/O psychology. *Annual Review of Psychology, 38,* 669–718.

Howard, A., & Bray, D. W. (1988). *Managerial lives in transition: Advancing age and changing times.* New York: Guilford Press.

Howell, W., & Fleishman, E. A. (1981). *Human performance productivity: Information processing and decision making.* Hillsdale, NJ: Erlbaum.

Hughes, H. M., Jr. (1972). Vocational choice, level, and consistency: An investigation of Holland's theory for an employed sample. *Journal of Vocational Behavior, 2,* 377–388.

Hunter, J. E. (1986). Cognitive ability, cognitive aptitudes, job knowledge, and job performance. *Journal of Vocational Behavior, 29,* 340–362.

Hunter, J. E., & Hunter, R. F. (1984). Validity and utility of alternative predictors of job performance. *Psychological Bulletin, 96,* 72–98.

Iachon, R. (1984). A measure of agreement for use with the Holland classification system. *Journal of Vocational Behavior, 24,* 133–141.

Institute for Personality and Ability Testing. (1986). *Administrator's manual for the 16 Personality Factor Questionnaire.* Champaign, IL: Author.

Irvine, S. H., & Berry, J. W. (1988). Abilities of mankind: A reevaluation. In S. H. Irvine & J. W. Berry (Eds.), *Human abilities in cultural context* (pp. 3–59). Cambridge, England: Cambridge University Press.

Ispa, M. M., Gray, M. M., & Thornburg, K. R. (1984). Childrearing attitudes of parents in person-oriented and thing-oriented occupations: A comparison. *Journal of Psychology, 117,* 245–250.

Jacklin, C. N., Wilcox, K. T., & Maccoby, E. E. (1988). Neonatal sex-steroid hormones and cognitive abilities at six years. *Developmental Psychobiology, 21,* 567–574.

Jackson, D. N., Ahmed, S. A., & Heapy, N. A. (1976). Is achievement a unitary construct? *Journal of Research in Personality, 10,* 1–21.

Jackson, D. N., Paunonen, S. V., & Rothstein, M. G. (1987). Personnel executives: Personality, vocational interests, and job satisfaction. *Journal of Employment Counseling, 24,* 82–96.

Jackson, I. (1982). The stability of selected personality factors across consecutive undergraduate student samples. *Journal of Psychology, 112,* 3–10.

Jacobs, A, & Dunlap, D. N. (1976). The clinical interpretation of the GZTS Scales. In J. S. Guilford, W. S. Zimmerman, & J. P. Guilford (Eds.), *The Guilford-Zimmerman Temperament Survey handbook* (pp. 287–301). San Diego, CA: EDITS.

Jamison, K. (1989). Mood disorders and seasonal patterns in British writers and artists. *Psychiatry, 52,* 125–134.

Jaskolka, G., Beyer, J. M., & Trice, H. M. (1985). Measuring and predicting managerial success. *Journal of Vocational Behavior, 26,* 189–205.

Jastak, S., & Wilkinson, G. S. (1984). *The Wide Range Achievement Test-Revised: Administration manual.* Wilmington, DE: Jastak Associates.

Jenkins, S. (1987). Need for achievement and women's careers over 14 years: Evidence for occupational structure effects. *Journal of Personality and Social Psychology, 53,* 922–932.

Johansson, C. B. (1970). Strong Vocational Interest Blank introversion-extraversion and occupational membership. *Journal of Counseling Psychology, 17,* 451–455.

Johansson, C. B. (1986). *Career Assessment Inventory: The enhanced version.* Minneapolis, MN: National Computer Systems.

Johnson, J. A. (1986, August). *Can job applicants dissimulate on personality tests?* Paper presented at the 94th Annual Convention of the American Psychological Association, Washington, DC.

Johnson, J. A., Cheek, J. M., & Smither, R. (1983). The structure of empathy. *Journal of Personality and Social Psychology, 45,* 1299–1312.

Johnson, R. C., & Nagoshi, C. T. (1985). Parental ability, education and occupation in Hawaii and Korea. *Personality and Individual Differences, 6,* 413–423.

Johnson, R. W. (1965). Are SVIB interests correlated with differential academic achievement? *Journal of Applied Psychology, 49,* 302–309.

Johnson, R. W., Flammer, D. P., & Nelson, J. G. (1975). Multiple correlations between personality factors and SVIB occupational scales. *Journal of Counseling Psychology, 22,* 217–222.

Judd, T. (1988). The varieties of musical talent. In L. K. Obler & D. Fein (Eds.), *The exceptional brain: Neuropsychology of talent and special abilities* (pp. 127–155). New York: Guilford Press.

Jung, C. G. (1923). *Psychological types*. London: Routledge & Kegan Paul.

Junge, D. A., Daniels, M. H., & Karmos, J. S. (1984). Personnel managers' perceptions of requisite basic skills. *Vocational Guidance Quarterly, 33*, 138–146.

Kamp, J., & Gough, H. G. (1986, August). *The big five personality factors from an assessment context*. Paper presented at the 94th Annual Convention of the American Psychological Association, Washington, DC.

Kanter, R. M. (1977). *Work and family in the United States: A critical review and agenda for research and policy*. New York: Russell Sage Foundation.

Kapalka, G. M., & Lachenmeyer, J. R. (1988). Sex-role flexibility, locus of control, and occupational status. *Sex Roles, 19*, 417–427.

Karma, K. (1982). Musical, spatial and verbal abilities: A progress report. *Psychology of Music, 10*, 69–71.

Karma, K. (1983). Selecting students to music instruction. *Bulletin of the Council for Research in Music Education, 75*, 23–32.

Karma, K. (1985). Components of auditive structuring: Towards a theory of musical aptitude. *Bulletin of the Council for Research in Music Education, 82*, 1–13.

Kass, R. A., Mitchell, K. J., Grafton, F. C., & Wing, H. (1983). Factorial validity of the Armed Services Vocational Aptitude Battery (ASVAB), Forms 8, 9, and 10: 1981 Army applicant sample. *Educational and Psychological Measurement, 43*, 1077–1087.

Katz, D., & Kahn, R. L. (1978). *The social psychology of organizations* (2nd ed.). New York: Wiley.

Kelso, G. I., Holland, J. L., & Gottfredson, G. D. (1977). The relation of self-reported competencies to aptitude test scores. *Journal of Vocational Behavior, 10*, 99–103.

Kemp, A. (1982a). Personality traits of successful music teachers. *Psychology of Music, 10*, 72–75.

Kemp, A. (1982b). The personality structure of the musician: III. The significance of sex differences. *Psychology of Music, 10*, 48–58.

Keown, C. F., & Keown, A. L. (1982). Success factors for corporate woman executives. *Group and Organization Studies, 7*, 445–456.

Kernan, M. C., & Lord, R. G. (1988). Effects of participative vs. assigned goals and feedback in a multitrial task. *Motivation and Emotion, 12*, 75–86.

Kets de Vries, M. F. R. (1985). The dark side of entrepreneurship. *Harvard Business Review, 63*, 160–168.

Keyser, D. J., & Sweetland, R. C. (1983). *Test critiques*. Kansas City, MO: Test Corporation of America.

Kiam, V. (1986, April). Are you an entrepreneur? *Reader's Digest*, pp. 105–109.

Kincel, R. L. (1986). Comparative study of Rorschach responses among art and dance students. *British Journal of Projective Psychology and Personality Study, 31*, 19–26.

Kincel, R. L., & Murray, S. C. (1984). Kinaesthesias in perception and the experience type: Dance and creative projection. *British Journal of Projective Psychology and Personality Study, 29*, 3–7.

King, A. S. (1985). Self-analysis and assessment of entrepreneurial potential. *Simulation and Games, 16,* 399–416.

Kinslinger, H. J. (1966). Applications of projective techniques in personnel psychology since 1940. *Psychological Bulletin, 66,* 134–150.

Kintner, M. (1933). *The measurement of artistic abilities: A survey of scientific studies in the field of graphic arts.* New York: Psychological Corporation.

Kirkcaldy, B. D. (1982). Personality profiles at various levels of athletic participation. *Personality and Individual Differences, 3,* 321–326.

Kirkcaldy, B. D. (1986). The relationship between occupational interests and personality variables in a psychiatric group. *Personality and Individual Differences, 7,* 503–508.

Klemp, G. L., Jr., & McClelland, D. C. (1986). What constitutes intelligent functioning among senior managers. In R. J. Sternberg & R. K. Wagner (Eds.), *Practical intelligence: Nature and origins of competence in the everyday world* (pp. 31–50). New York: Cambridge University Press.

Klimoski, R., & Brickner, M. (1987). Why do assessment centers work? The puzzle of assessment center validity. *Personnel Psychology, 40,* 234–260.

Kofodimos, J. R., Kaplan, R. E., & Drath, W. H. (1986). *Anatomy of an executive: A close look at one executive's managerial character and development* (Technical Rep. No. 29). Greensboro, NC: Center for Creative Leadership.

Kogan, N. (1990, August 12). *The performing artist: Some psychological observations.* Paper presented at the 98th Annual Convention of the American Psychological Association, Boston, MA.

Korman, A. K. (1968). The prediction of managerial performance: A review. *Personnel Psychology, 21,* 295–322.

Kotter, J. P. (1982). *The general managers.* New York: Free Press.

Krug, S. E. (1980). *Clinical Analysis Questionnaire manual.* Champaign, IL: Institute for Personality and Ability Testing.

Krutetskii, V. A. (1976). *The psychology of mathematical abilities in school children.* Chicago: University of Chicago Press.

Kuder, G. F. (1965). *Manual for General Interest Survey, Form E.* Chicago: Science Research Associates.

Kumar, P., & Mutha, D. N. (1985). Teacher effectiveness as related with intelligence, anxiety and ascendance-submission. *Journal of Psychological Researches, 29,* 24–29.

Lacey, D. W. (1971). Holland's vocational models: A study of work groups and need satisfaction. *Journal of Vocational Behavior, 1,* 105–122.

Lamont, L. M., & Lundstrom, W. J. (1977). *Journal of Marketing Research, 14,* 517–529.

Landy, F. (1989). *Test validity yearbook.* Hillsdale, NJ: Erlbaum.

Lehman, P. R. (1968). *Tests and measurements in music.* Englewood Cliffs, NJ: Prentice-Hall.

Lewerenz, A. S. (1927). *Tests in fundamental abilities of visual art.* Los Angeles: Research Service.

Likert, R., & Quasha, W. H. (1970). *Revised Minnesota Paper Form Board Test.* San Antonio, TX: Psychological Corporation.

Lindley, R. H., Smith, W. R., & Thomas, T. J. (1988). The relationship between speed of information processing as measured by timed paper-and-pencil tests and psychometric intelligence. *Intelligence, 12,* 17–25.

Lipman-Blumen, J., Handley-Isaksen, A., & Leavitt, H. J. (1983). Achieving styles in men and women: A model, an instrument, and some findings. In J. T. Spence (Ed.), *Achievement and achievement motives: Psychological and sociological approaches* (pp. 147–204). San Francisco: Freeman.

Lipman-Blumen, J., Leavitt, H. J., Patterson, K. J., Bies, R. J., & Handley-Isaksen, A. (1980). A model of direct and relational achieving styles. In L. J. Fyans (Ed.), *Achievement motivation* (pp. 135–168). New York: Plenum Press.

Livenh, H., & Livenh, C. (1989). The five-factor model of personality: Is evidence of its cross-measure validity premature? *Personality and Individual Differences, 10,* 75–80.

Lohman, D. F. (1979). *Spatial ability: Review and re-analysis of the correlational literature* (Tech. Rep. No. 8). Stanford, CA: Stanford University.

London, M. (1985). *Developing managers.* San Francisco: Jossey-Bass.

Lord, T. R. (1985). Enhancing the visuo-spatial aptitude of students. *Journal of Research in Science Teaching, 22,* 395–405.

Lounsbury, J. W., Bobrow, W., & Jensen, J. B. (1989). Attitudes toward employment testing: Scale development, correlates, and "known-group" validation. *Professional Psychology, 20,* 340–349.

Lowenkopf, E. L., & Vincent, L. M. (1982). The student ballet dancer and anorexia. *Hillsdale Journal of Clinical Psychiatry, 4,* 53–64.

Lowman, R. L. (1987). Occupational choice as a moderator of psychotherapeutic approach. *Psychotherapy, 24,* 801–808.

Lowman, R. L. (1988). Converting California Psychological Inventory protocols from 1957 to 1987 norms and variables. *Psychological Reports, 63,* 125–126.

Lowman, R. L. (1989). *Pre-employment screening for psychopathology: A guide to professional practice.* Sarasota, FL: Professional Resource Exchange.

Lowman, R. L., & Leeman, G. E. (1988). The dimensionality of social intelligence: Social abilities, interests and needs. *Journal of Psychology, 122,* 279–290.

Lowman, R. L., & Schurman, S. J. (1982). Psychometric characteristics of a Vocational Preference Inventory short form. *Educational and Psychological Measurement, 42,* 602–613.

Lowman, R. L., & Williams, R. E. (1987). Validity of self-ratings of abilities and competencies. *Journal of Vocational Behavior, 31,* 1–13.

Lowman, R. L., Williams, G. E., & Leeman, G. (1985). The structure and relationship of college women's primary abilities and vocational interests. *Journal of Vocational Behavior, 27,* 298–315.

Lubinski, D., Tellegen, A., & Butcher, J. N. (1983). Masculinity, femininity, and androgyny viewed and assessed as distinct concepts. *Journal of Personality and Social Psychology, 44,* 428–439.

Lundin, R. W. (1967). *An objective psychology of music* (2nd ed.). New York: Ronald Press.

Lundy, A. (1988). Instructional set and Thematic Apperception Test validity. *Journal of Personality Assessment, 52,* 309–320.

Lunneborg, P. W., & Lunneborg, C. E. (1985). Nontraditional and traditional female college graduates: What separates them from the men? *Journal of College Student Personnel, 26,* 33–36.

Lynn, R., & Gault, A. (1986). The relation of musical ability to general intelligence and the major primaries. *Research in Education, 36,* 59–64.

Lynn, R., & Hampson, S. (1987). Further evidence on the cognitive abilities of the Japanese: Data from the WPPSI. *International Journal of Behavioral Development, 10,* 23–26.

Maccoby, E. E., & Jacklin, C. N. (1974). The psychology of sex differences. Stanford, CA: Stanford University Press.

Maccoby, M. (1976). *The gamesman.* New York: Simon & Schuster.

Macher, K. (1986). The politics of people. *Personnel Journal, 65,* 50–53.

MacKinnon, D. W. (1962). The nature and nurture of creative talent. *American Psychologist, 17,* 484–495.

MacKinnon, D. W. (1970). The personality correlates of creativity: A study of American architects. In P. E. Vernon (Ed.), *Creativity* (pp. 289–311). New York: Penguin Books.

MacLeod, C. M., Jackson, R. A., & Palmer, J. (1986). On the relation between spatial ability and field dependence. *Intelligence, 10,* 141–151.

MacQuarrie, T. W. (1927). A mechanical ability test. *Journal of Personality Research, 5,* 329–337.

Maitra, A. K. (1983). Executive effectiveness: Characteristic thematic phantasy. *Managerial Psychology, 4,* 59–68.

Marlowe, H. A., Jr., & Bedell, J. R. (1982). Social intelligence: Evidence for independence of the construct. *Psychological Reports, 51,* 461–462.

Marmor, G. S. (1976). Mental rotation by the blind: Does mental rotation depend on visual imagery? *Journal of Experimental Psychology: Human Perception and Performance, 2,* 515–521.

Martin, J. D., Blair, G. E., Dannennaier, W. D., Jones, P. C., & Asako, M. (1981). Relationship of scores on the California Psychological Inventory to age. *Psychological Reports, 49,* 151–154.

Matarazzo, J. D. (1972). *Wechsler's measurement and appraisal of adult intelligence* (5th ed.). Baltimore: William & Wilkins.

Matthews, D. F., & Walsh, W. B. (1978). Concurrent validity of Holland's theory for non-college-degreed working women. *Journal of Vocational Behavior, 12,* 371–379.

Mayer, J. D., Caruso, D. R., Zigler, E., & Dreyden, J. I. (1989). Intelligence and intelligence-related personality traits. *Intelligence, 13,* 119–133.

Mayer, D., & Greenberg, H. M. (1964). Make makes a good salesman? *Harvard Business Review, 42,* 119–125.

McCammon, S., Golden, J., & Wuensch, K. L. (1988). Predicting course performance in freshman and sophomore physics courses: Women are more predictable than men. *Journal of Research in Science Teaching, 25,* 501–510.

McClelland, D. (1961). *The achieving society.* Princeton, NJ: Van Nostrand.

McClelland, D. (1975). *Power: The inner experience.* New York: Irvington-Wiley.

McClelland, D. (1985). *Human motivation.* Glenview, IL: Scott, Foresman.

McClelland, D. (1986). Characteristics of successful entrepreneurs. *Journal of Creative Behavior, 21,* 219–233.

McClelland, D., Baldwin, A., Bronfenbrenner, U., & Strodtbeck, F. (Eds.). (1958). *Talent and society: New perspectives in the identification of talent.* Princeton, NJ: Van Nostrand.

McClelland, D. C., & Boyatzis, R. E. (1982). The leadership motive pattern and long-term success in management. *Journal of Applied Psychology, 67,* 737–743.

McClelland, D. C., & Burnham, R. E. (1976). Power is the great motivator. *Harvard Business Review, 25,* 159–166.

McClelland, D., & Pilon, D. A. (1983). Sources of adult motives in patterns of parent behavior in early childhood. *Journal of Personality and Social Psychology, 44,* 564–574.

McClelland, D., & Winter, D. G. (1969). *Motivating economic acheivement.* New York: Free Press.

McCrae, R. R. (1987). Creativity, divergent thinking, and openness to experience. *Journal of Personality and Social Psychology, 52,* 1258–1265.

McCrae, R. R., & Costa, P. T. (1985). Comparison of EI and psychoticism scales with measures of the five-factor model of personality. *Personality and Individual Differences, 6,* 587–597.

McCrae, R. R., & Costa, P. T. (1986). Clinical assessment can benefit from recent advances in personality psychology. *American Psychologist, 41,* 1001–1003.

McCrae, R. R., & Costa, P. T. (1987). Validation of the five-factor model of personality across instruments and observers. *Journal of Personality and Social Psychology, 52,* 81–90.

McCrae, R. R., Costa, P. T., & Busch, C. M. (1986). Evaluating comprehensiveness in personality systems: The California Q-Set and the five-factor model. *Journal of Personality, 54,* 430–446.

McCutchen, D. (1986). Domain knowledge and linguistic knowledge in the development of writing ability. *Journal of Memory and Language, 25,* 431–444.

McGee, M. G. (1979). *Human spatial abilities: Sources of sex differences.* New York: Praeger.

McGue, M., Bouchard, T. J., Lykken, D. T., & Feuer, D. (1984). Information processing abilities in twins reared apart. *Intelligence, 8,* 239–258.

McKenna, F. P. (1984). Measures of field dependence: Cognitive style or cognitive ability. *Journal of Personality and Social Psychology, 47,* 593–603.

McLeish, J., & Higgs, G. (1982). Musical ability and mental subnormality: An experimental investigation. *British Journal of Educational Psychology, 52,* 370–373.

Megargee, E. I. (1972). *The California Psychological Inventory handbook*. San Francisco: Jossey-Bass.

Megargee, E. I., & Carbonell, J. (1988). Evaluating leadership with the CPI. In C. D. Spielberger & J. N. Butcher (Eds.). *Advances in personality assessment* (Vol. 7, pp. 203–219). Hillsdale, NJ: Erlbaum.

Mehrabian, A., & Epstein, N. (1972). A measure of emotional empathy. *Journal of Personality, 40*, 525–543.

Mehta, M., & Agrawal, R. (1986). Effect of need for achievement and repression sensitization dimension upon job satisfaction of bank employees. *Indian Journal of Applied Psychology, 23*, 39–44.

Meier, N. C. (1928). A measure of art talent. *Psychological Monographs, 39*(Whole No. 178).

Meier, N. C. (1939). Factors in artistic aptitude. *Psychological Monographs, 51*(Whole No. 231).

Meier, N. C. (1940). *The Meier Art Tests: I. Art judgment*. Iowa City, IA: Bureau of Educational Research and Services.

Meier, N. C. (1942). *Art in human affairs*. New York: McGraw-Hill.

Meir, E. I., & Erez, M. (1981). Fostering a career in engineering. *Journal of Vocational Behavior, 18*, 115–120.

Melamed, S., & Meir, E. T. (1981). The relationships between interests, job incongruity and selection of avocational activity. *Journal of Vocational Behavior, 18*, 310–325.

Melville, H. (1977). *Moby Dick*. New York: Easton Press. (Original work published 1851).

Metcalfe, R. J., & Dobson, C. B. (1983). Factorial structure and dispositional correlates of "locus of control" in children. *Research in Education, 30*, 53–63.

Metzler, B. E., Lewis, R. J., & Gerrard, M. (1985). Childhood antecedents of adult women's masculinity, femininity, and career role choices. *Psychology of Women Quarterly, 9*, 371–381.

Meudell, P. R., & Greenhalgh, M. (1987). Age related differences in left and right hand skill and in visuo-spatial performance: Their possible relationships to the hypothesis that the right hemisphere ages more rapidly than the left. *Cortex, 23*, 431–445.

Michael, W. B., Guilford, J. P., Fruchter, B., & Zimmerman, W. S. (1957). The description of spatial-visualization abilities. *Educational and Psychological Measurement, 17*, 185–199.

Miller, D., & Droge, C. (1986). Psychological and traditional determinants of structure. *Administrative Science Quarterly, 31*, 539–560.

Mills, J. I. (1984). The "pitch" subtest of Bentley's Measures of Musical Abilities: A test from the 1960s reconsidered in the 1980s. *Psychology of Music, 12*, 94–105.

Miner, J. B. (1978). Twenty years of research on role-motivation theory of managerial effectiveness. *Personnel Psychology, 31*, 739–760.

Miner, J. B. (1985). Sentence completion measures in personnel research: The development and validation of the Miner Sentence Completion Scales.

In H. A. Bernardin & D. A. Bownas (Eds.), *Personality assessment in organizations* (pp. 145–176). New York: Praeger.

Minogue, B. M. (1923). A case of secondary mental deficiency with musical talent. *Journal of Applied Psychology, 7,* 349–357.

Mintzberg, H. (1973). *The nature of managerial work.* New York: Harper & Row.

Misra, P., & Jain, N. (1986). Self-esteem, need-achievement and need-autonomy as moderators of the job performance-job satisfaction relationship. *Perspectives in Psychological Researches, 9,* 42–46.

Mitchell, J. V. (1985). *The ninth mental measurements yearbook.* Lincoln, NE: Buros Institute of Mental Measurement.

Modjeski, R. B., & Michael, W. B. (1983). An evaluation by a panel of psychologists of the reliability and validity of two tests of critical thinking. *Educational and Psychological Measurement, 43,* 1187–1197.

Mohan, J., & Tiwana, M. (1987). Personality and alienation of creative writers: A brief report. *Personality and Individual Differences, 8,* 449.

Mohan, V., & Brar, A. (1986). Motives and work efficiency. *Personality Study and Group Behavior, 6,* 37–45.

Moore, T. E., Richards, B., & Hood, J. (1984). Aging and the coding of spatial information. *Journal of Gerontology, 39,* 210–212.

Morris, L. W. (1979). *Extraversion and introversion: An interactional perspective.* New York: Hemisphere.

Morrow, R. S. (1938). An analysis of the relations among tests of musical, artistic, and mechanical abilities. *Journal of Psychology, 5,* 253–263.

Morrow, J. M., Jr. (1971). A test of Holland's theory of vocational choice. *Journal of Counseling Psychology, 18,* 422–425.

Moss, F. A., Hunt, K. T., Omwake, K. T., & Woodward, L. G. (1955). *Manual for the George Washington University Series Social Intelligence Test.* Washington, DC: Center for Psychological Services.

Mossholder, K. W., Bedeian, A. G., Touliatos, J., & Barkman, A. I. (1985). An examination of intra-occupational differences: Personality, perceived work climate, and outcome preferences. *Journal of Vocational Behavior, 26,* 164–176.

Mount, M. K., & Muchinsky, P. M. (1978a). Concurrent validation of Holland's hexagonal model with occupational workers. *Journal of Vocational Behavior, 13,* 348–354.

Mount, M. K., & Muchinsky, P. M. (1978b). Person-environment congruence and employee job satisfaction: A test of Holland's theory. *Journal of Vocational Behavior, 13,* 84–100.

Mumford, M. D., & Gustafson, S. B. (1988). Creativity syndrome: Integration, application, and innovation. *Psychological Bulletin, 103,* 27–43.

Murray, H. (1938). *Explorations in personality.* New York: Oxford University Press.

Murray, S. G. (1981). Personality characteristics of adult women with low and high profiles on the SCII or SVIB occupational scales. *Journal of Applied Psychology, 66,* 422–430.

Mursell, J. L. (1939). Intelligence and musicality. *Education, 59,* 559–562.

Myers, I. B. (1980). *Gifts differing*. Palo Alto, CA: Consulting Psychologists Press.

Myers, I. B. (1987). *Introduction to type*. Palo Alto, CA: Consulting Psychologists Press.

Myers, I. B., & McCaulley, M. H. (1985). *Manual: A guide to the development and use of the Myers-Briggs Type Indicator*. Palo Alto, CA: Consulting Psychologists Press.

Myers, P. B., & Myers, K. D. (1985). *A guide to the development and use of the Myers-Briggs Type Indicator*. Palo Alto, CA: Consulting Psychologists Press.

Nafzinger, D. H., Holland, J. L., & Gottfredson, G. D. (1975) Student-college congruency as a predictor of satisfaction. *Journal of Counseling Psychology, 22*, 132–139.

Naglieri, J. A., & Insko, W. R. (1986). Construct validity of the Matrix Analogies Test—Expanded Form. *Journal of Psychoeducational Assessment, 4*, 243–255.

Nagoshi, C. T., & Johnson, R. C. (1987). Cognitive abilities profiles of Caucasian vs. Japanese subjects in the Hawaii Study of Cognition. *Personality and Individual Differences, 8*, 581–583.

Naoumenko, S. I. (1982). Individual differences in musical ability. *Voprosy-Psikhologii, 5*, 85–93. [From *Psychological Abstracts*, 1982, *70*, Abstract No. 8036.]

Nash, A. N. (1965). Vocational interests of effective managers: A review of the literature. *Personnel Psychology, 18*, 21–37.

Nauss, A. (1973). The ministerial personality: Myth or reality? *Journal of Religion and Health, 12*, 77–96.

Neisser, U. (1983). Components of intelligence or steps in routine procedures? *Cognition,15*, 189–197.

Nichols, R. C. (1985). Comprehensive Ability Battery [Review]. In J. V. Mitchell, Jr. (Ed.), *The ninth mental measurements yearbook* (Vol 1, pp. 376–377). Lincoln, NE: Buros Institute of Mental Measurements.

Niebuhr, R. E., & Norris, D. R. (1982). The influence of individual characteristics on performance under varying conditions. *Journal of Social Psychology, 117*, 249–255.

Nieva, V. F., & Gutek, B. A. (1981). *Women and work: A psychological perspective*. New York: Praeger.

Norman, W. T. (1963). Toward an adequate toxonomy of personality attributes: Replicated factor structure in peer nomination personality ratings. *Journal of Abnormal and Social Psychology, 66*, 574–583.

Norris, S. P. (1988). Controlling for background beliefs when developing multiple-choice critical thinking tests. *Educational Measurement Issues and Practice, 7*, 5–11.

Nykodym, N., & Simonetti, J. L. (1987). Personal appearance: Is attractiveness a factor in organizational survival and success? *Journal of Employment Counseling, 24*, 69–78.

Obler, L. K., & Fein, D. (1988). *The exceptional brain: Neuropsychology of talent and special abilities*. New York: Guilford Press.

O'Connor, J. (1927). *Born that way*. Baltimore: Williams & Wilkins.

O'Connor, J. (1941). *The too many aptitude woman*. Boston, MA: Human Engineering Laboratory.

O'Connor, J. (1943). *Structural visualization*. Boston, MA: Human Engineering Laboratory.

O'Connor, N., & Hermelin, B. (1983). The role of general ability and specific talents in information processing. *British Journal of Developmental Psychology, 1*, 389–403.

O'Connor, N., & Hermelin, B. (1987). Visual and graphic abilities of the idiot savant artist. *Psychological Medicine, 17*, 79–90.

Oda, M. (1982). An analysis of relation between personality traits and job performance in sales occupations. *Japanese Journal of Psychology, 53*, 274–280.

Oda, M. (1983). Predicting sales performance of car salesmen by personality traits. *Japanese Journal of Psychology, 54*, 73–80.

Oldfield, R. C. (1971). The assessment and analysis of handedness: The Edinburgh Inventory. *Neuropsychologia, 9*, 97–113.

Olson, P. D., & Bosserman, D. A. (1984). Attributes of the entrepreneurial type. *Business Horizons, 27*, 53–57.

O'Malley, M. N., & Schubarth, G. (1984). Fairness and appeasement: Achievement and affiliation motives in interpersonal relations. *Social Psychology Quarterly, 47*, 364–371.

Orpen, C. (1983). The development and validation of an adjective check-list measure of managerial need for achievement. *Psychology: A Quarterly Journal of Human Behavior, 20*, 38–42.

Osborn, H. H. (1983). The assessment of mathematical abilities. *Educational Research, 25*, 28–40.

Osipow, S. (1983). *Theories of career development* (3rd ed.). Englewood Cliffs, NJ: Prentice-Hall.

Osipow, S. H. (1987). Counseling psychology: Theory, research, and practice in career counseling. *Annual Review of Psychology, 38*, 257–278.

Osipow, S. H., Ashby, J. P., & Wall, H. W. (1977). Personality types and vocational choice: A test of Holland's theory. *Personnel and Guidance Journal, 45*, 37–42.

Osipow, S. H., & Walsh, W. B. (1973). Social intelligence and the selection of counselors. *Journal of Counseling Psychology, 20*, 366–369.

O'Sullivan, M., & Guilford, J. P. (1975). Six factors of behavioral cognition: Understanding other people. *Journal of Educational Measurement, 12*, 255–271.

O'Sullivan, M., & Guilford, J. P. (1976). *Four Factor Tests of Social Intelligence (Behavioral Cognition): Manual of instructions and interpretations*. Palo Alto, CA: Consulting Psychologists Press.

Pagdiwalla, K. D., & Pestonjee, D. M. (1988). A study of need patterns in orphans, delinquents and physically handicapped. *Journal of Personality and Clinical Studies, 4*, 23–29.

Pallrand, G. J., & Seeber, F. (1984). Spatial ability and achievement in introductory physics. *Journal of Research in Science Teaching, 21*, 507–516.

Parsons, F. (1909). *Choosing a vocation.* New York: Houghton Mifflin.

Parvathi, S., & Natarajan, P. (1985). A study of the drawing abilities of children as related to abstract intelligence. *Journal of the Indian Academy of Applied Psychology, 11*, 21–24.

Parvathi, S., & Rama-Rao, P. (1982). Problem solving, need for achievement, expectancy of academic achievement and social desirability. *Journal of Psychological Researches, 26*, 88–92.

Patterson, D. G., Elliott, R. M., Anderson, L. D., Toops, H. A., & Heidbreder, E. (1930). *Minnesota Mechanical Ability Tests.* Minneapolis: University of Minnesota Press.

Paul, S. M. (1985–1986). The Advanced Raven's Progressive Matrices: Normative data for an American university population and examination of the relationship with Spearman's *g. Journal of Experimental Education, 54*, 95–100.

Pawlik, K. (1966). Concepts in human cognition and aptitudes. In R. B. Cattell (Ed.), *Handbook of multivariate experimental psychology* (pp. 535–562). Chicago: Rand McNally.

Peiser, C., & Meir, E. I. (1978). Congruency, consistency, and differentiation of vocational interests as predictors of vocational satisfaction and preference stability. *Journal of Vocational Behavior, 12*, 270–278.

Peraino, J. M., & Willerman, L. (1983). Personality correlates of occupational status according to Holland types. *Journal of Vocational Behavior, 22*, 268–277.

Peterson, J. M. (1979). Left-handedness: Differences between student artists and scientists. *Perceptual and Motor Skills, 48*, 961–962.

Peterson, J. M., & Lansky, L. M. (1980). Success in architecture: Handedness and/or visual thinking. *Perceptual and Motor Skills, 50*, 1139–1143.

Peterson, M. F. (1983). Co-workers and hospital staff's work attitudes: Individual difference moderators. *Nursing Research, 32*, 115–121.

Phillips, S. D., & Bruch, M. A. (1988). Shyness and dysfunction in career development. *Journal of Counseling Psychology, 35*, 159–165.

Pickman, A. J. (1987). Career transitions for dancers: A counselor's perspective. *Journal of Counseling and Development, 66*, 200–201.

Piechowski, M. M., & Cunningham, K. (1985). Patterns of overexcitability in a group of artists. *Journal of Creative Behavior, 19*, 153–174.

Plotkin, H. M. (1987). What makes a successful salesperson? *Training and Development Journal, 41*, 54–56.

Poltrock, S. E., & Brown, P. (1984). Individual differences in visual imagery and spatial ability. *Intelligence, 8*, 93–138.

Portegal, M. (1982). (Ed.). *Spatial abilities: Development and physiological foundations.* New York: Academic Press.

Posthuma, A. B., & Navran, L. (1979). Relation of congruence in student-faculty interest to achievement in college. *Journal of Counseling Psychology, 17*, 352–356.

Powell, J. L., & Brand, A. G. (1987). The development of an emotions scale for writers. *Educational and Psychological Measurement, 47,* 329–338.

Powers, S., Barkan, J. H ., & Jones, P. B. (1986). Reliability of the Standard Progressive Matrices Test for Hispanic and Anglo-American children. *Perceptual and Motor Skills, 62,* 348–350.

Prediger, D. J., & Cole, N. S. (1975). Sex-role socialization and employment realities: Implications for vocational interest measures. *Journal of Vocational Behavior, 7,* 239–251.

Prediger, D. J., & Hanson, G. R. (1974). The distinction between sex restrictiveness and sex bias in interest inventories. *Measurement and Evaluation in Guidance, 7,* 96–104.

Prediger, D. J., & Hanson, G. R. (1976a). A theory of careers encounters sex: Reply to Holland (1976). *Journal of Vocational Behavior, 8,* 359–366.

Prediger, D. J., & Hanson, G. R. (1976b). Holland's theory of careers applied to women and men: Analysis of underlying assumptions. *Journal of Vocational Behavior, 8,* 167–184.

Prothro, E. T., & Perry, H. T. (1950). Group differences in performance on the Meier Art Test. *Journal of Applied Psychology, 34,* 196–197.

Puglisi, J. T., & Morrell, R. W. (1986). Age-related slowing in mental rotation of three-dimensional objects. *Experimental Aging Research, 12,* 217–220.

Quinan, C. (1922). A study of sinistrality and muscle coordination in musicians, ironworkers and others. *Archives of Neurology and Psychiatry, 7,* 352–360.

Rachman, D., Amernic, J., & Aranya, N. (1981). A factor-analytic study of the construct validity of Holland's Self-Directed Search. *Educational and Psychological Measurement, 41,* 425–437.

Radecki, C., & Jennings, J. (1980). Sex as a status variable in work settings: Female and male reports of dominance behavior. *Journal of Applied Social Psychology, 10,* 71–85.

Rahimi, M., & Malzahn, D. E. (1984). Task design and modification based on physical ability measurement. *Human Factors, 26,* 715–726.

Randahl, G. J. (1990). *A typological analysis of the relationship between measured vocational interests and abilities.* Unpublished doctoral dissertation, University of Minnesota.

Rao, S., & Murthy, V. N. (1984). Psychosocial correlates of locus of control among college students. *Psychosocial Studies, 29,* 51–56.

Rao, T. V. (1981). Sales effectiveness. *Managerial Psychology, 2,* 1–12.

Ratcliffe, G. (1982). Disturbances of spatial orientation associated with cerebral lesions. In M. Portegal (Ed.), *Spatial abilities: Development and physiological foundations* (pp. 301–331). New York: Academic Press.

Raven, J. C., Court, J. H., & Raven, J. (1977a). *Manual for Raven's Progressive Matrices and Vocabulary Scales. Section 3. Advanced Matrices: Sets I and II.* London: H. K. Lewis & Co.

Raven, J. C., Court, J. H., & Raven, J. (1977b). *Manual for Raven's Progressive Matrices and Vocabulary Scales. Section 3: Standard Progressive Matrices.* London: H. K. Lewis & Co.

Reardon, R., Foley, J. M., & Walker, R. E. (1979). Social intelligence and vocational choice. *Psychological Reports, 44,* 853–854.

Reeve, J., Olson, B. C., & Cole, S. G. (1987). Intrinsic motivation in competition: The intervening role of four individual differences following objective competence information. *Journal of Research in Personality, 21,* 148–170.

Resnick, L. B. (1989). Developing mathematical knowledge. *American Psychologist, 44,* 162–169.

Resnick, S. M., Berenbaum, S. A., Gottesman, I. I., & Bouchard, T. J. (1986). Early hormonal influences on cognitive functioning in congenital adrenal hyperplasia. *Developmental Psychology, 22,* 191–198.

Reuman, D. A. (1982). Ipsative behavioral variability and the quality of thematic apperceptive measurement of the achievement motive. *Journal of Personality and Social Psychology, 43,* 1098–1110.

Reutefors, D. L., Schneider, L. J., & Overton, T. D. (1979). Academic achievement: An examination of Holland's congruency, consistency, and differentiation predictions. *Journal of Vocational Behavior, 14,* 181–189.

Revesz, G. (1953). *Introduction to the psychology of music.* London: Longsman, Green.

Richardson, A. G. (1986). Two factors of creativity. *Perceptual and Motor Skills, 63,* 379–384.

Riggio, R. E. (1986). Assessment of basic social skills. *Journal of Personality and Social Psychology, 51,* 649–660.

Riggio, R. E., & Sotoodeh, Y. (1987). Screening tests for use in hiring microassemblers. *Perceptual and Motor Skills, 65,* 167–172.

Ritchie, R. J., & Moses, J. L. (1983). Assessment center correlates of women's advancement into middle management: A 7-year longitudinal analysis. *Journal of Applied Psychology, 68,* 227–231.

Robbins, P. I., Thomas, L. E., Harvey, D. W., & Kandefer, C. (1978). Career change and congruence of personality type: An examination of DOT-derived work environment designations. *Journal of Vocational Behavior, 13,* 15–25.

Roe, A. (1946). The personality of artists. *Education and Psychological Measurement, 6,* 401–408.

Roe, A. (1951). A psychological study of eminent biologists. *Psychological Monographs, 65*(14, Whole No. 331).

Roe, A. (1952). *The making of a scientist.* New York: Dodd Mead.

Roe, A. (1956). *The psychology of occupations.* New York: Wiley.

Rosenblatt, E., & Winner, E. (1988). Is superior visual memory a component of superior drawing ability? In L. K. Obler & E. Fein (Eds.), *The exceptional brain* (pp. 341–363). New York: Guilford Press.

Rudocy, R. E., & Boyle, J. D. (1979). *Psychological foundations of musical behavior.* Springfield, IL: Charles C Thomas.

Ruth, J. E., & Birren, J. E. (1985). Creativity in adulthood and old age: Relations to intelligence, sex and mode of testing. *International Journal of Behavioral Development, 8,* 99–109.

Ryan, A. M., & Sackett, P. R. (1987). A survey of individual assessment practices by I/O psychologists. *Personnel Psychology, 40,* 489–504.

Rychlak, J. F. (1982). *Personalities and lifestyles of young male managers.* New York: Academic Press.

Salomone, P. R., & Slaney, R. B. (1978). The applicability of Holland's theory to nonprofessional workers. *Journal of Vocational Behavior, 13,* 63–74.

Salthouse, T. A. (1984a). Effects of age and skill in typing. *Journal of Experimental Psychology: General, 113,* 345–371.

Salthouse, T. A. (1984b). The skill of typing. *Scientific American, 250,* 128–135.

Salthouse, T. A. (1986a). Effects of practice on a typing-like keying task. *Acta Psychologica, 62,* 189–198.

Salthouse, T. A. (1986b). Perceptual, cognitive, and motoric aspects of transcription typing. *Psychological bulletin, 99,* 303–319.

Samson, G. E., Graue, M. E., Weinstein, T., & Walberg, H. J. (1984). Academic and occupational performance: A quantitative synthesis. *American Educational Research Journal, 21,* 311–321.

Sanders, B., Wilson, J. R., & Vandenberg, S. G. (1982). Handedness and spatial ability. *Cortex, 18,* 79–89.

Scanlan, T. J. (1980). Toward an occupational classification for self-employed men: An investigation of entrepreneurship from the perspective of Holland's theory of career development. *Journal of Vocational Behavior, 16,* 163–172.

Schacter, S. C., & Galaburda, A. M. (1986). Development and biological associations of cerebral dominance: Review and possible mechanisms. *Journal of the American Academy of Child Psychiatry, 25,* 741–750.

Schaefer, B. E. (1976). Holland's SDS: Is its effectiveness contingent upon selected variables? *Journal of Vocational Behavior, 8,* 113–123.

Schilit, W. K. (1986). An examination of individual differences as moderators of upward influence activity in strategic decisions. *Human Relations, 39,* 933–953.

Schmidt, F. L., & Hunter, J. E. (1977). Development of a general solution to the problem of validity generalization. *Journal of Applied Psychology, 62,* 529–540.

Schmidt, F. L., Hunter, J. E., & Pearlman, K. (1981). Task differences as moderators of aptitude test validity in selection: A red herring. *Journal of Applied Psychology, 66,* 166–185.

Schmitt, N., Goodding, R. Z., Noe, R., & Kirsch, M. (1984). Meta-analyses of validity studies published between 1964 and 1982 and the investigation of study characteristics. *Personnel Psychology, 37,* 407–438.

Schmitt, N., Noe, R. A., & Fitzgerald, M. P. (1984). Validity of assessment center ratings for the prediction of performance ratings and school climate of school administrators. *Journal of Applied Psychology, 69,* 207–213.

Schmitt, N., White, J. K., Coyle, B. W., Rauschenberger, J., & Shumway, S. (1978). Prediction of post-high school labor force decisions. *Human Relations, 31*, 727–743.

Schmitt, N., & White, J. K. (1978). Relationships between job motivation variables and interest measures. *Journal of Vocational Behavior, 12*, 333–341.

Schneider, B. (1987). The people make the place. *Personnel Psychology, 40*, 437–453.

Schneider, B., & Schmitt, N. (1986). *Staffing organizations* (2nd ed.). Glenview, IL: Scott, Foresman.

Schneider, D. E. (1979). *The psychoanalyst and the artist*. East Hampton, NY: Alexa Press.

Schroth, M. L. (1987). Relationships between achievement-related motives, extrinsic conditions, and task performance. *Journal of Social Psychology, 127*, 39–48.

Schroth, M. L., & Andrew, D. F. (1987). Study of need-achievement motivation among Hawaiian college students. *Perceptual and Motor Skills, 64*, 1261–1262.

Schuldt, D. L., & Stahmann, R. F. (1971). Interest profiles of clergymen as indicated by the Vocational Preference Inventory. *Educational and Psychological Measurement, 31*, 1025–1028.

Schutz, W. (1978). *FIRO Awareness Scales manual*. Palo Alto, CA: Consulting Psychologists Press.

Seashore, C. E. (1939). *Psychology of music*. New York: McGraw-Hill.

Seashore, C. E., Lewis, D., & Saetveit, J. G. (1960). *Seashore Measures of Musical Talent test manual*. New York: Psychological Corporation.

Sedge, S. K. (1985). A comparison of engineers pursuing alternate career paths. *Journal of Vocational Behavior, 27*, 56–70.

Shaffer, L. H. (1986). Skilled typing performance and keyboard design. *Current Psychological Research and Reviews, 5*, 119–129.

Shanley, L. A., Walker, R. E., & Foley, J. M. (1971). Social intelligence: A concept in search of data. *Psychological Reports, 29*, 1123–1132.

Sharf, R. (1970). Relative importance of interest and ability in vocational decision making. *Journal of Counseling Psychology, 17*, 258–262.

Sheehan, E. P., & Smith, H. W. (1986). Cerebral lateralization and handedness and their effects on verbal and spatial reasoning. *Neuropsychologia, 24*, 531–540.

Sherman, J. (1983). Factors predicting girls' and boys' enrollment in college preparatory mathemathics. *Psychology of Women Quarterly, 7*, 272–281.

Shettel-Neuber, J., & O'Reilly, J. (1983). Handedness and career choice: Another look at supposed left/right differences. *Perceptual and Motor Skills, 57*, 391–397.

Shuter, R. (1968). *The psychology of musical ability*. London: Methuen.

Shuter-Dyson, R., & Gabriel, C. (1981). *The psychology of musical ability* (2nd ed.). London: Methuen.

Sid, A. K., & Lindgren, H. C. (1982). Achievement and affiliation motivation and their correlates. *Educational and Psychological Measurement, 42,* 1213–1218.

Silver, E. M., & Bennett, C. (1987). Modification of the Minnesota Clerical Test to predict performance on video display terminals. *Journal of Applied Psychology, 72,* 153–155.

Sincoff, J. B., & Sternberg, R. J. (1987). Two faces of verbal ability. *Intelligence, 11,* 263–276.

Sipps, G. J., Berry, W., & Lynch, E. M. (1987). WAIS-R and social intelligence: A test of established assumptions that uses the CPI. *Journal of Clinical Psychology, 43,* 500–504.

Slaney, R. B. (1980). An investigation of racial differences on vocational variables among college women. *Journal of Vocational Behavior, 16,* 197–207.

Smart, J. C. (1975). Environments as reinforcement systems in the study of job satisfaction. *Journal of Vocational Behavior, 6,* 337–357.

Smith, I. M. (1964). *Spatial ability: Its educational and social significance.* San Diego: Knapp.

Smith, K. E. (1986). Sex-typed occupational roles and self-image among teachers. *Psychological Reports, 58,* 73–74.

Smith, P. C., Kendall, L. M., & Hulin, C. L. (1969). *The measurement of satisfaction in work and retirement.* Chicago: Rand McNally.

Solan, H. A. (1987). The effects of visual-spatial and verbal skills on written and mental arithmetic. *Journal of the American Optometric Association, 58,* 88–94.

Spence, J. T. (Ed.). (1983). *Achievement and achievement motives: Psychological and sociological approaches.* San Francisco: Freeman.

Spence, J. T., & Helmreich, R. L. (1978). *Masculinity and femininity: Their psychological dimensions, correlates and antecedents.* Austin: University of Texas Press.

Spence, J. T., & Helmreich, R. L. (1983). Achievement-related motives and behaviors. In J. T. Spence (Ed.), *Achievement and achievement motives: Psychological and sociological approaches* (pp. 7–74). San Francisco: Freeman.

Spokane, A. R., & Derby, D. P. (1979). Congruence, personality pattern, and satisfaction in college women. *Journal of Vocational Behavior, 12,* 145–154.

Spokane, A. R., & Walsh, W. B. (1978). Occupational level and Holland's theory for employed men and women. *Journal of Vocational Behavior, 12,* 145–154.

Sprowl, J. P., & Senk, M. (1986). Sales communication: Compliance-gaining strategy choice and sales success. *Communication Research Reports, 3,* 64–68.

Stahl, M. J. (1983). Achievement, power and managerial motivation: Selecting managerial talent with the job choice exercise. *Personnel Psychology, 36,* 775–789.

Stahl, M. J., & Harrell, A. M. (1982). Evolution and validation of a behavioral decision theory measurement approach to achievement, power, and affiliation. *Journal of Applied Psychology, 67,* 744–751.

Stankov, L. (1986). Kvaschev's experiment: Can we boost intelligence? *Intelligence, 10,* 209–230.

Stanley, J. C., & Benbow, C. P. (1982). Huge sex ratios at upper end. *American Psychologist, 37,* 972.

Steinberg, R., & Shapiro, S. (1982). Sex differences in personality traits of male and female master of business administration students. *Journal of Applied Psychology, 67,* 306–310.

Stericker, A., & LeVesconte, S. (1982). Effect of brief training on sex-related differences in visual-spatial skill. *Journal of Personality and Social Psychology, 43,* 1018–1029.

Sternberg, R. J. (1982a). A componential approach to intellectual development. In R. J. Sternberg (Ed.), *Advances in the psychology of human intelligence* (Vol. 1, pp. 413–463). Hillsdale, NJ: Erlbaum.

Sternberg, R. J. (Ed.). (1982b). *Handbook of human intelligence.* Cambridge, England: Cambridge University Press.

Sternberg, R. J. (1988). *The triarchic mind: A new theory of human intelligence.* New York: Viking Press.

Sternberg, R. J., & Smith, C. (1985). Social intelligence and decoding skills in nonverbal communication. *Journal of Social Cognition, 3,* 16–31.

Sternberg, R. J., & Wagner, R. K. (Eds.). (1986). *Practical intelligence: Nature and origins of competence in the everyday world.* New York: Cambridge University Press.

Stewart, D. W., & Latham, D. R. (1986). On some psychometric properties of Fiedler's contingency model of leadership. *Small Group Behavior, 17,* 83–94.

Strong, E. K., Jr. (1931). *Change of interests with age, based on examination of more than 2,000 men between the ages of 20 and 60 representing 8 occupations.* Stanford, CA: Stanford University Press.

Strong, E. K., Jr. (1943). *Vocational interests of men and women.* Stanford, CA: Stanford University Press.

Super, D. E., & Crites, J. O. (1962). *Appraising vocational fitness* (rev. ed.). New York: Harper & Row.

Super, D. E., & Hall, D. T. (1978). Career development: Exploration and planning. *Annual Review of Psychology, 29,* 333–372.

Taylor, C. W. (Ed.). (1964). *Creativity: Progress and potential.* New York: McGraw-Hill.

Taylor, C. W., Albo, D., Holland, J., & Brandt, G. (1985). Attributes of excellence in various professions: Their relevance to the selection of gifted/talented persons. *Gifted Child Quarterly, 29,* 29–34.

Taylor, J., Hunt, E., & Coggan, P. (1987). Effect of diazepam on the speed of mental rotation. *Psychopharmacology, 91,* 369–371.

Taylor, M. C., & Hall, J. A. (1982). Psychological androgyny: Theories, methods, and conclusions. *Psychological Bulletin, 92,* 347–377.

Teevan, R. C., Heinzen, T. E., & Hartsough, W. R. (1988). Personality correlates between need for achievement and subscales of the F-scale of authoritarianism. *Psychological Reports, 62,* 959–961.

Tenopyr, M. (1967). Social intelligence and academic success. *Educational and Psychological Measurement, 27*, 961–965.

Tenopyr, M., Guilford, J. P., & Hoepfner, R. (1966). *A factor analysis of symbolic-memory abilities* (Research Rep. No. 38). Los Angeles: University of Southern California Psychological Laboratory.

Terpstra, D. E. (1983). An investigation of job-seeker preferences through multiple methodologies. *Journal of Employment Counseling, 20*, 169–178.

Thomas, L. E., & Robbins, P. I. (1979). Personality and work environment congruence of mid-life career changes. *Journal of Occupational Psychology, 52*, 177–183.

Thompson, C. E. (1942). Motor and mechanical abilities in professional schools. *Journal of Applied Psychology, 26*, 24–37.

Thorndike, E. L. (1920). Intelligence and its use. *Harper's Magazine*, pp. 227–235.

Thorndike, R. L. (1985). The central role of general ability in prediction. *Multivariate Behavioral Research, 20*, 241–254.

Thorndike, R. L., & Stein, S. (1937). An evaluation of the attempts to measure social intelligence. *Psychological Bulletin, 34*, 275–285.

Those button-down, baby boomer blues: Counseling can help career related depression. (1989). *Duke Health Line, 4*, 2–3.

Thurstone, L. L. (1938). Primary mental abilities. *Psychometrika Monographs, 1*, 1–121.

Tiebout, C., & Meier, C. (1936). Artistic ability and general intelligence. *Psychological Monographs* (Whole No. 313).

Tinker, M. A. (1944). Speed, power, and level in the Revised Minnesota Paper Form Board Test. *Journal of Genetic Psychology, 64*, 93–97.

Torrance, E. P. (1965). *Rewarding creative behavior*. Englewood Cliffs, NJ: Prentice-Hall.

Townsend, A. (1986). The inner critic, the creative, and the feminine. *Psychological Perspectives, 17*, 49–58.

Tsui, A. S., & Gutek, B. A. (1984). A role set analysis of gender differences in performance, affective relationships, and career success of industrial middle managers. *Academy of Management Journal, 27*, 619–635.

Tuck, B. F., & Keeling, B. (1980). Sex and cultural differences in the factorial structure of the Self-Directed Search. *Journal of Vocational Behavior, 9*, 31–42.

Turnbull, A. A. (1976). Selling and the salesman: Prediction of success and personality change. *Psychological Reports, 38*, 1175–1180.

Turner, R. G., & Hibbs, C. (1977). Vocational interest and personality correlates of differential abilities. *Psychological Reports, 40*, 727–730.

Turner, R. G., & Horn, J. M. (1975). Personality, husband-wife similarity, and Holland's occupational types. *Journal of Vocational Behavior, 10*, 111–120.

U.S. Employment Service. (1957). *Estimates of worker trait requirements for 4,000 jobs*. Washington, DC: U.S. Government Printing Office.

U.S. Department of Labor. (1970). *Manual for the USES General Aptitude Test Battery: Section III. Development*. Washington, DC: U.S. Government Printing Office.

U.S. Department of Labor. (1979). *Manual for the USES General Aptitude Test Battery: Section II. Occupational aptitude pattern structure*. Washington, DC: U.S. Government Printing Office.

Utz, P., & Korben, D. (1976). The construct validity of the occupational themes on the Strong-Campbell Interest Inventory. *Journal of Vocational Behavior, 16*, 105–114.

Vandenberg, S. G., & Kuse, A. R. (1979). Spatial ability: A critical review of the sex-linked major gene hypothesis. In M. A. Wittig & A. C. Petersen (Eds.), *Sex-related differences in cognitive functioning: Developmental issues* (pp. 67–95). New York: Academic Press.

Vernon, P. E. (1950). *The structure of human abilities*. London: Methuen; New York: Wiley.

Vernon, P. E. (1970). *Creativity*. New York: Penguin Books.

Virmani, K. G., & Mathur, P. (1984). Intelligence to use intelligence: Managerial trait theory revisited. *Abhigyan, 4*, 39–48.

Viscott, D. S. (1970). A musical idiot savant. *Psychiatry, 33*, 494–515.

von Bergen, C. W., & Shealy, R. E. (1982). How's your empathy? *Training and Development Journal, 36*, 22–28.

Waddell, F. T. (1983). Factors affecting choice, satisfaction, and success in the female self-employed. *Journal of Vocational Behavior, 23*, 294–304.

Wagner, R. K., & Sternberg, R. J. (1985). Practical intelligence in real-world pursuits: The role of tacit knowledge. *Journal of Personality and Social Psychology, 49*, 436–458.

Wakefield, J. A., Jr., & Cunningham, C. H. (1975). Relationships between the Vocational Preference Inventory and the Edwards Personal Preference Schedule. *Journal of Vocational Behavior, 6*, 373–377.

Walker, R. E., & Foley, J. M. (1973). Social intelligence: Its history and measurement. *Psychological Reports, 33*, 839–864.

Wallace, T., & Walberg, H. J. (1987). Personality traits and childhood environments of eminent essayists. *Gifted Child Quarterly, 31*, 65–69.

Wallbrown, F. H., Mcloughlin, C. S., Elliott, C. D., & Blaha, J. (1984). The hierarchical factor structure of the British Ability Scales. *Journal of Clinical Psychology, 40*, 278–290.

Waller, J. D., & Rothschild, G. (1983). Comparison of need for achievement versus need for affiliation among music students. *Psychological Reports, 53*, 135–138.

Walsh, W. B., Bingham, R., Horton, J. A., & Spokane, A. (1979). Holland's theory and college-degreed working black and white women. *Journal of Vocational Behavior, 15*, 217–223.

Walsh, W. B., Horton, J. A., & Gaffey, R. L. (1977). Holland's theory and college degreed working men and women. *Journal of Vocational Behavior, 10*, 180–186.

Walters, J. M., & Gardner, H. (1986). The theory of multiple intelligences: Some issues and answers. In R. J. Sternberg & R. K. Wagner (Eds.), *Practical intelligence* (pp. 163–192). Cambridge, England: Cambridge University Press.

Ward, G. R., Cunningham, C. H., & Wakefield, J. A. (1976). Relationships between Holland's VPI and Cattell's 16PF. *Journal of Vocational Behavior, 8,* 307–312.

Warrier, S. K. (1982). Values of successful managers: Implications for managerial success. *Management and Labour Studies, 8,* 7–15.

Watson, G., & Glaser, M. (1980). *Watson-Glaser Critical Thinking Appraisal: Manual.* San Antonio, TX: Psychological Corporation.

Wechsler, D. (1981). *WAIS–R manual.* San Antonio, TX: Psychological Corporation.

Weeda, W. L., & Drop, M. J. (1985). The discriminative value of psychological characteristics in anorexia nervosa: Clinical and psychometric comparisons between anorexia nervosa patients, ballet dancers and controls. *Journal of Psychiatric Research, 19,* 285–290.

Weekley, J. A., & Gier, J. A. (1987). Reliability and validity of the situational interview for a sales position. *Journal of Applied Psychology, 72,* 484–487.

Wehner, W. L. (1985). Australian Test for Advanced Music Studies [Review]. In J. V. Mitchell (Ed.), *The ninth mental measurements yearbook* (pp. 119–120). Lincoln, NE: Buros Institute of Mental Measurement.

Weinrach, S. G. (1984). Determinants of vocational choice: Holland's theory. In D. Brown, L. Brooks, & Associates, *Career choice and development* (pp. 61–93). San Francisco: Jossey-Bass.

Werner, J. E. (1969). A study of vocational choice as it applies to selected working women. (Doctoral dissertation, State University of New York at Buffalo, 1969). *Dissertation Abstracts International, 30,* 1832A.

Westbrook, M. T., & Nordholm, L. A. (1984). Characteristics of women health professionals with vertical, lateral, and stationary career plans. *Sex Roles, 10,* 743–756.

White, K. R. (1985). Comprehensive Ability Battery [Review]. In J. V. Mitchell, Jr. (Ed.), *The ninth mental measurements yearbook* (Vol 1, pp. 377–379). Lincoln, NE: Buros Institute of Mental Measurements.

White, P. A. (1988). The structured representation of information in long-term memory: A possible explanation for the accomplishments of "idiots savants." *New Ideas in Psychology, 6,* 3–14.

Whittington, J. E. (1988). Large verbal-non-verbal ability differences and underachievement. *British Journal of Educational Psychology, 58,* 205–211.

Wiener, Y., & Vaitenas, R. (1977). Personality correlates of voluntary mid-career change in enterprising occupations. *Journal of Applied Psychology, 62,* 706–712.

Wiggins, J. D. (1976). The relation of job satisfaction to vocational preferences among teachers of the educable mentally retarded. *Journal of Vocational Behavior, 8,* 13–19.

Wiley, M. G., & Eskilson, A. (1982). The interaction of sex and power base on perceptions of managerial effectiveness. *Academy of Management Journal, 25,* 671–677.

Wiley, M. G., & Eskilson, A. (1983). Scaling the corporate ladder: Sex differences in expectations for performance, power and mobility. *Social Psychology Quarterly, 46,* 351–359.

Williams, E. D., Winter, L., & Woods, J. M. (1938). Tests of literary appreciation. *British Journal of Educational Psychology, 8,* 265–284.

Williams, S. W., & McCullers, J. C. (1983). Personal factors related to typicalness of career and success in active professional women. *Psychology of Women Quarterly, 7,* 343–357.

Wills, G. I. (1984). A personality study of musicians working in the popular field. *Personality and Individual Differences, 5,* 359–360.

Wing, H. (1941). A factorial study of musical tests. *British Journal of Psychology, 31,* 341–355.

Wing, H. (1960). *Manual for Standardised Tests of Musical Intelligence.* Windsor, Berkshire, England: National Foundation for Education Research.

Wing, H. (1968). *Tests of musical ability and appreciation: An investigation into the measurement, distribution, and development of musical capacity.* Cambridge, England: Cambridge University Press.

Winter, D. G. (1973). *The power motive.* New York: Free Press.

Witkin, H. A., Moore, C. A., Goodenough, D. R., & Cox, P. W. (1977). Field-dependent and field-independent cognitive styles and their educational implications. *Review of Educational Research, 47,* 1–64.

Wittkower, R., & Wittkower, M. (1963). *Born under Saturn: The character and conduct of artists.* New York: Norton.

Wolfe, L. K., & Betz, N. L. (1981). Traditionality of choice and sex-role identification as moderators of vocational choice in college women. *Journal of Vocational Behavior, 18,* 43–53.

Wolff, L. K., & Frey, P. W. (1984). A note on the correlations of visual-spatial ability and the acquisition of game skill. *Educational Research Quarterly, 9,* 4–5.

Wolman, B. B. (1985). *Handbook of intelligence: Theories, measurements and applications.* New York: Wiley.

Wong, P. T., Kettlewell, G. E., & Sproule, C. F. (1985). On the importance of being masculine: Sex roles, attribution, and women's career achievement. *Sex Roles, 12,* 757–769.

Wood, L. E., & Stewart, P. W. (1987). Improvement of practical reasoning skills with a computer game. *Journal of Computer-Based Instruction, 14,* 49–53.

Yogev, S. (1983). Judging the professional woman: Changing research, changing values. *Psychology of Women Quarterly, 7,* 219–234.

York, D. C., & Tinsley, H. E. A. (1986). The relationship between cognitive styles and Holland's personality types. *Journal of College Student Personnel, 27,* 535–541.

Zagar, R., Arbit, J., Stuckey, M., & Wengel, W. W. (1984). Developmental analysis of the Wechsler Memory Scale. *Journal of Clinical Psychology, 40*, 1466–1473.

Zaleznik, A. (1974). Charismatic and consensus leaders: A psychological comparison. *Bulletin of the Menninger Clinic, 38*, 222–238.

Zaleznik, A. (1977). Managers and leaders: Are they different? *Harvard Business Review, 55*, 67–78.

Zaleznik, A. (1989). *The managerial mystique: Restoring leadership in business.* New York: Harper & Row.

Zeidner, M. (1988). Age as a factor in scholastic aptitude: Some Israeli findings. *Journal of Applied Developmental Psychology, 9*, 139–149.

Zenatti, A. (1985). The role of perceptual-discrimination ability in tests of memory for melody, harmony, and rhythm. *Music Perception, 2*, 397–403.

Zytowski, D. G., & Hay, R. (1984). Do birds of a feather flock together? A test of the similarities within and the differences between five occupations. *Journal of Vocational Behavior, 24*, 242–248.

Appendix

Some Psychological Tests Relevant for Career Assessment

The following list identifies many of the tests mentioned in this book. For page numbers on which the tests are discussed in the text, please consult the index. Note that the list is *not* an exhaustive list of career-relevant tests.

Vocational Interest Measures

Career Assessment Inventory
Self-Directed Search
Strong Vocational Inventory Blank (formerly called Strong-
    Campbell Interest Inventory)
Vocational Preference Inventory

Ability Measures

Australian Test for Advanced Music Studies
Bennett Mechanical Comprehension Test
Brick Uses test
Bulley & Burt Art Judgement Test
Reproductive Drawing Ability
Comprehensive Ability Battery (CAB)
Differential Aptitude Test
Dvorine Color Vision Test
Farnsworth-Munsell 100-Hue Test for the Examination of Color
    Discrimination
Flexibility of Closure test of the CAB
Four Factor Tests of Social Intelligence
General Ability Test Battery
Guilford-Zimmerman Aptitude Survey

Hidden Shapes test
Horn Art Aptitude Inventory
Interpersonal Problem-Solving Ability Test
Iowa Tests of Educational Development
Kuhlman-Anderson Test
Kwalwasser-Dykema Music Tests
Match Problems III
McAdory Art Test
Meier Art Judgment Test
Minnesota Clerical Test
Minnesota Mechanical Ability Test
Minnesota Paper Form Board
Minnesota Rate of Manipulation Test
Object-Question test
O'Connor Finger Dexterity Test
O'Connor Tweezer Dexterity
O'Connor Wiggly Block
Perceptual Memory Test
Purdue Pegboard
Raven Progressive Matrices
Seashore Measures of Musical Talents
Stenquist Assembly Test
Things Categories Test
Torrance Tests of Creative Thinking
Watson-Glaser Critical Thinking Appraisal
Wechsler Adult Intelligence Scale–Revised (WAIS–R)
Welsh Figure Preference Test
Wide Range Achievement Test–Revised (WRAT–R)
Wing Standardised Tests of Musical Intelligence
Wonderlic Personnel Test
Word Associates test

Personality Measures

Bem Sex-Role Inventory (BSRI)
Bernreuter Personality Inventory
Clinical Analysis Questionnaire (CAQ)
FIRO-B (Fundamental Interpersonal Relations
    Orientation-Behavior)
Hogan Personality Inventory
Hogan Personnel Selection Series
L-BLA Achievement Styles Inventory
Motivation Analysis Test
Myers-Briggs Type Indicator
NEO Personality Inventory
Personal Attributes Questionnaire
Rorschach
Self-Description Inventory
Sixteen Personality Factor Questionnaire (16PF)
Social Intelligence Test: George Washington University Series
Thematic Apperception Test (TAT)
Work and Family Orientation Questionnaire

Miscellaneous

Minnesota Importance Questionnaire

Index

Abilities, 11–12, 51–131, 177–181, 183–184, 232, 235–245. *See also* Specific abilities
spatial ability and personality, 177, 178–181
contribution to applied psychology, 51–52
history, 51–52
interests, 177, 183–184
measurement issues, 51–52, 53–56
neuropsychology of, 52
primary abilities, 57
test selection criteria, 53–56
Ability–interest relationships, 44, 177, 183–184
Ability–interest–personality relationships, 185, 186–187
Ability–personality relationships, 177, 178–181
Accounting, 68, 80
Achievement motivation, 119, 121, 134, 135, 137–138, 142–150, 158, 173, 180
and mechanical ability, 61
and productivity, 148–149
career relevance, 147–149
changeability of, 146–147
defined, 142–143, 143–144
measurement issues, 149–150
sex differences, 145–146
racial differences, 145
Acting, 102
Action inhibition, 158
Activity level, 169
Actors, 119, 152, 163
Adjustment, 105–106, 141, 161–164, 213, 248–249
artistic occupations, 162–163
career relevance, 162–164
correctabilty, 163

factor structure, 161
measurement issues, 164
Aesthetic ability, 95–97, 240
definition, 95
Affective disorders, 104
Affiliation, need for, 148, 158, 169, 173
Agreeableness, 141, 169, 180, 213, 249
Ambiguity, tolerance of, 103, 203
Androgyny. *See* Masculinity-femininity
Armed Forces Vocational Ability Battery (ASVAB), 78
Architecture, 68, 70, 116, 162, 167
Art education, 162
Artistic vocational interests, 20–27, 33, 28, 68–69, 81, 83, 88, 103, 104, 117, 162–163, 165, 167, 181, 182, 184. *See also* Specific artistic abilities
and achievement, 103
and independence, 23, 104
and intelligence, 81
and narcissism, 21–22, 103
and neurosis, 20–27, 104, 162–163
and nonconformity, 21–23
and self-centeredness, 103
and spatial ability, 68–69
creativity, 83
masculinity–femininity of, 167
openness of, 181
related abilities, 184
Artists, 152, 153, 159, 167. *See also* Artistic vocational interests
Ascendance. *See* Dominance
Assertiveness. *See* Dominance
Assessment centers, 125
Assessments, career, xii
as a clinical activity, 8–9, 13–14

309

About the Author

Rodney L. Lowman, PhD, is founder and Chief Executive Officer of the Career & Personal Development Laboratories, headquartered in Houston. In addition to numerous journal articles on the Interdomain Model of Career Assessment and on professional practice issues, he is the author of *Pre-Employment Screening for Psychopathology: A Guide to Professional Practice* and editor of the *Casebook on Ethics and Standards for the Practice of Psychology in Organizations*. Dr. Lowman has served on the faculties of the Institute for Social Research, University of Michigan, the University of North Texas, and Duke University Medical Center. He trained in industrial–organizational and clinical psychology at Michigan State University, completing his clinical psychology internship at the Texas Research Institute of Mental Sciences. He has served on the Ethics Committee and Board of Professional Affairs of the American Psychological Association, is on the editorial board of *Professional Psychology*, and actively consults on individuals and organizations, especially on career, work, and occupational mental health issues.